CONTROVERSIAL TOPICS

FOR YOUTH GROUPS

CONTROVERSIAL TOPICS
FOR YOUTH GROUPS

Edward N. McNulty

Group Books

Loveland, Colorado

Controversial Topics for Youth Groups

Copyright © 1988 by Edward N. McNulty

First Printing

Credits
Edited by Nancy M. Shaw
Designed by Judy Atwood

Scripture quotations are from the Holy Bible, New International Version. Copyright © 1973, 1978, 1984 International Bible Society. Used by permission of Zondervan Bible Publishers.

Library of Congress Cataloging-in-Publication Data
McNulty, Edward N., 1936-
   Controversial topics for youth groups.

   1. Church group work with youth. 2. Youth—Religious life. 3. Youth—Conduct of life. I. Title.
BV4447.M38   1987   268'.433   87-27913
ISBN 0-931529-51-4 (pbk.)

Printed in the United States of America

Dedication

To my youth groups in Indianapolis, Indiana;
Bottineau, North Dakota; Parkersburg, West
Virginia; Bethel Park, Pennsylvania; and
Westfield, New York. Thanks for the fond
memories.

Acknowledgments

T his book has been almost a year in preparation—a long and meaningful year filled with the usual activities of a pastor. I have learned again that a book is not just the product of one person. It is the result of a long process arising from an author's interaction with and learning from a host of other people, what the author of Hebrews calls "a cloud of witnesses."

I am grateful to Lee Sparks for first suggesting that I tackle this project and then insisting the first draft needed more revisions. He and his associates at Group Books deserve credit for helping mold the final form of this work. Nancy Shaw and Cindy Hansen suggested program ideas that lightened the load considerably as I struggled to produce fresh thoughts for each topic. I shall miss Nancy's encouraging letters and cheerful phone calls. My family, Sandra in particular, has had to endure my long sessions at the word processor, but they have sustained me through thick and thin. In conclusion, I would mention the youth groups to whom I've been privileged to minister over the years. They are the ones for whom this book ultimately is written. Without their involvement in the church and in my life, I would never have written this book. I hope this book will be one way of returning to youth ministry a little of what I have received over the years.

Contents

Preface

*C*ontroversial Topics for Youth Groups helps young people
study and discuss controversial topics. This book is intended
for that stalwart crew of youth workers, Sunday school
teachers and pastors who believe youth ministry means
more than keeping the kids busy with games and cookies. I
strongly believe youth ministry not only prepares young
people for leadership in the church of tomorrow, but also
engages and challenges kids with the difficult issues of
today.

Why involve young people in controversial topics? Because controversy flows through their church and the
world in which they live. We need to help young people
consider the issues they may face each day. We need to
help kids form their own opinions and listen to other opinions on each issue. We need to help kids handle controversy in creative and loving ways so they can grow and
mature in their faith. Instead of shielding young people
from controversy, we need to equip them to handle their
differences without hostility or bitterness.

Controversial Topics for Youth Groups provides leaders
with study material, background information, programming
ideas and resources to help young people deal with controversial topics. This book covers 40 issues such as abortion,
biblical interpretation, homosexuality, predestination and
rock music.

The Issues

Each of the 40 issues begins with two vignettes (or
conversations) presenting opposite positions:

- Yes—agreement with the question at hand.
- No—disagreement with the question at hand.

The Yes/No vignettes within each issue provide examples of how people operate when they support a particular
position. Ask two people to read the different stories to in-

troduce an issue, or use these as skits or stimuli for role plays. Encourage your young people to include the vignettes in their debates to illustrate the different positions.

Introductory material following the vignettes offers reasons and evidence supporting each position. Even though I have strong opinions on many of these issues, I've written both extremes for each issue as vigorously as possible. This kind of intensity provides strong, clear arguments for each position. Neither I nor the publisher necessarily endorses either extreme. Extreme positions present opposite ends of a continuum. People's opinions usually fall somewhere between the two extremes. The purpose of these essays is to help kids and leaders decide where they stand on each continuum. The extreme positions should stimulate "creative juices" in both leaders and their young people, producing opportunities to develop their own ideas.

Programming

Following the introductory material are programming plans designed to help kids respond to the issue and clarify their own values. Programming ideas for each issue include the following:

● Preparation tips.

Editor's note: Some preparation requires you to rent a video and show it to your youth group. Typical video stores rent movies and films for home use only. Videos rented from typical distributors (for example, Mass Media Ministries) are for group viewing. Secure permission to show a "home-use-only" video to a large group by calling or writing the producer. Ask the video store owner for the address and phone number of the movie's producer. Most videos contain the producer's name and address.

● Program ideas such as role plays, panels, Bible studies, continuums and discussions. The introductory material can be used to initiate formal debate—a lively and fun method for groups to look at two sides of an issue and still come away friends. (See the Appendix for suggestions on how to use debate in your program.)

● Ways to help kids respond to the program.
● Optional ideas to explore the topics.
● Resources to help young people research the issues.

Although these programming ideas offer easy-to-follow plans for each issue, the programs shouldn't mislead you into thinking you can leaf through this book an hour before meeting time and generate a winning session. Most projects require planning for both the leader and the young people. Like everything else, the more you put into a program, the more rewards you and your kids will reap. Once teenagers learn how to use and practice the techniques suggested in the following pages, they will find that no issue is too hot to handle.

HELPING YOUNG PEOPLE DEAL WITH CONTROVERSIAL TOPICS

S ince you are reading *Controversial Topics for Youth Groups,* you probably believe youth ministry is more than fun and games. The "fun-and-games" approach to youth ministry relies primarily on entertaining young people. Meetings consist of lots of active games and a brief Bible devotion. The youth leader joins in like a real pal. This approach keeps kids and parents happy for a while. It gets the teenagers into the church building and keeps them off the streets. But it offers little long-term fulfillment for both the kids and the youth leader. It settles for what Isaiah called "that which is not bread" (Isaiah 55:2).

Controversial Topics for Youth Groups provides "bread," or study material, for 40 controversial topics. This book guides kids and leaders beyond a fun-and-games routine. Learning how to deal with controversial topics is an important part of each person's maturation process. This material helps leaders make the church youth group a training ground or a laboratory for developing Christian leaders.

Despite young people's frequent complaints about adults' attitudes toward their dress and music, teenagers often demonstrate the least tolerance among God's creatures. The very intolerance they hate in others often appears in their own cutting remarks at the school lunch table or during peer-group gossip sessions. Many criticize their classmates who don't fit in, while virtually enslaving themselves to their friends in their quest for conformity. Taking cues from current rock or film idols, some teenagers dress alike, talk alike and listen to the same records and radio stations. Their peer groups allow little room for individuality or differences. For example, in the numerous polls I have taken among teenagers concerning their tastes in music, no one has listed classical music or jazz as his or her favorite. One teenager shared privately that he really enjoyed classical music, but he refused to discuss it with the group for fear others would put him down.

Teenagers need to learn how to deal constructively and creatively with each other's differences; they need to learn how to "agree to disagree." Youth groups then can become what few really are—an accepting, caring community, rather than just another program unit of the church. Developing such a community isn't easy, but it's certainly worth the effort for all concerned—the teenagers, their youth group and the adult youth workers.

Controversy in the Church

Controversy is as old as the human race, or at least as old as temptation and sin. Imagine Eve repeating the tempter's lies while she argued with Adam over the forbidden fruit. We can picture Adam weakly reminding her of God's command not to eat the fruit of that particular tree.

As long as there are two human beings, Christian or otherwise, there will be controversy. Anyone who thinks that true Christians never argue should read "between the lines" in Paul's letters to the Corinthians and the Galatians.

Some people imagine the church as a gathering of smiling saints who live continuously in harmony. When these people encounter the first signs of disharmony, some leave the congregation and look for another "more Christian" church. Others pine for the "good old days" of the New Testament church when Christians were "afire" with their new faith and lived in "peace and perfect love."

But this view cannot survive a careful reading of the New Testament. The disciples quarreled among themselves even while Jesus was still with them. They were jealous of each other and wanted a place of power and prestige in the coming kingdom, which they mistakenly thought would be like other earthly kingdoms (Mark 10:35-45).

Acts records the continuous controversies and struggles of the New Testament church. Most Christians were natives of Judea and Galilee and spoke Aramaic, but some lived in areas where Greek was spoken. In Acts 6, the Greek-speaking Christians complained to the apostles that their widows were not getting a fair share of the daily distribution of food and clothing. The apostles then called the church together and declared that their first duty lay in studying and preaching the Word of God. They decided to create a new body of leaders to deal with the mundane matters of the church. These new leaders looked after the church's internal affairs. Later, these leaders were called deacons.

Acts 15 records more controversy in the early church. Paul discovered the Holy Spirit leading more Gentiles than Jews into the church. Because of this situation, a new and more serious controversy erupted. Some of the Christians with a Jewish background could not accept the new Christians unless they agreed to be circumcised and promised to follow the Torah. Paul disagreed with this barrier. He argued that in Christ the law was fulfilled and now everyone had free access to the love of God. Acts 15 describes the meeting of the great council of apostles at Jerusalem to decide the outcome of the issue. Any group planning to study controversy in the church should start here to see how the apostles handled this issue. The apostles used experience, scripture and logic to guide their decision.

After the first apostles were gone and the church had

been legalized by the emperor, the bishops of the local churches represented the faithful to discuss controversies. We usually think of church leaders as dignified and holy. But during the early controversies, spiritual passion ran so high that bishops and their followers often came to blows. At one council meeting, they brought swords and daggers beneath their cloaks. Prominent bishops would also excommunicate their opponents from the church. The bishop of Rome did this when the eastern bishops refused to accept his date for the observance of Easter. These actions were a long way from the Prince of Peace who taught love and forbearance!

The church moved further away from Jesus' gentle ways as it grew in political power. Often it demanded the arrest and torture of those who disagreed with an official practice or teaching and attempted to make them change their minds. During the Middle Ages church officials started the Inquisition—first, to look into heretical beliefs, and second, to punish erroneous believers if they would not admit their errors. They justified torture on the basis that the opponent's soul was at stake. For if this believer persisted in his error, so the church argued, he would go to hell.

Roman Catholics weren't the only people who dealt with their opponents in such brutal ways. Protestants seized Catholics in England and burned them at the stake. Michael Servetus was strangled and then burned in Calvin's Geneva because of heresy. Baptists were drowned in Europe and New England. Quakers were imprisoned or hanged in New York and Virginia. Almost every church of the 17th and 18th centuries refused to tolerate dissent or any questioning of its practices.

The 19th century saw a great series of divisions in the church over a host of issues. Slavery. Free will vs. predestination. The place of the slave and freedman in the church. The role of women. The use of musical instruments in worship. The meaning of the Lord's Supper. Baptism by immersion or sprinkling. The use of wine or grape juice. Sending missionaries to foreign countries. The use of creeds. The teaching of evolution. The nature of the Bible as a reliable book of science or a book of faith. These and other issues continue to split the church today, not to mention all of the personal animosities and issues that are a part of God's people simply because they are people. People of God—redeemed, but still human.

The history of the church has many dark moments when controversies led to persecution, torture and death. Some people have become cynical about the church because mistakes are all they can see—the terrible massacre of Protestants in France, the bloody Thirty Years' War, the Spanish Inquisition, the strife between Protestants and Catholics in Ireland, the blood feuds between Christians and Moslems in Lebanon, and the smug denunciations of denominations within American churches.

No wonder today's church leaders shy away from anything controversial. They know how conflicts can destroy. So, for the peace and unity of the church, they ignore many important issues.

In light of all this historical data, it may be difficult to see the constructive as well as destructive aspects of controversy. But controversy can be properly handled and approached with right attitudes.

Developing Tolerance

If we regard the church as a family, we can see a growing and changing group of individuals. And we may begin to see faith in terms of relationships with both God and neighbors. With this perspective, our faith becomes a matter of trust in God and each other rather than strict adherence to a list of beliefs. In our families we expect disagreements, even arguments and fights at times. But the combatants are still family. We may not always be on best terms, but no one denies the relationship.

Like many families who develop tolerance to make their holiday gatherings pleasant, the Christian family must learn the same skill. John Wesley, the founder of Methodism, once wrote: "I have no more right to object to a man holding a different opinion from mine than I have to differ with a man because he wears a wig and I wear my own hair . . . The thing which I resolved to use every possible method of preventing was a narrowness of spirit . . . that miserable bigotry which makes many so unready to believe that there is any work of God but among themselves."

This kind of attitude can help us deal with controversy in creative ways, for tolerance is based on several premises:

1. No one has *all* the truth. We are finite beings. Only one person could *justly* claim, "I am the way and the truth and the life . . . " (John 14:6). The rest of us are still discovering new aspects of truth every day of our lives.

2. Every person, no matter how disagreeable, can teach us something. Accepting criticism or correction from our friends, let alone our enemies, is hard. But if we realize truth doesn't always come in pleasant and agreeable packages, we have the potential to grow even during a painful encounter.

3. We may recognize more sides to an issue than just one or two. When Soviet and American politicians quarrel over areas in the Middle East, Africa or Central America, they often hurl mutual accusations about encroaching on other nations and usurping their power. Many times leaders native to these less-powerful countries denounce both of these powerful countries for seeing the situation only from a communist vs. capitalist perspective. Most real life issues are more complex than an "us vs. them" or a "right side vs. a wrong side" attitude allows.

4. When all parties have a chance to openly express their feelings and understandings of the facts, we "actively listen" to one another and see that there are other sides of an issue. Active listening is a skill anyone can develop. This technique requires listeners to check frequently with the speaker to make sure that what they think they hear is really what the speaker is saying. The listeners should use questions and then reword the responses they hear back to the speaker. This process takes time, but the time is well-spent for understanding each other.

An interchange of active listening might sound like this:

"You Americans are always so smug and superior. You come here with your fancy clothes, cameras and money and you think we 'peons' should be grateful. You expect us all to speak English when you are in our country! And when we don't, you call us stupid and lazy."

"You've apparently met a lot of people from my country, and obviously they weren't always courteous or friendly."

"No, they weren't. Some even bought large portions of our land for almost nothing and then hired us at slave wages to work it. Then if any of us voiced protest against the inhumane treatment or the poor working conditions, you called us communists and threatened to call in your military forces!"

"It must feel really bad when people from my country don't treat you as valuable, especially when you are working for them in your own country. Believe it or not, most Americans know very little about this, and what we do know is probably pretty slanted. Tell me more from your viewpoint."

"I'd like to, but how do I know I can trust you to listen and understand my position? How do I know you won't turn around and report me to the authorities?"

"I can understand your hesitancy and fear. If I were you, I'm not sure I would know whom to trust either. All I can say is that I'm here, and I would be glad to listen. There's no way I can prove my concern other than to let you know that I hear what you are saying."

5. We need to *listen* to what a person is saying, not discredit or ridicule him or her. Too often we resort to the old tactic of attacking and discrediting a person so no one will believe what he or she has to say, even if the statement is true. This kind of tactic destroys trust and respect; it builds walls rather than bridges.

6. We must work to keep our emotions under control and focus only on the facts and the issues.

Only opinions based on facts are acceptable, not opinions based on prejudice or hearsay. Controversy generates strong emotions that need release, but they must not be used as "clubs" against our "opponent."

The Youth Worker's Role

The youth group whose leader willingly guides the members into the thicket of controversial topics develops into *more* than just a training ground for church leaders. The youth group becomes an arena for discipleship, not just preparation for some unknown ministry. We can be so future-oriented toward young people that we often forget the importance of their present lives.

Just what is the youth worker's role in this process of developing Christian leadership within young people? How can the youth worker guide young people to become an accepting community of thinking adolescents? What skills and responsibilities must the youth worker use to teach his or her young people how to handle conflict within the church? Your role, as a youth worker, is at least fourfold:

1. *Lead*, don't spoon-feed. Help young people learn how to examine and weigh facts, find scripture relevant to the issue, sift applicable but conflicting values and arrive at personal conclusions. This type of responsibility isn't easy. Leaders, like parents, often want their young people to arrive at the "right" answer, so they steer them away from the "wrong" approach. Some leaders even keep disagreeable facts or arguments away from their kids, "so as not to confuse them." Of course, this "hiding of facts" short-circuits the learning process, which requires free investigation.

It is extremely important to help young people look for the facts of a situation, apply the scripture and ask hard questions, even of the church and faith itself. This type of programming will provide teenagers with a strong and tested faith. We can send these young people to college or into the world with little fear that some smart-aleck philosophy professor or self-appointed guru will plunder their tender,

unexamined faith and throw them into the ranks of confused agnostics.

**2. Help adolescents learn how to accept varying
viewpoints so they can listen to those with whom
they disagree.** Listen to young people and accept them
just as they are, regardless of their "mixed-up" values and
contradictory opinions. This acceptance includes their
choice of music and clothing. It doesn't mean the leader
pretends to like their choices. He or she certainly should
not fall into the trap of trying to dress, talk and think like
the kids. For in that case, who would be leading whom?
The youth leader should lead, not try to be a pal.

Unconditional acceptance of young people is possible
for the Christian leader because of the reconciling work of
Christ: "But now in Christ Jesus you who once were far
away have been brought near through the blood of Christ.
For he himself is our peace, who has made the two one and
has destroyed the barrier, the dividing wall of hostility, by
abolishing in his flesh the law with its commandments and
regulations. His purpose was to create in himself one new
man out of the two, thus making peace, and in this one
body to reconcile both of them to God through the cross,
by which he put to death their hostility" (Ephesians
2:13-16).

The "oneness" that Paul declared in this scripture is
just as important today as when the Jews and Gentiles felt
separated by the Law of Moses.

**3. Help the youth group move into an active, ex-
periential learning environment.** Look for a variety of
ways to air an issue—formal debates, role plays, simulation
games or activities, discussion groups and video presentations. Invite speakers to participate in panels, debates or
educational presentations. As the group's leader, be careful
that your young people hear many sides of an issue. You
are responsible to see that things don't get out of hand. Be
especially careful how you structure your programs for sensitive issues that may become emotional.

4. Provide quality resources for the group and

give directions on how to find other facts and materials within the community. Numerous magazines present one side or another of important issues. Christianity Today, The Christian Century, The Other Side and Sojourners are the better Christian publications for dealing with social and international issues. You can find the latter two at any peace and justice center or in denominational offices and resource centers. GROUP Magazine provides articles dealing with controversial matters. Many churches subscribe to one or more of these publications, so check around.

Denominations usually take a stand on a large variety of issues—abortion, capital punishment, homosexuality, the arms race, racism, etc. Official papers and pamphlets give background information for the church's stand and are available for a small charge. Check the denominational catalog in your church office for the names and prices of these publications and where to send for them. Since not all denominations agree officially, check to see if information from other denominations is also available. Many denominations publish family magazines. These publications, along with Sunday school curricula and supplements, may also contain helpful articles.

School and public libraries are good sources for secular magazines and books. Time, Newsweek, US News and World Report, The New Republic, The National Review, The Atlantic Monthly and many other publications often produce articles for debate topics. Examine the editorials in USA Today, since this newspaper always provides pro and con voices on important issues. Although these articles are short and rarely deep in content, they can prove useful in initiating arguments and ideas. Various special interest groups also issue brief and factual public affairs statements, which are usually stored in the library's pamphlet section.

Set up an information center in your youth room or other location in your church. Display back issues of magazines, denominational publications and various pamphlets on a table or bookshelf. Find out what publications your teenagers' parents subscribe to and ask the group to form a clipping service. You can even include parents in this activity. Ask individuals to look for articles on the issues your group chose to deal with, and cut the articles out (after the owners are through with the magazines, of course). Remind everyone to be sure the source and the date are attached to every article. Ask your group members to bring their articles to church and file them in folders. Label each folder with the name of the controversial topic and include all articles on that topic, no matter what viewpoint they represent.

The debate format (see the Appendix) offers a convenient way to present two sides of any issue. No group using this book, however, should feel compelled to debate each issue. Your teenagers might not feel comfortable with this method, or they might want more variety in their presentations. You can use role plays, games, art projects, speakers, panel presentations and on-site visits. For a change of pace, show a film or videotape on a particular issue. Both the school and public library are likely sources for materials on some of these controversial topics. Many denominations produce films or filmstrips presenting information on various issues. A search through the subject index of either the Ecufilm or Mass Media Ministries catalogs will reveal more films on controversial topics than you can schedule in a year. As youth leader, you should help your group adapt this material to its interests and needs.

You can't do everything suggested in the following pages, and you wouldn't want to. But you will certainly find enough ideas to challenge your group and encourage the kids to grow in understanding and love—even in their differences.

5. Inform parents and other adults about the youth group's plans to explore controversial topics. If your program is to run smoothly, you must consider how to work with parents and the other adults in your church who will hear about what you are doing. With no introduction or explanation of your plans, an adult's reaction could be something like the following:

"Did you hear what the kids talked about last night? Homosexuality! Someone spoke in favor of letting homosexuals help run the church, and her adviser didn't even step in to put a stop to it."

Publicize your program through the church newsletter. Hold an informative meeting for parents and adults to explain your plans. Help them see the special needs their teenagers have to freely explore and express their views and feelings.

Utilizing this type of programming may take some persuasion in churches, especially those accustomed to an authoritarian approach with their young people. In fact, you may be tempted to skip this informative process altogether. But neglecting the concerns of the adults in your church would be unwise. Word *will* get out, and it is far better that the facts come from you so you can present the whole picture.

6. Encourage the qualities of faith, hope and love. We must believe in the God who unites all people through the cross. We must hope for solutions that reconcile many parties. Because we have experienced a loving relationship with our Savior, he expects us to establish the same kind of love with everyone, including people with whom we disagree.

To paraphrase Paul's "love" chapter in 1 Corinthians: "Though I debate in the tongues of men and of angels, but have not love, I am only a resounding gong or a clanging cymbal. And if I have all the facts straight and understand all the arguments but have not love, I am nothing."

All of us should read this scripture passage before we engage in controversy. For long after the arguments have faded away, " . . . these three (will) remain: faith, hope and love. But the greatest of these is love" (1 Corinthians 13:13).

FAMILY ISSUES

Young people struggle with family issues even though they don't always acknowledge this concern to their peers or families. Teenagers come from different kinds of family structures and need to work constantly through their feelings within those relationships. No longer children, but not yet adults, teenagers continually readjust their views and roles in the family. Conflicts develop as values and viewpoints change.

Some teenagers rebel. Others quietly accept their parents' rules and desires, but anticipate the day they can function on their own. Some have parents who listen to them and help them work through their differences and changes as they occur. Probably at no other point in their lives is it harder for children to honor their father and mother than during the teenage years. Debating and discussing the following issues might not make life any easier for you or your teenagers, but it might clarify the different positions and facilitate understanding for everyone involved.

ISSUE 1
Should young people always obey their parents?

YES, children should always obey their parents.

At school, Bob and Jim compared notes. "Boy, my parents stepped in the house and immediately jumped on me about my hair! They've given me until Saturday to make it all one color—or else my dad will buzz it."

"Sounds familiar. My folks attacked me after church too. They say I have to get rid of my rock albums, and I can't buy any more!"

"Parents can sure be a pain. They just don't understand us."

"They're hopelessly lost in another world! But what can we do?"

The Sixth Commandment tells us to "Honor your father and your mother, so that you may live long in the land the Lord your God is giving you" (Exodus 20:12). Biblical interpretation of this passage includes obeying parents' orders and wishes. Paul continues support for this position when he says, "Children, obey your parents in the Lord, for this is right" (Ephesians 6:1).

The family should be the cornerstone of our society. Within this institution parents need to hand down the faith and values of the church and the community. Society expects parents to provide order and discipline since respect for authority begins with respect for parents and both are essential for a strong family. Proverbs 13:24 says, "He who spares the rod hates his son, but he who loves him is careful to discipline him."

Parents have experienced more of life than their children. Having made mistakes themselves, they recognize the possible consequences of certain actions. Having gained wisdom from their own experiences, parents know better than their children what is right and wrong.

Parents also deserve obedience from their children because they brought them into this world. They cared for them through their infancy and spent long hours nursing them through their illnesses. They have provided all the essentials like food, clothing and shelter. They often make great sacrifices for their children's education and for their participation in sports, music and other pursuits. Therefore, when parents say, "As long as we're paying the bills and you're living in this house, you must follow our rules," they are well within their rights, regardless of how the teenager feels.

Society requires children to obey their parents. When rebellious children threaten the authority of their parents, they create an unstable community in which they reject law and order. The chaos of civil war that occurred during the latter part of King David's reign resulted from his son Absalom's willful disobedience and his attempts to seize his father's power (2 Samuel 15—18). Many attribute the miserable chaos of the '60s to the breakdown of American parents' authority. Because the law holds parents responsible for their children's actions, it is reasonable to subject teenagers to the authority of their parents.

Most importantly, children should obey their parents because God's Word tells them to. The Ten Commandments are not just the opinions of a man called Moses; they are direct orders from God and should be followed.

NO, young people shouldn't always obey their parents.

Martha's parents divorced a few months ago. This 16-year-old girl lives with her mother and visits her father every other weekend. After her latest visit with her dad, she talked to her best friend at school.

"It's getting so I don't want to come home after I've been with Dad. Mom always quizzes me. In fact, this week she *ordered* me to find out more about the woman Dad's been seeing—her name, her age, what she's like, where she lives. I feel like a spy sent on a mission. I just can't do this!"

"So, what are you going to do?"

"I tried to tell Mom how I feel, but she got mad. She wouldn't listen. She told me I'd better do what she says or I'd be sorry!"

Most of the time children should obey their parents, for parents typically care about the welfare of their children. But the Bible's commandments refer to parents who obey God's Word, and unfortunately not all parents do this. Within our society is the drunken mother who beats her child or the father who demands his daughter to come close so he can sexually abuse her. We also have parents who tell their children to lie to callers at the door or to scout for police cars while they exceed the speed limit. These are just a few instances in which children struggle with how to obey both their parents and God.

Since God commands that we have no other gods before him, God must come first and parents second. In Ephesians 6:1, Paul says children are to obey their parents "in the Lord." This means that children are to obey what their parents command, as long as their demands are in accord with the Lord's directions. Paul clarifies this idea in the fourth verse when he says, "Fathers, do not exasperate your children; instead, bring them up in the training and instruction of the Lord." In this way the apostle sets limits on the authority of parents. They are not to overstep their bounds and command their children to do something against God's will.

Jesus implied that there were limits to parental authority when he told his disciples: "For I have come to turn a man against his father, a daughter against her mother . . . Anyone who loves his father or mother more than me is not worthy of me" (Matthew 10:35-37). Within these verses Jesus describes what happens in a non-Christian home when a child accepts Christ over the objections of the parents. He warns us that there will be conflict or a "sword" between parents and their children. But no child should surrender his or her allegiance to Christ because the parents say to. This struggle occurred in Jesus' day, and it continues today.

In most instances children, especially young ones, should obey their parents. But when parents' commands oppose the Lord's, children must choose their direction and take the consequences. They can follow the Sixth Commandment *only* when the First Commandment has been properly obeyed.

Programming Ideas for Issue 1

Preparation—Inform parents that the group will discuss this issue. A letter or phone call will defuse reactions from parents and allay any fears they might have about their authority being undermined.

Read the materials ahead of time. On 3×5 cards write the five situations in the Program section. Gather Bibles, paper, pencils and an offering plate. Prepare several copies of Chart 1.

Opening—Ask for a show of hands of those who have had a disagreement with a parent within the past week. Ask individuals to share arguments they had over family rules or the authority of their parents.

Parental authority has always been a difficult issue for both parents and teenagers. Parents find it difficult to determine when their children pass from childhood into adulthood. And even when parents do recognize their kids' growth, it's still hard to stop making decisions for them. Teenagers naturally push against their parents' restraints, not only to make their own decisions, but also to test their abilities to function as independent adults.

Program—Divide into pairs and let each pair choose one of the situation cards you prepared ahead of time. (If your group has more than 10 kids, prepare more situation cards.) Encourage each team to read the card, talk about the situation and work out a role play based on the incident. Allow 15 to 20 minutes for this activity, and then have each team present its role play.

● A lawyer talks with his son about college. He wants his son to go into law, but his son wants to pursue a career as a commercial artist.

● A mother doesn't like her daughter's girlfriend. They talk over the situation, with the mother trying to convince her daughter to give up this particular friend.

● A parent smokes, but he is upset to learn his child was caught smoking at school. He orders the child to stop smoking, but . . .

● While cleaning her son's room, a mother finds a condom in her son's drawer. She confronts him with it and tries to find out what he's been up to. She orders him to change his ways, but he resists.

● The family has always had a strict midnight curfew for weekend events. Mike's friends get to stay out until 1 or

2 a.m. This Friday night he gives in to his friends' taunts and pleas and goes home at 1:30 a.m. His angry and frightened parents hear him come in and confront him.

At the end of each role play, ask the group members to comment and make suggestions about how they would resolve the conflict. Invite them to suggest other situations where teenagers run into conflict with their parents' authority. Talk about ways these conflicts have been resolved.

Response—Ask everyone to follow you as you read Ephesians 6:1-4. Then ask the groups to clarify the following concerns.

● To whom are these lines addressed?

● Why is "in the Lord" crucial to understanding what Paul means?

● What other restriction is placed on the father's authority?

● Why is this restriction necessary?

After this information has been clarified, allow about 20 minutes for the small groups to discuss the questions in Chart 1.

Pass out paper and pencils to each small group. Ask individuals to write one disagreement or complaint they have with their parents. Then ask them to write something they like or appreciate about their parents. Ask them to put their paper in the offering plate in the center of the room and form a circle around it. Ask your young people to thank God for those qualities they appreciate about their parents and pray for guidance and patience in working with problems that concern them.

Offer a brief prayer with a long moment for silent prayer. Close with a group "Amen."

Options:

1. Invite parents to join the youth group to debate the topic. Assign parents one side of the issue, and assign teenagers the other side. Proceed with the debate. Then continue the debate with parents and teenagers taking opposite sides of the issue.

Chart 1
Relationships With Parents

1. Which commandment do you think is most important: the First, "You shall have no other gods before me" or the Sixth, "Honor your father and your mother"?

2. Do you agree that sometimes these two commandments can conflict? If you or your friends have experienced this situation, share as much of an incident as you can.

3. How can we use this argument to justify disobeying our parents and merely satisfying our own desires? Jesus said, "For I have come to turn 'a man against his father, a daughter against her mother, a daughter-in-law against her mother-in-law—a man's enemies will be the members of his own household.' Anyone who loves his father or mother more than me is not worthy of me; anyone who loves his son or daughter more than me is not worthy of me" (Matthew 10:35-37). How have these words been misused, especially by cults? What do you think Jesus meant by this statement?

4. Have you done something against family rules and later discovered that your parents were right after all? Describe this experience.

5. If you are caught in a conflict with your parents, to whom do you turn for help? a brother, sister, grandparent, close relative, friend, neighbor, pastor, youth leader, teacher or some other person? What does this person offer you that you can't receive from your parents? Why *can't* you receive this from your parents?

6. If everyone in the family always did what he or she wanted and disregarded the parents, what would family life be like? What would happen to our society?

7. What rules or expectations in your home make sense? Which rules seem to be nothing but a lot of bother? How does your family deal with complaints or questions about rules? How would you like to see your family handle this kind of disagreement or discussion?

2. Invite grandparents to discuss the different views toward parental authority when they were parents. What was parental authority like when they were children? Ask the grandparents to share their opinions about parental authority today.

3. Use a panel of parents and teenagers to answer the discussion questions in Chart 1.

ISSUE 2

Should parents accept the reality of drinking, but make a covenant with their children not to drive after drinking?

YES, parents should accept the reality of drinking and come to an agreement with their children about how to handle their drinking habits.

"You mean your mom and dad know we're drinking?"

Lou was just ready to dial the phone, but responded to Brad: "Sure. We had a long talk about this when I turned 16. We agreed that I may drink as long as I don't get drunk. And if I have more than two drinks, I'm to call home for a ride."

"That's incredible. But it's after midnight. Won't they be mad?"

"No, that's part of the deal. They said they'd rather have *me* drag them out of bed than to have a policeman knock on their door to tell them I'd been in a wreck."

Drinking is part of our lives today. It's all around us, even at the high school level. Most teenagers have tried alcohol, and many drink regularly. Adults and adolescents alike have few parties without some form of alcoholic beverage.

Parents can try to deny the reality of their teenagers' drinking, but they are fighting a losing battle. If young people can't get alcohol at home, they will obtain it through their friends. Thus, parents should accept the reality of drinking rather than exert their energies to fight against its use.

Instead of making strict rules about not using alcohol or being around people who do, parents need to concern themselves with alcohol abuse. Try to establish rules like "No driving after two or more drinks." Parents and teenagers should work together and agree upon their expectations. Any violation should result in a loss of driving privileges or being grounded for a period of time.

Parents may agree to a covenant where they will provide safe transportation any time teenagers need assistance. The parents also agree to no lectures or hassles when they pick up their intoxicated children, no matter if their own teenagers or their driving friends have been drinking. However, parents and teenagers expect to talk with each other the next day about the problem. Sometimes young people agree to travel with a non-drinking designated driver who can drive them home. Teenagers can alternate this responsibility within their group.

This type of parental cooperation and understanding reduces the hypocrisy of both parents and teenagers. Young people will feel no need to sneak around or lie about their drinking habits. Sons and daughters will see that their parents can understand and support their efforts to handle alcohol responsibly.

NO, parents shouldn't accept the use of alcohol by their teenagers.

"Come on, Jan, have some fun. Just one little drink."

"No, thanks. I'm enjoying this ginger ale."

"But a drink will help you cut loose. You'll relax more and can enjoy the party."

"I *am* enjoying the party. Look, I don't have to drink alcohol to have fun. Besides, I don't need the hassle of getting caught or having an accident."

"Aw, nothing like that's going to happen. You really ought to have something instead of being so 'uptight' about it."

"Looks like *you're* the one who's 'uptight.' You seem a lot more bothered by my *not* drinking than I am by your drinking. I'll be all right, not just tonight, but tomorrow morning as well. And I won't have to lie to my parents if they ask what I did tonight."

Alcohol creates enough difficulties for adults. Whether parents drink or not, they should not allow their children to use alcohol. In fact, parents could present a more consistent position to their children if *they* would give up drinking.

At parties where beer and liquor flow freely, teenagers can be influenced easily. With their inhibitions lowered by alcohol, young people may do things they will regret later. It's one thing to decide at home that you will have only one or two drinks. But it's something else at a party where your friends urge you to have another. Comments such as "Come on. Don't be chicken!" are difficult for teenagers to brush aside.

Half of all automobile accidents involve drinking drivers, and a large percentage of these drivers are teenagers. Most high schools have at least one tragic story about a fatal car accident involving drunk teenagers.

Drinking leads to an easy loss of self-control, and the scripture warns us about this state. "Like a city whose walls are broken down is a man who lacks self-control" (Proverbs 25:28). Even if you aren't drinking but others in your group are, you may receive blame for something a member of your group did during a drunken moment. Thus, it's best not to attend such parties. To avoid even the appearance of evil can be a high price for teenagers to pay for being Christian, but perhaps this is what Jesus meant when he said to take up your cross daily (Luke 9:23). In the long run you will find that bearing your cross is worth much more than bearing the disease of alcoholism.

Programming Ideas for Issue 2

Preparation—Make arrangements for the youth group to attend an open meeting of Alcoholics Anonymous (AA), Al-Anon or Ala-Teen. Talk with a member of your local chapter to see which day is best and what to expect. Arrange transportation ahead of time and make sure all drivers know where you are going and how to get there.

Gather some pamphlets on alcohol and drinking from your local health and social service offices. Spread these out on a table for the kids to see as they come in to the meeting.

Prepare several copies of Chart 2.

Opening—Explain to the young people that they will soon be meeting people who have been through some difficult times because of alcohol abuse. Share some of the effects of addiction and how it touches the lives of individuals and their families. Ask God to support those who are about to share their stories and offer a prayer that each young person will be open to what he or she is about to hear.

Program—Ask the teenagers to divide in pairs and sit among the audience. Encourage kids and leaders to take notes for later reference. If there is a question-and-answer period during the AA meeting, encourage the young people to ask questions.

Be sure to stay for the refreshment and social period. Encourage your teenagers to mingle with the adults during this time and to listen carefully. Watch for shy teenagers who gather in cliques and link these young people up with an AA member.

Response—Plan to have a brief reaction period right after the meeting while the young people's thoughts are fresh. If there was no refreshment period, stop at a fast-food restaurant for a snack and some conversation. Ask the group members to discuss their experiences by using questions like these: Did any stories stand out for you? Which ones? Why? Did you hear any common themes running through the stories? When did the alcoholics *begin* to drink? When did alcohol become a problem for them?

Before dispersing, close with a brief prayer of thanksgiving for what everyone experienced.

Use the discussion questions in Chart 2 and the following Bible study suggestions for the next youth fellowship meeting. First read 1 Corinthians 6:12 and 1 Thessalonians 5:16-22. Divide the group into small groups of four to six people to facilitate discussion.

Options:

1. Invite speakers from organizations like SADD, MADD, AA or your local alcoholism information and treatment centers. These people are usually well-prepared to handle questions and discussions after their presentations.

For information from Mothers Against Drunk Driving

Chart 2
What Are You Thinking About Drinking?

1. How widespread is drinking among your classmates? Would you call it a problem? Why or why not? Are there parties where no alcohol is served? When alcoholic beverages are served, do parents know or condone this?

2. What starts teenagers drinking? What is the image of the drinker as seen by your peers? as portrayed in magazine ads? in films and on television? Do you or your friends drink to fit any of these images? How does drinking help to create that image?

3. Do you have an arrangement with your parents or friends to protect yourself if the driver of the car you are in begins to drink? What could you or your youth group do to foster a more mature attitude toward drinking and driving? What do you know about Students Against Driving Drunk (SADD) and Mothers Against Drunk Driving (MADD) and how they operate? Would these programs work for your group of friends?

4. Should parents or the church "lay down the law" on drinking? Do you think this position is necessary or hopeless in our society? What should the church do or say about drinking?

and Students Against Driving Drunk write:
- MADD, 669 Airport Freeway, Suite 310, Hurst, TX 76053.
- SADD, 110 Pleasant St., Marlboro, MA 01752.

2. In some areas there is a youth branch of these organizations in which teenagers are trained in psychodrama. Their brief dramas deliver their point without preaching and can lead to in-depth discussions within your group.

ISSUE 3

Should parents be responsible for the child of their minor-age adolescent?

YES, if a young mother wants to keep the baby, her parents should assume some basic responsibility for both the adolescent and her child.

When Laurel admitted she was pregnant, her parents were stunned. They realized something was wrong and had tried to get her to talk with them. She had been unusually tired and moody, her interest in school and extracurricular activities had dropped, and she had often burst into tears. After several weeks of this strong behavior, her mother scheduled a visit to the doctor—"just to find out if something is wrong." Laurel finally realized she had to tell.

"What do you want to do, Laurel?" her mom asked.

"I . . . I've been thinking about that a lot. I don't want to get an abortion, and I don't think I could stand to give the baby up for adoption. I think I want to keep it."

"What about Stewart? Is he willing to get married? Does he want to be a father and take on all those responsibilities?"

"No, I don't think so. We haven't seen much of each other since I told him I was pregnant. And I don't think I really love him.

"Mom . . . Dad, if I do decide to keep this baby, will you stand by me? I know I shouldn't have done what I did, and yet the baby may be the one good thing that comes from all this. I just don't feel I can give it away!"

The teenager has paid a price for her transgression: the shame and embarrassment of her unwed pregnancy. She will experience feelings of helplessness over what to do and criticism from her friends and relatives. Even if the father is still in the picture, the young couple probably cannot make it financially without help from their parents.

Parents are responsible for their child's welfare until she reaches 21. This responsibility includes helping her resolve her mistakes, as well as basking in the success of her worthwhile achievements.

Christian parents can positively influence both their daughter and their grandchild. Parents should refrain from an "I-told-you-so" attitude and genuinely forgive their child. Instead of offering unwanted advice, parents should make it clear they are willing to offer moral support or financial help whenever the child needs assistance. Above all, parents should provide prayerful support for the welfare of both the young mother and her child and seek God's will and guidance in the situation.

If the young parent cannot or will not raise her child, parents need to consider the situation prayerfully, especially if the baby is "dumped" on them. They will need to balance their feelings against their age, health, disposition and finances. Being responsible may mean giving up their daughter's child for adoption, if this action seems best for the baby's welfare.

Like it or not, parents are legally responsible for their child until age 21, even if she becomes a parent.

NO, parents should not be responsible for the child of their minor-age adolescent.

"Beth . . . Jim," Mr. Morgan began as he and Mrs. Morgan settled into their living room chairs. Their 16-year-old daughter sat on the couch with her young boyfriend. "It's good that you two finally told us what has happened. Your mother and I are tempted to launch into our I-told-you-so lecture, but we know that wouldn't do any good now."

"But," continued Mrs. Morgan, "we can at least help

you so you won't make an even greater mistake."

"Mom, getting married so that the baby will have a family isn't a mistake!" Beth interjected.

"Oh yes, it would be, young lady," her father replied. "Neither of you could finish high school, much less go on to college. And neither of you is prepared for *all* the responsibilities of being a parent or of being a husband or a wife."

"Dad, we think we are. We know it wouldn't be easy, but with your help . . . "

"That's just it. We won't help you make an even greater mistake. The sensible thing to do is to put up the baby for adoption and then get on with the rest of your lives. We will not help you financially if you keep on with this pipe dream of yours. If you get married, you'll have to assume responsibility and pay for the consequences on your own."

Part of growing up is accepting responsibility for our actions, good or bad. If a teenager becomes pregnant and decides not to marry the father of her child, she should relinquish the child for adoption. She is seldom in a stable emotional or financial position to care for a child. If she and the father decide to marry, they should accept full financial responsibility for themselves and their new baby, even if this means dropping out of school.

Overindulgent parents have spoiled too many young adults by bailing them out of their difficulties. These young people grow up to be adults who think the world owes them something. Since their parents' intervention saved them each time they made a mistake, they have never had to face the consequences of their bad decisions. This is not the way to build strong character.

Parents need to let their children know they love them, but at the same time they should refuse to step in and make it easy for their children to go against their training and advice. This might seem harsh at first, but in the long run it is best for everyone concerned, especially the young people.

Programming Ideas for Issue 3

Preparation—Recruit four or five adults to participate in a panel presentation on teenage pregnancy. Try to include some of the following professionals: a doctor, lawyer, youth counselor, psychologist, pastor, staff member for an adoption agency or counselor at a pregnancy clinic. A parent and a teenage mother who have experienced this issue would contribute greatly to such a panel. Make sure you provide a list of expectations for your panel members and give them ample time to prepare their material. Alert them to the type of audience they will have.

Ask each panel member to speak to the issue for five to eight minutes. Let the panel members know that a moderator will keep track of their time. Inform them that a card will be held up when they have one minute left and again when 30 seconds remain. Remind them that there will be a question-and-answer session after all the speakers have made their presentations.

Before you introduce your panel members, check with them to reconfirm their names and the positions they hold.

Investigate the current statistics for teenage pregnancy and the options available to these young people. Write this information on a sheet of newsprint to use during the opening.

Gather paper and pencils, and pass these out as your group members arrive so they can take notes and write their questions or comments as they listen to the panel. Prepare several copies of Chart 3. You will also need a doll.

Opening—Ask the group members to talk about the options available to teenage girls who find themselves pregnant. Some get married and begin their families right away. Others decide on abortions. Many have their babies and give them up for adoption. Some stay single and keep their babies. Remind the group that this is a serious subject affecting more and more teenagers.

Program—Present the current statistics about teenage pregnancies, and then introduce the panel members. After the panel's presentations, give the group a few minutes to write questions they would like to ask the panel. If some are more comfortable asking their questions aloud, offer that option, too.

Response—After the question-and-answer session, divide the group into smaller groups of four to six individuals to discuss the questions in Chart 3.

After 20 minutes ask the small groups to bring their chairs and form a circle. Bring a doll to the circle. Ask that each person think about how wonderfully formed an infant is, how tremendously helpless, and how totally dependent upon others for every need.

Ask one of the young people to read Romans 5:6. Say, "Just as Christ died for us while we were helpless to save ourselves, so parents must 'die' to their own needs so that a

---

Chart 3
Who Is Responsible?

1. In what way should we be responsible for our own actions?

2. Does it really help when parents bail us out every time we get into trouble? How can parents help without destroying our integrity?

3. Do you know someone who has had a baby and kept it? How is she handling the situation? What has she had to give up? What has she gained?

4. If you're in a tempting situation with your boyfriend or girlfriend, what can you do to curb the passionate feelings that arise? What can give you the strength or courage to say "No" and stick to that decision?

5. Do you think the emphasis on sex in films, television and ads is part of the problem? Why or why not? What can the church or the youth group do to prepare teenagers better for dating and courtship?

child can grow into a whole and healthy human being."
Offer a prayer of thanksgiving for those young people who
have small children. Ask that God will help those present to
recognize their responsibility for their own lives and the
lives of those they choose to bring into this world.

Options:

1. Instead of using the panel presentations, give each
young person an egg, a balloon or a 5-pound bag of flour
the week before this session. Instruct the teenagers that for
the next week they are to pretend that this object is their
baby. They cannot leave the "child" untended night or
day. They must either take it with them or arrange to pay
for a babysitter when they go out.

Suggest that the kids keep a journal to register their
feelings and experiences. Talk about this at the next meeting. Then use the questions from Chart 3 to facilitate discussion.

2. This issue often neglects the responsibilities and
needs of the adolescent father. Investigate the parents'
responsibility for the young man who is struggling with
"doing what is right." The issue is still parental responsibility, but the needs are different.

The young father may be struggling with several decisions—marriage, adoption, abortion and even parenthood, if
the girl doesn't want to keep the child and he does. Parents
will need to examine their feelings and responsibilities in relation to both financial and emotional support.

3. Invite a nurse to your group to discuss the cost and
care of raising a baby. Be sure to explain the purpose for
your request, including any specific information your group
needs or wants.

4. A social worker could add insight into the growing
problem of teenage pregnancy. Ask this person to present
some of the social issues involved as well as speak to the
emotional struggles we have already mentioned.

5. Assign individuals in the group to go to a supermarket and the infant section of a department store. Have them

price baby food, diapers, clothing, infant furniture and a car seat.

Ask someone else to contact a medical clinic to discover the typical costs for prenatal care, delivery and infant care for one year, including checkups, shots and medication. Share this information at a meeting and discuss the questions in Chart 3.

ISSUE 4

Should youth workers, teachers, counselors or doctors ever tell parents what a teenager told them in confidence?

YES, those working with young people should let parents know if a teenager shares something that is harmful to his or her life.

"Jenny, I'm pleased that you came to talk with me about your problem. You don't need to deal with this alone."

"It's just that I haven't been able to tell anyone, except Terri, my best friend. She's the one who urged me to come see you."

"Well, she's right. I had noticed at the fellowship meetings that you weren't as cheerful and outgoing as usual. But you should have come several weeks ago, rather than carry this burden around all this time."

"I know. Right now I just wish I'd never gone to dinner with Tom that night so I wouldn't have seen my dad with that woman."

"But you did. And now we have to think about what to do. Have you talked to your father about what you saw?"

"Oh no! I can't say anything to him. I don't even like to look at him!"

"But is it fair to assume something was going on without even talking to your dad? You're destroying your relationship with him without knowing the facts. And if there *is* a problem between your parents, this experience may help them decide to get help.

"Why not talk with your dad first, Jenny? I'll go with you, if you'd like."

There are times when an adult working with a teenager needs to break the code of confidentiality and let the parents in on a teenager's concern. The young person may be on drugs or alcohol. He or she may be part of an unwanted pregnancy. The adult might suspect the teenager is suffering from some form of a mental disorder. Perhaps a serious problem at home is affecting the son or daughter in ways the parents don't suspect.

The relationship between parents and their children is primary. Both scripture and society make parents responsible for their children until they are legally adults. Parents also have the right to know about something important to their children's physical, emotional and spiritual well-being, including their children's sexual activity.

Parents should handle this knowledge in a mature way. The adult working with the young person could offer some helpful advice and assistance to the parents, but the parents have the main burden of dealing with their teenager. At a time when much parental authority and responsibility is threatened, those working with young people should not add to the trend by withholding information.

The adult should talk with the teenager first and suggest that he or she talks with his or her parents. Together they should explore the consequences of telling versus not telling. They should also consider the consequences of delay. When the teenager is aware of his or her choices, he or she can see more clearly what has to be done. The adult can volunteer to accompany the teenager to help explain or calm the situation, but the teenager must recognize the fact that one way or another, the parents must know.

If the teenager still refuses to talk with his or her parents, the adult can find more than one way to inform them. For example, he or she could invite all parents to a youth meeting where that young person's concern or problem would be presented by a speaker or a film. The experience may stimulate conversation between the child and his or her parents so resolution can begin.

In extreme cases, the adult might talk with the parents and make them promise they will not tell their child that they know about the problem. This alternative helps the parents be more sensitive to the situation and quietly allows them to find a way of correcting the situation. No matter how this is handled, the parents must be brought into the picture, since it is their troubled child.

NO, when a young person shares something in confidence, there is no excuse for breaking that confidence, even if parents should know.

"Matt, you see a lot of our son Larry in your work with the youth group. Lately, he's been excessively moody and hard to live with. Have you heard anything about what might be troubling him?"

"Yes, I've noticed the change in him, too, Mr. Johnson. In fact, Larry dropped by several times to talk. He is troubled. I've been urging him to talk with you about his concerns."

"Larry and I haven't hit it off too well the past few years. We seem to get on each other's nerves. I suppose it isn't too surprising that he hasn't come to me, but I am his father and I do love him. Can you tell me what it is that's bothering him so?"

"I'm sorry, Mr. Johnson. But before Larry would open up to me about his problem, I had to promise that I wouldn't tell anyone, not even you."

"Look, Matt, I realize your position. Promises are important, but right now it's more important that I know what's bothering my own son. Now either tell me, or I'll go to Pastor Lowry about this!"

Nothing would destroy a teenager's trust more quickly than to have the adult betray his or her confidence, no matter how well-intentioned the act might be. A young person needs to have an adult outside the home with whom he or she can talk. That individual needs to be someone who will not lecture or laugh at him or her and certainly will not tell someone else what he or she has shared in confidence.

Betraying a confidence would also destroy the effectiveness of the adult with the rest of the group. Word of what happened would soon spread. The teenagers might forgive the adult, but they wouldn't forget. Nor would they be likely to open up to that person again.

In this case, two valid principles clash—the right of parents to know about their children and the right of a youth worker to have a confidential relationship with a young person. Both rights are important and should be upheld. But in this case the right of the person working with the young person should prevail over that of the parents.

The adult should continue to talk with the teenager and try to convince him or her that the parents should be brought into the situation. But if the teenager doesn't want to do this, the youth worker must respect his or her wishes.

Without a young person's permission, betraying a confidence can only worsen the problem. There are situations in which a young person needs help and doesn't realize it or cannot admit it; however, telling the parents is not the solution. Young people must not look at their adult leaders, doctors or confidants as policemen or paid informers.

Programming Ideas for Issue 4

Preparation—Gather the following items: a tape recorder, a tape player, a blank tape, paper and markers. Record songs like "Help!" by the Beatles, "You've Got a Friend" or "Stand by Me" by various artists.

Prepare individual signs, approximately 8½ × 11 inches, for each of the following people: Mom, Dad, teacher, coach, youth leader, Sunday school teacher, doctor, nurse, pastor, scout leader, employer, neighbor, boss, relative, other. Tape these signs onto the walls around the meeting room. Make copies of Chart 4.

Opening—Play the tape of songs you prepared as the group gathers. Begin the meeting by saying: "At times we all get into situations where we need help. Tonight we will explore the topic of whom we can turn to for help."

Program—Ask the group to look at the signs around the room. Say: "These are some of the adults with whom you have frequent contact. Choose the one you would go to first if you had a drug problem." After everyone has chosen a sign, ask individuals to spend three to five minutes telling the others in the group why he or she chose this person. If there is no one else at the sign, have the person talk with someone from another category where there are just a few people.

Next, ask everyone to move to the sign that indicates who he or she would talk to if he or she had a sexual problem. Again ask the small groups to take a few minutes to share with each other *why* that individual was chosen.

Ask the groups to move to the front and share some of the reasons for the choices they made. Have the kids talk about *why* they would turn to these adults for help and not to others. Write these reasons on a sheet of newsprint large enough for all to see. Ask the group to rank these reasons in order of importance.

Point out whether the list mentions confidentiality and trust. Ask how many think these two qualities are important when they need to talk with someone about something serious.

Ask the group to recall if parents were first on anyone's list. Talk about why parents might be or might not be first on most kids' list. How would you feel if the person you confided in told your parents? Could you go to that person again with a problem? Why or why not?

Ask the young people to divide into small groups of four or five to discuss the questions found in Chart 4.

Response—Tell the group: "All of us have times when our troubles seem overwhelming. The Psalmist reminds us we can trust God." Ask one of your young people to read Psalm 27:1, 7-10.

Continue: "God meets us in the scripture and in our prayers, but he also comes to us through our relationships with other people, especially through an experienced or trained adult whom we can trust." Play the song "Stand by Me" or "You've Got a Friend."

Tell the kids: "An adult can be this kind of friend. Rather than trying to face a serious problem alone, reach out for others' understanding and the help they can bring."

Close with a prayer like the following: "Lord God, you are our shepherd, our light and our salvation. Thank you that you do not call us to walk our lonesome valleys alone. Thank you for giving us caring people to help us understand and wrestle with our difficulties. When we have troubles, give us the courage to seek out these caring individuals and find the strength to share our heartaches.

"Remove any barriers that separate us from those close to us. Make us one with each other and with you. We ask

---

Chart 4
Secrets and Confidentiality

1. Why do parents believe they have the right to know everything about their children? Why do children resist this? Who do you think is right? Why?

2. Does the need for confidentiality apply to a doctor-teenage patient relationship? What about the relationship between a teenager and the youth worker or pastor?

3. If a son or daughter chooses to keep a secret, what does this do to the family relationship? Is this choice in conflict with the commandment, "Honor your father and mother"? How?

4. If you can't tell your parents you're in trouble, would you keep it to yourself and try to work it out? How does Galatians 6:1-2 relate to this situation? Do you think your church or your youth group is this kind of burden-sharing fellowship? Why or why not?

this in the name of him who died that all barriers might come down, Jesus Christ, our Lord. Amen.''

Options:

1. Arrange for a panel composed of a parent, a counselor and two teenagers. Ask these individuals to present their views on the issue. Allow each person five minutes to speak. Let the panel members react to one another, and then open the discussion to the audience. Invite parents to this session.

2. Is there a point where doctors who believe in confidentiality with their patient can or must change their stance on this issue? What should a physician do when an adolescent's sexual experiences have produced a health problem that may be critical if treatment is not immediate and that treatment requires parental permission?

ISSUE 5

Should parents limit their child's stressful activities?

YES, parents should exercise some control over their child's stressful activities.

"Mom, I feel better. I think I'll be able to go to school tomorrow."

"Don't count on it, Mary Ann. You're still weak from the flu. You've been running just too much."

"But the tryouts for cheerleading are tomorrow! And there's a dance at school I'm supposed to help with."

"I'm sorry, but you're not going. In fact, you'll be dropping out of everything but two activities."

"What? You must be kidding."

"No, I'm not kidding, young lady. This year you've spread yourself through the drama club, the Spanish club, your sorority, the volleyball team and everything else. You obviously don't know when to say 'No,' so I'm saying it for you. I'd much rather have you angry with me than ruin your health."

High school offers numerous activities—band, sports, drama, clubs and a host of opportunities for socializing. Then there are homework, part-time jobs, hobbies, church, friends and leisure activities. Many teenagers become so busy they could use a social secretary, which is what the rest of the family members become since they are the ones taking messages and marking the calendar for appointments and events.

This kind of involvement may not be a problem unless illness occurs or activities generate anxiety. The teenager may experience concern about grades or huge amounts of homework. He or she may worry about a problem within a relationship or may struggle with how he or she can get everything done. This anxiety results in stress and may produce poor performance. If the stress intensifies, it can spill over into other areas of life as well. The family may notice this anxiety in the teenager's irritability or withdrawal.

Since the teenager may not recognize what is going on, the parents must step in. They might risk their child's displeasure, but for the sake of his or her health, sometimes parents must intervene and take their child out of an activity or insist that he or she turn down a new one.

Many times the teenager wants to back out of an activity, but feels embarrassed to do so. He or she doesn't want to incur the displeasure of a teacher or peers. The teenager may not admit this to his or her parents, but may be secretly relieved when the parent says "No." He or she now is free to point to the parent as the cause for dropping out or declining an invitation.

NO, parents should not interfere with their child's stressful activities.

"Lyle, aren't you going to eat supper with us?"

"Sorry, Mom, I forgot about play practice."

"But Lyle, we never see you any more, not even at supper time."

"That's the way it goes. There's so much to do. See

you la—"

"No, Lyle, sit down! Play practice can wait. Your mother and I are worried about you."

"Dad, I'm fine. Don't worry about me. I can handle things. Now I really must go. See you later."

"Okay, but remember we're both available when and if you want to talk about your heavy schedule. If the pace gets to be too much for you, we're here to help you sort things out."

Part of growing up is learning to make decisions for oneself. Parents should advise their teenagers, but not take over their decisions. The teenage years have always been a stressful time with new knowledge to learn, body changes that occur at an alarming rate, increased expectations from teachers and family, and the problems of living in a crazy world that seems to care and then blames that generation for most of its problems. Teenagers don't need the additional stress of parents trying to run their lives.

Instead of stepping in and telling teenagers what to do, parents should sit down and talk with their children about their schedules. They could point to situations where stress is affecting grades, relationships with other family members, or levels of performance in activities. Parents might suggest that their teenagers chart their activities for a week, including their preparation time. This chart may help teenagers realize why their parents are concerned and allow them to recognize how over-scheduled they really are.

By sharing their concern and using reason, parents will probably get further with their teenagers than by forcing changes. In this way teenagers can grow as they learn how to evaluate their situation; they may even accept the results more easily. The decision to alter their schedules will be based on a shared concern rather than a unilateral decree from parents.

Programming Ideas for Issue 5

Preparation—Invite a doctor or other expert to talk

about stress. Ask him or her to explain what stress is and how it affects young people and their families. Perhaps he or she can offer suggestions on how to avoid stress and how to cope with it when it occurs. Set a time limit on this talk of no more than 15 minutes.

Gather the following items: Bibles, paper, pencils, newsprint and markers. Prepare a sheet of newsprint for the opening with the following headings: "I worry about . . . " List two or three items that you know your kids worry about such as taking tests, getting into college, getting along with friends and so on.

Opening—As your young people arrive, encourage them to add to the list of things they worry about. Before the program begins, look over the list together and add any additional concerns the kids may have.

Program—Say: "All of us have been under stress, no matter how old we are. Our speaker tonight will talk to us about what stress is and how it affects us. He (or she) will also tell us how to avoid stress and how to deal with it when it occurs."

Introduce your speaker.

Response—Pass out paper and pencils and have the members of the group list all their activities in a typical two- or three-week period.

● Ask them to star those activities that are most enjoyable.

● Have them underline those activities or situations that create problems. Ask the group to share some of the problems these activities cause. List the problems on newsprint. Looking at others' problems may help young people recognize their own struggles.

● Ask individuals to rank activities according to their importance. If there is a need to cut back on activities, this ranking will indicate which activities they could give up.

How can our faith help in stressful situations? Divide the group into two parts. Ask one part to scan the Gospel of Mark and see what a hectic life Jesus and his disciples led. In one instance Mark says they were surrounded by so many people that they didn't have a chance to eat (Mark 3:20). Notice how often that impatient word "immediately" comes up. What did Jesus do to keep his equilibrium? (See Mark 1:40-45; 2:1-12; 3:7-12.)

Ask the second part of the group to scan the Psalms to see if they present any insights into the problem of stress. One way to cover the book of Psalms is to ask individuals to look through five to 20 Psalms, the number depending on how many people you have. After 15 minutes, ask individuals to report back to their small group and share their findings.

Bring both groups together, listing the relative verses on a sheet of newsprint for all to share.

Ask the expert to lead the group on a fantasy journey of relaxation or introduce them to biofeedback techniques. Or instruct the group in some relaxation or meditation techniques. Ask the group members to think about ways they can work prayer and quiet time into their own schedules.

Read Psalm 46 while the group members sit or lie down with their eyes closed. Join hands in a circle and pray the Lord's Prayer. Sing "Be Still, My Soul" from *Songs* (Songs and Creations) to close this session.

Options:

1. After all of this, young people's opinions may still vary considerably on whether parents should limit their children's activities. A debate would be an effective way to clarify individuals' positions and would provide group members a way to see how this issue applies to them.

2. Instead of merely presenting an expert and his or her opinions, some groups may be more receptive to a panel of two parents, two teenagers and an expert. Some groups may respond more to this form of personal involvement and fewer facts and recommendations. With some guidance and planning, the panel can present as much information, but the format may be more interesting, especially to younger groups.

FRIENDSHIP ISSUES

Next to parents, friends are the most important people in a teenager's life. In fact, many perplexed parents find that their child's friends seem more important to him or her than they are. Certainly the opinions and ideas of other teenagers count for more at this stage of a child's life. It is a rare teenager who would choose to spend an evening with his or her parents if friends are available.

In a recent survey, Dr. Peter Benson of Search Institute found that teenagers spend 55 percent of their time with their friends and only 13 percent of their time with their parents. Because of the intensity of peer relationships, a teenager's friends can work good or wreak havoc in his or her life. Many teenagers have been misled into smoking, drinking, drugs or sex because of the influence of their friends. Others have been helped by their friends to uphold their convictions and strengthen their resolve in the midst of personal trials. The following issues provide opportunities for your young people to explore the important topic of friendship in the context of their Christian faith.

ISSUE 6
Should a Christian acknowledge or report his or her friend's actions when the friend cheats at school?

YES, a Christian should take a stand against his or her friend's cheating at school.

"Did you see Bill sneak in his notes for the test?"

"Yes, I sure did, and this time I'm going to call him on it. I'm fed up with his cheating!"

"Are you kidding? You'll only get him mad at you."

"Maybe so, but I don't think it's right. I also want him to know that he's not fooling anyone."

"Don't be stupid! He'll not only get down on you, but he'll get everyone else to think you're crazy, too. Do you want him to turn the whole senior class against you?"

Christians must always hold the highest moral standards. We cannot go along with friends who cheat nor can we just look the other way. Cheating is wrong; it damages the cheater as well as the rest of the class. A successful cheater will be tempted to take shortcuts throughout life without spending the time and energy needed to gain what he or she wants in a legitimate way.

Classmates are also injured when the cheater receives the same reward they do without any of the same effort. If the class operates on a curve, the cheater's actions may alter the curve so that classmates' grades may be lowered.

A Christian friend should go first to the cheater to let him or her know that people are aware of what is going on. The friend should point out to the cheater how wrong his or her actions are and urge him or her to stop. If the cheater agrees, promises to stop and then follows through with this decision, the matter should end there. But if the cheater scoffs at the friend's efforts and continues to cheat, the Christian should take further action. He or she should warn the cheater that if the cheating continues, he or she will report the action to the teacher or school authorities.

At first it is probably best not to give the name of the cheater to the teacher. An anonymous note suggesting that the teacher keep close watch on the class should be enough to discourage the cheater. The Christian friend could also enlist some mutual friends to talk with the cheater, urging him or her to quit. There are numerous creative ways for a Christian to help his or her friend put an end to the cheating.

If other classmates go along with the cheating, either by approving it or keeping quiet out of fear, the Christian should still take a stand. Even though it is difficult to stand up against a group and refuse to go along with what is wrong, it is necessary to protect schools and society from immoral practices.

NO, a Christian is responsible for no one's actions other than his or her own.

"Mark, thanks for staying to talk with me. You sit next to Bill in this class. Did you notice anything unusual or not quite right yesterday?"

"What do you mean, Mrs. Hancock?"

"Well, I've just graded the test papers for this chapter. Bill answered 23 out of 25 questions correctly. Yesterday he was failing; now he's at the top of the class. I'm also suspicious now about the disturbance he created yesterday during the test."

"I don't know anything about that. We did study together the night before. I guess we just went over the right material."

"Maybe so, Mark. But I must tell you I'm concerned, not just about this one test, but I'm really concerned about Bill. If he's getting away with something now, his cheating could alter his behavior from this point on. You're his friend; I know because I see you both in Sunday school together. I don't want to put you under any pressure, but I do want you to know I care—about both of you."

"Well, I . . . uh . . . I . . . "

"Mark, are you aware of something I need to know?

"Uh, no. I don't . . . I . . . I can't say anymore 'cause I don't know anything! Really!"

Cheating is so widespread among young people that the best a Christian can do is refuse to participate. Many students receive little training at home and have no church connections, so they become easy prey for the "anything-goes" philosophy.

There will always be cheating and other forms of wrongdoing; it's simply human nature. The Christian has to get along in this world without indulging in its evil practices. We should say "No" to those who want to look at our tests or who ask for answers during a test. We should also talk with them after the test to tell them why we think cheating is wrong.

But we should not go beyond this point to report the cheater. This action would create even more problems than it would solve. "No one likes a tattletale!" We've heard this statement all our lives. Even our parents have told us this because it's true! Since people look down on tattletales, we should not tell on someone who cheats. We can pray for the cheater and hope for the best, but in the long run cheating is the cheater's problem. His or her actions damage only himself or herself. In the end the cheater will be found out and receive a just reward.

Programming Ideas for Issue 6

Preparation—Prepare a 20-question Bible quiz to read or duplicate ahead of time. Use questions like the following:

1. How many books are in the Old Testament? (39)

2. How many books are in the New Testament? (27)

3. Name the first five books of the Bible. (Genesis, Exodus, Leviticus, Numbers, Deuteronomy)

4. Name the four Gospels. (Matthew, Mark, Luke, John)

5. Who received the Ten Commandments from God? (Moses)

6. Out of what country did Moses bring his people to freedom? (Egypt)

7. Who became the leader of the Hebrews when Moses died? (Joshua)

8. Name the wizard called to curse Israel. (Balaam)

9. Who was the second king of Israel? (David)

10. What were the men called who denounced the sins of the kings and the people? (Prophets)

11. Name three of these critics. (Among others, Isaiah,

Jeremiah, Ezekiel, Elijah, Samuel, Daniel, Amos, Hosea)

12. What was an agreement between God and his people called? (A covenant)

13. Where was Jesus born? (Bethlehem)

14. Who came before Jesus to prepare his way? (John the Baptist)

15. What was Jesus' Hebrew title? (The Messiah)

16. What was Peter's and Andrew's profession before Jesus called them to be his disciples? (Fishermen)

17. What does Cephas or Peter mean? (Rock)

18. Who is Beelzebub? (The prince of demons, also the name Jesus' enemies called him)

19. Who became the great apostle to the Gentiles? (Paul)

20. Were the first witnesses to the Resurrection men or women? (Women; see the last chapter of each of the Gospels)

On a small card, prepare a crib sheet for the cheater. Ask one of your young people to "cheat" on the Bible quiz so that only one or two other people notice. Give the card to the person *before* the actual meeting so no one sees you talking to the cheater ahead of time.

Gather newsprint, markers, paper, pencils, Bibles and the prize for the winner of the Bible quiz. Be sure the prize is something that can be divided among the group members at the end of the session such as a box of candy bars or a case of soft drinks.

On newsprint, prepare the list of experiences in which cheating can occur from the Program section of this issue. Leave space after each idea for students' responses. Post this list on the wall prior to the meeting and cover with a blank piece of newsprint.

Opening—Announce the Bible quiz and display the prize for the winner. Pass out pencils and paper, and ask everyone to number from one to 20.

Give the quiz. The "cheater" should quietly steal a look at the crib sheet ever so often. Some may notice the cheating and try to inform you about what is going on. Ignore these warnings or defend the cheater, saying you're sure he or she wouldn't do such a thing.

Have the young people exchange papers and place a check next to the answers that are wrong. Read the questions again and let the students answer the questions. Offer the correct answer only if no one else can come up with the answer. Collect the answer sheets immediately. Without spending much time looking through the papers, announce the winner—the cheater, of course, and give him or her the prize.

Now, deal with the objections others may have. There should be plenty. If no one caught the cheater, have him or her lay the crib sheet down or place it in an obvious location so someone will see it. Deal with the other group members' feelings. Ask what would happen if this occurred at school. Would anyone have publicly objected? Why or why not?

Program—Remove the cover sheet and ask the group members to look over the list of experiences in which cheating can occur. Ask the group members to think of ways people could cheat in each of the experiences listed. Record these ideas on the newsprint you have posted on the wall.

Ways people could cheat:

On a school test
On a boyfriend or girlfriend
On a construction project
In a political office
On an income tax form
On an expense-account report
In a construction project

In a sports contest
At the auto garage
At a checkout register
As a treasurer of a club or organization
In a laboratory experiment
In a survey of public opinion

Ask the group questions such as the following: In what ways are others hurt by such cheating? What would it do to public trust if such cheating became widespread? What kind of a society would we become if cheating became acceptable? What are some forms of cheating we see in the news today? How have these actions affected our society?

Response—Ask everyone to turn to Exodus 20:1-17. Ask which of the Ten Commandments cheating violates. Have the kids explain their answers.

Conclude this part by discussing these questions: If cheating is stealing, why is the person who reports the cheater more likely to be looked down on than the cheater? Is this true in your school? What can be done about it? Can you think of ways to stop a person from cheating without "telling on" the person?

Divide the candy bars or soft drinks among all the group members. Remind them that when we value honesty and display the courage to speak out for what is right, we all become winners. Close with a prayer of thanksgiving for those who follow the path of honesty regardless of the consequences. Pray for those who struggle with the easy way out. Ask for God's guidance as the group members strive to model Christ's values.

Options:

1. Invite an experienced teacher or teachers to talk about what they have seen and done over the years about cheating. Ask them to talk about what has happened to some of the students they knew as cheaters, without naming names, of course! Ask the teacher or teachers to respond to the issue of the tattletale and how responsible students should handle the cheater.

2. Instead of beginning with a Bible quiz, divide the group into two competing teams for games and activities. Quietly let one team know they should do everything they can to win all the games and relays. Ask them to be subtle, but consistent in their efforts to win. Shower the cheaters with prizes. Discuss everyone's feelings.

ISSUE 7
Is it right for Christians to date non-Christians?

YES, it is right for Christians to date non-Christians.

"Grace, don't hang up! Please! Last night I did get carried away. I know how you feel about making out. You made that clear from the beginning. I *am* sorry, but you looked so good in that green dress, and we had been having such a great time. I just wanted to let you know that I really cared about you. If you can forgive me, I promise I'll never try anything again. Grace, I don't know what else I can say. I'm just really sorry I upset you."

"I want to believe you, David. In fact, I do believe you. It's not that I didn't *want* to go all the way with you, but I just can't do that yet. I've been raised to believe that sex should be saved for marriage, for that special relationship of commitment and respect. You know I feel very deeply for you, but I just can't share that part of me until marriage. I guess I panicked because my feelings were strong, too."

"I know, and I respect you for your stand. Your faith was one of the things that attracted me to you. It made you stand out from the other girls I was dating. I want to talk more about what you believe, but I feel uncomfortable talking about this over the phone. Can I come over or meet you at the pizza place? You've never pushed religion on me, and I've never asked about it. But I'd like to hear more now. Whatever kept you on an even keel last night must be something."

It is often difficult for students at school to know whether the person they are attracted to is a Christian or not. Our society promotes many Christian values, but individual choices and commitments may not be evident immediately. Christians are responsible for maintaining their faith and moral values in all relationships.

If Christian youth date only other believers, they may make their religion seem narrow, smug or even self-righteous to those outside the church. Sometimes the only view others have of the church occurs within their dating relationships with Christian young people. The Christian partner has an excellent opportunity to witness to the truth and power of the Christian faith, but he or she should be careful not to push religion on the non-Christian. There will be many opportunities during a date to share one's faith—after a movie or TV program, while listening to or talking about a new song, and when sharing stories about friends or school situations. All kinds of experiences provide opportunities for the Christian to share his or her faith with the non-Christian.

There are too many barriers in the world now. Walls divide races, classes and nationalities. The church must not erect another wall to relationships by forbidding its young people to date those who are not Christians. Recognizing the problems of such barriers ahead of time can help Christian young people prepare for dating non-Christians.

NO, it is not right for Christians to date non-Christians.

"No, Steve, you know I can't go out tonight."

"Aw, come on, Sharon. Brad's having a big party."

"No, it's youth fellowship night. I've already missed the last two meetings in order to see you. They'll think I've dropped out."

"So what? Who needs that group? Brad's is where the real action will be tonight. His parents will be gone, and we'll have the whole place to ourselves."

"I . . . I don't think that's such a good idea—not with all the drinking. Tom will probably be there passing out drugs, too.

"Steve, it's obvious we don't want the same things. Perhaps if you came to youth fellowship you could see why it's important to me. For now, though, I think we'd better just agree to be good friends."

There are enough problems for teenagers in dating relationships without adding further complications. Paul's command to the Corinthians is still valid today: "Do not be yoked together with unbelievers. For what do righteousness and wickedness have in common? Or what fellowship can light have with darkness?" (2 Corinthians 6:14).

The non-Christian may weaken or corrupt the faith and

morals of the Christian so that the latter falls away from the faith. Because the dating experience is often an emotional one, Christians may be tempted to do things they know are not right out of fear for losing their partners.

Christian young people should look for their dating partners within the church. In this way they can be reasonably certain they will find someone who shares a common love for God that results in a relationship that will bind them together rather than separate them. When young people share similar priorities in their lives, they may find they also have similar beliefs about sex, marriage, commitment, responsibilities, family, etc. Christians definitely should not date non-Christians, for their stakes in the future are far too high to take such risks in relationships.

Programming Ideas for Issue 7

Preparation—For about a month before this meeting, ask your group members to bring magazines from home. Ask them to include some of those written specifically for teenagers, plus some of the glamor, sports and men's adventure publications. (It's a good idea to collect and keep various magazines—they provide lots of programming possibilities.)

Gather newsprint, markers, pens and a Bible for each participant. Cut two strips of newsprint, each about 7 feet long.

Opening—Place magazines around the room for the kids to peruse when they arrive. Ask your young people to look through several publications for articles or advertisements that describe the ideal man or woman in our society.

After about 10 minutes let each person share his or her findings with the others. Use the following questions to stimulate further discussion: According to these publications, what is important in life? Are any Christian values upheld or negated? Explain. How could a Christian relate to a person who "bought" the values of these magazines? What can a Christian do in the world depicted in these publications?

Program—Ask for a show of hands of those who have

dated non-Christians as well as Christians. Discuss the fact that in today's world many people have no connection with a church. Let the group know this session will deal with some of the concerns that can arise when Christians and non-Christians are attracted to each other as dating partners.

Divide the group into boys and girls and ask the groups to meet on opposite sides of the room. Have a member of each group lie down on a long sheet of newsprint while the others make an outline of his or her body. Tape the boy's body outline on the girls' side of the room and the girl's body outline on the boys' side of the room. Ask the two groups to list the qualities they look for in a prospective date on the body outlines. For example, on the boy's hand, the girls might list "friendly," to indicate they like guys who reach out to be friendly. Or on the girl's head, the boys might list "intelligent," to indicate they like girls who are smart.

After the groups have completed their lists, have them circle those qualities that are desirable for the ideal boy or ideal girl.

Bring the boys and girls back together and compare lists. Don't worry if some of the clowns have listed some funny items; allow them to express themselves. Suggest that if those items are what they're really looking for, that's their choice. Ask the groups to respond to each other's lists. How valid do the various items seem? Did anyone mention the faith of the person—whether or not he or she is a Christian? Why or why not? Are most of the items on the lists physical? If there are general terms like "nice personality," press the groups to define these more specifically. What about characteristics that are associated with being a Christian such as truthfulness, compassion, caring, gentleness, purity, loyalty and so on?

Response—Ask one of your young people to read aloud Galatians 5:19-24. Ask the group:

1. How many "works of the flesh" are glamorized in today's society and regarded as positive qualities? Share some specific examples.

2. What are the problems of dating a non-Christian? Can these be handled by a teenager? (Some teenagers who are dating may want to share their experiences at this point.)

3. Read 2 Corinthians 6:14—7:1. Why would Paul give such a command to the Christian church in Corinth? What does this scripture say to us now? Is Paul's viewpoint too narrow for today? How can we avoid falling into intolerance and smug self-righteousness?

4. How can dating be a means of presenting a positive image of what it is to be a Christian?

After briefly summarizing the discussion, ask the group to form a prayer circle. Invite the young people to pray silently for the friends they are dating or those individuals who are special to them. Offer thanks for these relationships and ask for strength and guidance in how to glorify God within these friendships. Close the session by singing, "They Will Know We Are Christians by Our Love" from *Songs* (Songs and Creations).

Options:

1. Videotape a typical Friday or Saturday evening of TV commercials. Use the videotape to introduce the session in place of the magazines.

2. Divide the group into smaller groups of three to five people, including both boys and girls. Have them cut out examples from the magazines to create the ideal man and the ideal woman. Have them glue heads, bodies, arms and legs on a sheet of newsprint to represent these ideal people. Ask the groups each to talk about their creations. Ask them to talk about what's missing from these pictures. Discuss the fact that "ideal" can be a relative term.

ISSUE 8

Should a Christian remain loyal to his or her friends when they want to do something the Christian thinks is wrong?

YES, the Christian should stay with his or her friends when they intend to do something wrong, and try to influence them in the right direction.

"Come on, Forest, are you in on this or not?"

"I don't know. I don't like Old Man Sanders either, but spray painting his new car doesn't sound like a good idea."

"What do you mean? He's had it coming for a long time. Now come on, we need you. He lives on the other side of town, and you're the only one with a car today."

"I'd rather not. You'd better count me out on this one."

"Do you want us to beg you? Okay, please, please, pretty please! We'll buy you some gas, and I might even introduce you to that gorgeous girl that sits next to me in history class."

"Well, I would like to do something with you guys this afternoon. And I'm all for toilet-papering his trees or taping his doors. Those things are fun! But spray painting his car, that's vandalism! And I don't think any of us really want to do that. Why don't we go swimming at the beach or girl watching at the mall? We could make plans for a Saturday morning surprise that Sanders would never forget."

Loyalty is an important part of friendship; it's the glue that holds friendships together. Loyalty means accepting friends the way they are and encouraging them to be the best they can be.

Being a loyal friend also means that you won't tell anyone else what your friends have shared with you. "Ratting on a friend" pretty well sums up the general feeling about someone who shares another friend's secrets. Any breach of confidence could destroy the trust you have established within your group.

When your friends choose to do something wrong, pray for them and try to influence them to do what is right. If and when they are caught, stand by your friends and offer your support. For it is within difficulty that we meet the true test of friendship.

Being a friend can get complicated and costly, but friendship is worth extra effort and expense. Surviving a period of disagreement and trial can be the test of true friendship. Even when you know a friend is in the wrong, stick with him or her, for that's what friendship is all about.

NO, a Christian's ultimate loyalty must be to truth and right even if it means rejecting friends and their actions.

"Gary, that's a really mean thing to do!"

"Aw, Sue, when did you get so tenderhearted? All I want to do is put a sign on his locker that says 'Hey! Hey! I'm gay!' "

"You know that'll embarrass him, and this is just the second week he's been in class."

"Yeah, and he's the weirdest new student we've ever had. I say if he walks like a queer, talks like a queer and looks like a queer, then he must be a queer."

"Stop it . . . all of you! How can you be so cruel? None of us even know him yet. Which one of you has talked with him or tried to get to know him?"

"Well, look who's preaching; Miss Goody-Goody."

"Cut it out, Gary! If you do this, I'll rip that sign off and tape it to *your* locker!"

"Sue, if you do that, you'd better forget hanging around with us. Isn't that right, guys?"

You should be loyal to your friends, but you also have a loyalty to God that goes beyond other loyalties. Friendships, parental and family relationships and allegiance to your country must give way to your loyalty to God as you see him in Jesus Christ. Therefore, when your friends talk about doing something you believe is wrong, oppose them as strongly as possible.

This opposition can take the form of reasoning or arguing at first. Try to convince your friends that what they intend to do is wrong, that it hurts others and themselves, or simply that it's against God's Word.

If you can't talk your friends out of their intentions, then leave, not in a self-righteous or "holier-than-thou" manner, but with an attitude of, "I'm sorry, but I can't be part of this." Your stand might bring your friends around, or it might result in their derision, taunts and hostility toward you. That's part of the price you pay—the "cross" you bear—for accepting Christ as your Lord.

If what your friends plan to do is so bad that it will really hurt someone, tell some person in authority what is going on. Talk with an understanding parent, your pastor or youth leader or a teacher you can trust. This individual may be able to think of a creative way to deal with your friends without involving the police or other authorities. But even if the situation comes to this point, don't keep the knowledge of your friends' wrongdoing to yourself.

Opposing your friends at any time won't be easy. It won't win you any popularity contests and it could result in the breakup of friendships. But in the long run you will be able to live with yourself and with God. Standing up for what you believe will probably result in people respecting you more as someone who is willing to pay the price to stand up for principles. But regardless of the outcome, stand up to your friends and refuse to go along with them when they are in the wrong.

Programming Ideas for Issue 8

Preparation—Gather newsprint, markers, 3×5 cards, masking tape, a small box, Bibles, a record player or tape player and recordings of friendship songs like "You've Got a Friend," "Stand by Me" and "Bridge Over Troubled Water." Prepare copies of Chart 5.

Opening—Play the tape or record of friendship songs as the group arrives. Talk about how important it is to have friends. Mention that sometimes friends' values may conflict with what Jesus taught.

On a sheet of newsprint, have the group members list some wrong actions that their group of friends might persuade them to do. The list could include:

getting drunk	smoking
taking drugs	watching a pornographic
destroying property	movie

cursing   gossiping
threatening or hurting someone   lying
stealing a car   cheating on a test
engaging in sex   gambling
putting down others

Ask the young people to rank the items on their list in order from the most serious to the least serious. Ask the group members to give reasons for their rankings.

Program—Write each item on a separate index card, and put the cards in a small box. Divide the group into teams of three or four people. Ask a member from each team to draw one of the cards. Instruct the teams to talk over the situation and come up with one or more ideas on how they would resolve this situation with their friends. Distribute a copy of Chart 5 to each small group. Have them write their ideas on the sheet.

Chart 5
Resolving an Issue

Issue: _____

We resolve to avoid this problem by:

1.

2.

3.

4.

5.

Within the small teams, talk about what pressure is hardest to withstand when the group is doing something you think is wrong: ridicule, curses, insults, arguments or reasons for going ahead, threats of being ostracized by group force, etc.

Ask what gives individuals the motivation to withstand such pressure: fear of getting caught, a desire not to let your parents down, faith in God, etc.

Response—Bring the teams together and ask them to share their issue sheets. Post the sheets on the wall around the newsprint listing the wrong actions friends might persuade them to do. Ask individuals to list the pressures their group found hardest to resist and the motivations they selected to resist these pressures. Discuss the following scriptures:

1. Read Matthew 5:10-16. What does this scripture say about choosing friends? What should we look for in prospective friends besides loyalty and common interests?

2. Listen to one of the friendship songs you played earlier. Would this person lead a friend astray? Describe the chief characteristics of this friend. Compare such friendship to 1 Corinthians 13.

Pass a 3×5 card to each group member. Ask everyone to write on the card the friendship characteristic that is most important to him or her. Have individuals tape their cards to the newsprint. Suggest they arrange their cards in a stick figure to represent their special friends.

Summarize the discussion and offer a prayer of thanksgiving for friends who stand by us and to whom we can offer our love and loyalty.

Option:

1. Plan a friend-appreciation banquet. Ask young people to bring their friends to the youth group. Give an award to each friend such as Great Listener, Super Attitude, Always Available, Happy Helper or Great Friend. Let the kids design and create their own awards the week before the banquet.

ISSUE 9
Is it right to have sex outside of marriage?

YES, there is nothing wrong with sex outside of marriage if two people truly love each other.

"Donna, you know I love you and you love me. You're wearing my engagement ring; we belong to each other right now. Why should we wait for a year before we express our love physically?"

"Because we learned a long time ago that it just isn't right. My faith says a woman should present herself to her husband as a virgin."

"But those rules were made a long time ago by people whose marriages were arranged by their parents, not by people who chose their partner. We have already promised ourselves to each other, and you *would* be a virgin for me right now. How can that piece of paper make any difference in the way we feel about each other?"

Promiscuous sex is always wrong because it cheapens the love relationship. But sex between two people who have promised mutual devotion and loyalty can be a beautiful thing.

We live in an age when we no longer have to fear unwanted pregnancies and disease. With our medical knowledge, a modern man and woman can enter a responsible intimate relationship with confidence and joy.

Because of college expenses and the intensive demands for beginning a career, many young adults are postponing marriage until their late 20s. Yet their bodies are at the peak of their sexual appetites. It is unreasonable to expect healthy young men and women to withhold sexual intimacy until marriage. This kind of frustration merely adds to the intense pressure young people already have in every other area of their existence.

The sexual experience is a couple's most intimate form of communication. Through it a man and a woman can offer intense pleasure by using their whole bodies to express their love for each other. A couple makes a statement of love and loyalty through the sexual experience that a marriage license merely recognizes but does not create. The love is already there before the marriage ceremony takes place. Commitment and love should be justification enough for a couple's deepest expression of their relationship; they need not wait for a ceremony to legalize this physical expression of their love.

NO, a couple should not engage in sexual intercourse before marriage.

"Look, Charlie, you know I love you. When you asked me to marry you, I said 'Yes' and I wear your ring here to show that I am committed to our relationship."

"But I want us to express our love in the deepest way possible."

"We will, when the time is right. And for me, that will be on our wedding night. I want something special to look forward to. If I give in to our passions now, it would be like opening our Christmas presents a month before the holiday. You say that if I love you, I would give in tonight. But I say that *because* I love you so much, I want to wait. You can show me your love by realizing how important this is for me."

When a couple is not married, the concept of going "too far" is still valid, even though today's birth control methods are extremely effective. The sexual act is an expression of our emotions more than a statement of our reason and loyalty. Therefore, this emotional expression of love needs the stability of a formal commitment "before God and these witnesses" to put it in perspective. A marriage service is more than just a legalization of sex. Christian marriage is based on the biblical understanding of a covenant— a binding commitment that God and humans make with each other that they will love and be faithful to one another, no matter what happens.

As a covenant relationship, marriage provides the stable

framework within which a couple may grow in their relationship with God and with each other. Feelings that are often sublime during moments of courtship and sex can quickly change during times of stress or disagreement. But because of personal commitments to the relationship, the couple will not walk out on each other or hurt each other unnecessarily, even though their feelings might tell them to do so at the moment. When a couple recognizes God as a part of their covenant with each other, their marriage relationship has the bedrock that both individuals need to develop a mature married life.

Christian couples can control their desires and passions. Contrary to the popularized expressions of love in films, television and songs, sex before marriage is usually initiated by a selfish partner. An inability to wait and increased pressure to fulfill one's physical urge declare, "I want what I want, and I want it right now!" When a person manipulates his or her partner into intercourse, the other person may begin to feel resentment or guilt about what has happened. And the relationship may begin to deteriorate before it has even begun, for it's impossible to build a lasting relationship on passion alone.

Even if those who wait for marriage are a minority in our instant-gratification culture, Christian couples should still follow this proper course. Their love relationship will be more precious because both people sacrificed their own desires for the other, and both people reserved a part of themselves until their commitment to each other was made complete before God, family and friends. The piece of paper *does* make a difference, and the support that comes from others definitely affects a relationship.

Programming Ideas for Issue 9

Preparation—The week before this program, ask your young people to look for ways our society talks about love and sex. Ask them to pay attention to how love is expressed while they listen to their records, watch television and movies, and read current novels and magazines. Encourage them to bring their findings to the meeting. Some may want to bring records or videotapes of TV programs or movies. Others may want to bring their books or magazines to illustrate what they have discovered. Let them know you will spend some time sharing their findings at the beginning of the meeting next week.

Prepare a letter for parents to explain what you are doing and send this early in the week with a reminder for students to bring their findings to the next meeting.

Do some research on your own. Bring magazines and books. Tape songs and parts of TV shows. Attend some popular movies that you know your young people have seen and talked about.

In addition to examining the media presentations of love and sex, research current surveys and statistics on teenage sexual practices and pregnancy. Be prepared to share relevant information with your group.

Gather newsprint, markers, paper, easy-to-remove labels, pens and a Bible for each person. Bring a record player, a tape player, a VCR and a television set to the meeting. Be sure all machines are set up and ready to use.

Prepare a sign that reads, "Sex Before Marriage—Yes or No?" Ask your pastor if you may borrow his or her service manual or liturgical handbook to make copies of the marriage vows used in your church. Some pastors may be willing to visit with your group about the marriage service, the meaning of the vows and what is included in premarital counseling.

Before the meeting, tape a long strip of newsprint across the front of the room. Draw a line down the middle, labeling the left side Yes and the right side No. Fix the sign you made directly above the line. (See Chart 6 for an example.)

Place tables below each side of the sign to hold the items your kids bring. Put labels and pens on the tables so your young people can label their items and identify them easily.

Opening—As your young people arrive for their meeting, ask them to label their tapes, records, magazines or

---

Chart 6
Sex Before Marriage—Yes or No?

Y   N

E   O

S

---

books. If their materials support the Yes position, ask them to put them on the table beneath the Yes position; if their materials support the No position, have the kids place them on the other table. If the kids have other facts or experiences they want to share, have each one write his or her name on a sheet of paper and place that paper on the appropriate table.

After everyone has arrived, ask the group to look at the tables to see where most of the items have been placed. Talk about the impact media play in our lives and how we are influenced without realizing it.

Program—Have the kids think about what they brought to the meeting and ask them to share for one to two minutes a piece, depending on how many brought something. Ask the group to watch the videos for how sex is portrayed—as an appetite to be satisfied, as a sign of deep commitment, as a self-centered experience, as a self-giving opportunity, as a method of manipulation, etc.

As the group members listen to tapes and records, ask them to listen for what each song says about love. Is it merely an emotional high? Is commitment involved? Is it simply a momentary thrill? Is there mention of more than a physical relationship? Is physical love used as a justification for existence or purpose in life? Is there a threat of death without the love of another? Is there a concept of balance within the relationship?

As people share, ask the group to decide which position each item supports and write that item on the newsprint on the appropriate side.

After everyone has shared, talk about what you have discovered. Do most items portray the Yes or the No position? How many items portray a balanced position? How many items mention a relationship beyond the physical experience?

Ask your group members to think about what they have seen and heard. Have individuals suggest reasons for and against sex before marriage, and write these on the newsprint at the front of the room. Compare the lists. Which reasons are based on concern for one's personal needs and feelings? Which reasons are based on concern for others?

Response—Pass out copies of the marriage vows used in your church. Talk about the church's expectations for a love relationship. If your pastor is willing, ask him or her to spend a few minutes with your young people, explaining the vows and clarifying any questions the kids might have. Here are some of the concerns your group might have:

1. Why is it important for a couple to pledge themselves to each other before God and witnesses?

2. How does the word "covenant" affect the marriage relationship?

3. Why is it important to promise "until death do us part," or until death separates us?

Ask your young people to read 1 Corinthians 13:4-13 together. Talk about the concept of love as it is presented here. How can this scripture relate to sex before marriage?

Close this session by celebrating God's love and commitment to all of us. Sing, "I Love You With the Love of the Lord" from *Songs* (Songs and Creations).

Options:

1. The subject of sex before marriage is a hot issue with young people today and would make an excellent debate topic. Your young people could debate the issue at the beginning of the session, introducing the emotional and logical stances of both positions, or they could use the debate

forum as a way to finalize their study of this issue. Either way, it will be important to stress acceptance and love for each other, even if there are differences of opinion.

2. Show one of the following films: *The Great Chastity Experiment, When, Jenny, When?* or *The Sex Game.* These 25-minute films present dramatic stories that raise many issues about sexual relationships among teenagers. They are Christian films, but not in the "preachy" sense. Rent these films from your local film distributor or directly from Paulist Productions (write: Box 1057, Pacific Palisades, CA 90272). Use these films to stimulate discussion about sex before marriage and close with the Response section.

3. After sharing examples from media and scripture from 1 Corinthians 13, divide the group into two parts to create collages—one depicting love from the standpoint of the world and the other illustrating the Christian understanding of love and marriage. Collect two large sheets of corrugated cardboard cut from a packing crate for an appliance or a piece of furniture. Let artistic individuals sketch a design while others look through magazines and newspapers for suitable images and words. Provide paste, scissors, poster paints and brushes, markers and other items the groups might need.

Play love songs on the record and tape players as the groups work. After about 45 minutes have the groups stop and discuss what they have created. What do the images say about love and sex? Close with the Response section.

LIFE ISSUES

L ife is a precious gift from God. We cannot create it from nothing, even though we can set up conditions for it to thrive in a laboratory. We can end life. We also have the power to enrich life or empty it of joy and meaning. But how and when life begins and ends is still a mystery.

Because of our inability to determine *exactly* when life begins, we have numerous controversies about abortion. During the years between birth and death, human beings can be afflicted with dreadful diseases. Job's so-called "comforters" regarded his afflictions as God-sent punishments for past sins, but Job refused to accept this easy answer. Many years later Jesus also rejected such an explanation from his disciples. Learned theologians and people in the pew, including teenagers, continue to debate the question of God's use of physical illness as punishment.

The termination of life can be just as perplexing. We talk about the life of a pain-wracked patient with no possibility for recovery, or we discuss the right-to-life of a young murderer-rapist on death row. If we have the right to end life, then under what circumstances can we exercise this right? These life issues have no easy answers. They should provide challenging discussions for our teenagers.

ISSUE 10
Should abortion be outlawed?

YES, abortion should be outlawed.
Sally and Bill had been going steady for over two years.

Everyone regarded them as the perfect couple and expected them to get married after high school. Convinced of their future together, the couple decided to go "all the way" one night after a dance. They repeated their sexual experience several times during the next few weeks.

When Sally discovered she was pregnant in spite of their precautions, she was panicky. So was Bill. Graduation was just a few months away, and it looked as though he would receive a partial athletic scholarship for college. Sally had already received a scholarship from the state university and looked forward to a teaching career. They both knew they couldn't afford to get married if they were to attend college. And yet a baby was on the way.

The couple scarcely spoke to each other during the next few days. Sally couldn't bring herself to talk to her parents either. They had argued with her over so many things during the past few years—her clothes, her choice of music and friends, her goals in life and even her church.

After talking with a doctor, Sally decided to have an abortion. She was told the operation was quick and painless. Most importantly, it could be performed without anyone knowing. With some financial help from Bill, she went through the procedure. When she walked out of the clinic, instead of feeling relieved, she felt strangely empty inside. She saw less and less of Bill. And when they did meet, they seemed to have little to say to each other. Sally began to have trouble sleeping, and her prayers seemed formal and useless.

One night she went with a friend to a pro-life meeting. The speaker showed slides of a fetus in various stages of development. Sally finally realized why the workers at the clinic hadn't wanted her to see what they had removed from her uterus. She had no idea how *human* an eight-week-old embryo appears. She began to feel even worse about what she had done. That night she cried herself to sleep and asked: "God, can you ever forgive me? How long will I feel this way?"

It is wrong to take a life, especially when a person is completely defenseless. And no life is more defenseless than that of an unborn baby. Life begins at conception, and it doesn't matter whether a child is conceived out of love or lust. Once a child is conceived, a human being begins to take shape. This miracle of cell reproduction in the uterus is guided by the genetic code particular to this sperm and this egg. Our loving Creator designed the uterus to be the safest place for a child's development, but now it may be one of the most dangerous places in the world, especially if the mother decides she doesn't want to have this child.

Abortion is wrong. Contrary to feminists who claim the right to control their own bodies, a woman who decides to have an abortion is dealing with more than just her own body. The body of another human being, the fetus, is involved. The Sixth Commandment states, "You shall not murder" (Exodus 20:6). Snuffing out another life, no matter how therapeutic the process or how young the fetus, is still killing, no matter how we label it.

Although on occasion aborting a child may be necessary to save a mother's life, we shouldn't use words to cover up what is done. A hard decision had to be made between two human lives. Those who made the decision decided to sacrifice the life of the child for that of the mother. Sally has a right to feel guilty. How long she feels that way will depend on how soon she asks for forgiveness from her loving Creator and how easily she can forgive herself.

Using abortion as a method of birth control or a way to eliminate the inconvenience of a pregnancy cheapens our view of all life. This attitude could easily lead to our society's acceptance of taking other lives deemed "useless"—the mentally retarded, the handicapped, the elderly and the hopelessly insane. It happened once before in a so-called "civilized" country. The German people accepted the arguments of Hitler as he strived to create the perfect race by eliminating "inferior specimens." It could happen here also.

We need to affirm life, not cheapen or destroy it. The

Bible shows us a God who protects and cares for the weak and the oppressed. Surely in this fight to save the lives of more than a million babies a year, God is calling us to take a stand. Even when a mother has been raped and doesn't want the child, we can guide her to find an alternative like adoption. Christians should support the victim as she struggles with her predicament. They can surround her with their love, care for her and see that her baby receives a proper home. The trauma of going through a pregnancy and birth isn't nearly as great as facing the guilt of an abortion.

NO, abortion should not be outlawed.

Sarah looked at the doctor in fear and confusion while her mother quietly wept in the corner of the room. She still didn't understand what was happening to her and why her father had been put in jail. When the doctor said she was going to have a baby, Sarah wasn't even sure he was talking about her. Only married people have babies, she thought.

"But she's only 11 years old," her mother sobbed. "She's never even had a period. How could she be pregnant?"

"Your husband said he'd been having relations with her since she was 7 years old, Mrs. Turner. It's obvious she became pregnant the first time she ovulated."

"But why didn't she tell me what was going on? Sarah, why didn't you tell me what Daddy was doing to you?"

"Daddy said it was a secret. He told me you would leave if I told you. I didn't want you to leave again. I just wanted us to be a family like everybody else at school. I'm sorry, Mom. Please don't leave!"

After Sarah left the room, Mrs. Turner looked at the doctor and asked, "What should we do about Sarah? She's just a baby herself."

In another city, Mary looks at the calendar and shudders. Today is the 16th anniversary of Sue's death. She always dreads this time of year. Her mind again relives the circumstances of her best friend's death. Even after all these years, the events are vividly etched in her memory.

Sue had been in love with her special guy, a dream-boat. They became intimate, and . . . In those days a girl with an enlarged abdomen didn't graduate from high school. She would have been rejected by the college that had just given her a scholarship. Sue's dreams of becoming a nurse would have been destroyed forever. Marriage was out of the question. Not only was it frowned on by the college authorities and her parents, but the boy dropped her as soon as he learned of her condition. Sue was so frightened she couldn't think.

In those days there were no clinics or advisers who could help, so Sue turned to her friends and acquaintances. One girlfriend's older brother told Sue about a place where she could get help for a price. It was located on a back street in the seamy section of town.

Mary sold some of her clothes and jewelry to help Sue raise the money she needed for the operation. The price was several times what her well-off friends claimed was charged in countries where abortion was legal. But traveling to another country wasn't an alternative for Sue.

When they arrived at the run-down building, Mary almost grabbed Sue's arm and ran off with her. She wondered if she would spend the rest of her life regretting that she hadn't. The last time she saw Sue alive was on that brown-stained wooden table the "butcher" used for his operations.

Mary eventually returned to her studies after her friend's funeral. Several years later, she met a politician who campaigned to work for the legalization of abortion so abortion mills would become a thing of the past. Mary volunteered to work for his re-election. She supported women's rights movements and continued to serve on the board of a rape-crisis counseling center. She wished her friend Sue could have benefited from such an enlightened service. She would be alive today with her laughter and love for life. As Mary walked through the Pro-Life picket line on her way to the board meeting, she shuddered.

Didn't these people know what would happen to thousands of women like Sue if safe abortions were not available in this country?

Before the Supreme Court legalized abortion, numerous women died in abortion mills each year because they couldn't obtain legal abortions in our hospitals. Only the wealthy could afford to travel to other countries where abortions were performed by qualified medical personnel. Outlawing abortion would create more problems than it would solve.

A woman should be free to choose her own alternative to an unwanted pregnancy. Conditions under which women may seek an abortion do need to be examined so that mere inconvenience is not a viable excuse for requesting this procedure. Christian counselors can continue to encourage pregnant women to look at other alternatives, but abortion itself should not be outlawed.

When a sperm fertilizes an egg, cell division begins immediately. But during the first few months the fetus is not human; it merely holds the potential for becoming so. Medical opinions vary, but most assume a fetus is not viable until the 24th to the 28th week of development. By then it has the capacity to live on its own and can continue to develop outside the uterus. In some people's minds, this is the point at which the fetus becomes human.

Other people feel that to be human requires more than just a physical birth. A fetus' development into a human being requires nurturing and a bonding relationship. To support this stance, these individuals point to the neglected infants discovered within our society. Not only have their physical bodies failed to thrive, but their emotional development has been stunted. Many cannot overcome this lack of human interaction and die. Others seem to fight for survival, but are slow to develop human traits even after intense therapy. We actually *learn* to be human by growing up within a human community.

If the development of a fetus threatens a mother's

physical life, there is rarely much debate over whether or not to terminate the pregnancy. Therapeutic abortions that preserve the life of the mother over the life of the undeveloped fetus are not illegal. But there are times when emotional health must be considered. Can an 11-year-old understand a pregnancy and all the bodily changes this experience will require? Is it fair to ask a rape victim to carry a child that will continually remind her of the horror of this experience? Therapy may need to go beyond the physical to the emotional scars this experience can bring.

Our increasing genetic knowledge brings even more difficult choices. What do we do when it is certain that a fetus will be severely mentally retarded or physically handicapped as in the thalidomide scare during the '60s? Although it would be wrong to eliminate those handicapped individuals who are alive and living in institutions, allowing such births when we have the means to prevent them would be even more cruel.

We now have the ability to prevent a great deal of this family and personal anguish. One hundred years ago we allowed nature to take its course. But today's increased medical knowledge brings increased moral responsibility in its wake. There are times when abortion is the moral decision and to forbid this practice under these circumstances would be wrong.

To outlaw abortion completely would throw our society back to the days of the abortion mill. Thousands of desperate women would die each year at the hands of unqualified, hack surgeons. The rich could still obtain this operation, but the poor would be trapped. The unscrupulous would thrive again on the misfortune of others, and the death toll of women would rise once more. This must not be allowed to happen.

Programming Ideas for Issue 10

Preparation—Because this is a highly charged, emotional issue, you will need to involve parents in planning and carrying out this program. Many parents may want to attend if you use a film or panel. If your young people are giving the presentation, however, the parents' presence could be intimidating. Talk it over with your minister first and decide what type of presentation you would like to use.

Since there are many disputed facts on this issue, open with an educational session of outside speakers. Try to include professionals such as a physician, a counselor from a rape-crisis center, a social worker, an adoption counselor and your minister. Invite these people several weeks in advance. Ask them to speak about the issue of abortion for about five to seven minutes. Be sure to reconfirm their acceptance about one week before your meeting. Remember to ask if they need any special equipment for their presentations such as film projectors, tape recorders, newsprint, markers, and other things.

Gather posterboard, 3×5 cards, masking tape, markers, newsprint and a basket. On three separate sheets of posterboard print one of the following words: NEVER, DEPENDS, ALWAYS. Use large block letters that people can read easily.

Write each of the following statements on a 3×5 card. If your group is large, prepare a duplicate set of situation cards since individuals may answer the questions differently.

1. You are not married.

2. Your pregnancy is the result of sexual abuse by your father.

3. Your life is in danger if the fetus continues to grow.

4. Medical tests indicate the fetus is physically deformed.

5. Medical tests indicate the fetus will be severely mentally handicapped.

6. You were raped by a man who is criminally insane.

7. You already have six children. All of them are under 10 years of age and you're having trouble coping now. You know another child will create problems for you emotionally.

8. You are a single parent with three children, and

you are living on welfare. After extensive retraining you are excited about going back to work next month when your youngest child enters first grade.

9. You are not temperamentally suited to have or raise a child. In fact, you really don't like little kids.

10. You are in the first semester of your senior year in college. Your husband is planning on your financial support so he can complete his degree next year.

Write the discussion questions for the last part of the Response session on newsprint. Use large letters so participants can read the questions from any position around the room.

Immediately prior to your meeting, arrange your meeting room so that everyone can see and hear your speakers. Remind your speakers of the time limit for their presentations. Be sure you have all the equipment everyone will need, and put it in place. Tape the three signs that say NEVER, DEPENDS and ALWAYS in that order along one wall of your meeting room. Place the 3×5 cards you prepared in a basket. Have the discussion questions ready to tape onto the wall. Cut sheets of newsprint and provide markers for the small groups to record their thoughts.

Opening—It is extremely important to set a tone of acceptance at the beginning of your meeting. Remind the group members of the intensity of this issue, but reassure them that everyone has something valuable to say. Tell them: "We can learn only if we listen with respect to what everyone has to say. Now is the time to listen carefully to what someone is *actually* saying, not what you *think* he or she will say."

Program—Introduce your speakers and describe their qualifications. After the presentations allow about 10 minutes to clarify any questions or misunderstandings. Take care that this time does not become a time for debate with the audience. Remind the group merely to seek understanding of what the speakers are saying.

Response—Thank your speakers for their presentations and explain the next activity. Tell the group: "To make this issue personally relevant, each person will assume you are a woman and have just discovered you are pregnant. If you have trouble identifying with this idea, assume that your sister has just discovered she is pregnant. Take a situation card from the basket as it passes you and read it to determine the circumstances of your particular pregnancy. Spend the next few moments thinking about how *you* would respond to this predicament. Then ask yourself, 'Would I have an abortion in this situation?'

"After you have made a decision, move yourself and your chair to some place along the wall that indicates how you feel about this particular pregnancy. If you are absolutely sure you would not have an abortion, place your chair under the NEVER sign. If you are *not* absolutely sure, but feel you *probably* would choose an abortion, place your chair somewhere between DEPENDS and ALWAYS."

While the group members are making their decisions, tape the newsprint with the discussion questions onto the wall at the front of the room. Cover it with a second sheet of newsprint until it is time for the small group discussions.

Once everyone has taken a position along the wall, ask each person to read his or her card aloud and then explain the reason for his or her decision. Allow no more than 30 to 45 minutes for this sharing.

After all individuals have shared their cards and their decisions, ask them to meet in small groups of three to five people. Pass out newsprint and markers and ask the groups to discuss the following questions printed on the newsprint at the front of the room:

1. List the rights of the woman and the rights of the fetus on your newsprint.

2. Identify the ways these rights are in conflict.

3. As you listened to and examined the arguments for both sides, what problems did you see with either extreme?

4. Can there be one easy answer to the issue of abortion? Why or why not?

Allow about 20 minutes for discussion. Ask one person from each group to report on the group's discussion.

Ask the groups to bring their chairs to the front. Allow about 15 minutes for the small groups to report on their discussions. Then have different young people read the following scripture passages one at a time: Psalm 139:13-16, Matthew 25:40, Genesis 1:28, Deuteronomy 30:19. Discuss how these passages relate to the abortion issue.

After the discussion, lead the group members to form a circle with their arms around each other. Thank everyone for sharing. Express your appreciation for the group's willingness to listen and learn from the other side. Then offer the following prayer:

"Dear God, you are our creator and the sustainer of our lives. Out of the mystery of your love, we have been created. For the wonder and joy of life, we give you thanks. For the opportunity to explore this difficult issue, we praise your name. Whether we have decided or are still wavering with what we know is right, continue to guide us and open our minds to even more of your truth.

"Save us from self-righteousness and the arrogance of identifying *our* will too easily with *yours*. Help us to remember to listen to those with whom we disagree and to continue in fellowship with them.

"But above all, be with those who are hurting from the wounds of an unwanted pregnancy. Guide and heal them. Use our prayers and outstretched hands in your service so these people will know they are not alone. In Jesus' name, Amen."

Conclude by singing, "They'll Know We Are Christians by Our Love" from *Songs* (Songs and Creations).

Options:
1. If you plan to use a film or a combination of films, contact groups like Life Ministries, Americans Against Abortion, Planned Parenthood, your local hospital, county services and student health services at your nearby universities. Tell them what you are looking for and ask for their help in locating video presentations from both points of view. Always preview these presentations ahead of time to see if

they are appropriate for the maturity level of your group.

Once you decide which films are appropriate, reserve them and prepare your program around them. Many films include a study guide to help you with your discussions, but tailor your programming to fit the needs of your particular group.

Remember to reconfirm your film reservations about one week ahead of your actual presentation, and be sure you also reserve the video equipment you will need.

2. Instead of asking the professionals to make short educational presentations, make your meeting less formal by setting up a professional panel for questions from a moderator. Help your group prepare a list of questions ahead of time, and send each panelist a copy. Preparing questions ahead of time can help in several ways. It curbs the tendency to ask repetitive questions, it helps control the emotions of the group and it guides the professionals as they prepare to answer your group's questions.

3. Use a debate to conclude the study of this issue. After your young people have listened to professionals or videos with varying opinions, they may be inspired to do further research on their own. Debate offers a controlled situation where young people can present their ideas and agree to disagree.

4. A corollary to this issue is to talk about the other options available to women who find themselves pregnant with unwanted or even dangerous pregnancies. Abortion is certainly not the only choice, but it is the one that is legislated by the courts rather than the individual. By discussing the positive and negative aspects of keeping the child or adoption, kids have to struggle with the consequences of their choices as they mature into young adults. No longer do their choices affect only themselves.

ISSUE 11

Should human life be prolonged by heroic means?

YES, human life should be sustained by heroic means whenever possible.

As Betty stood beside her husband's bed in the intensive care ward, she released a sob she had been holding in while she was with the rest of her family. Pete had shown no sign of recognition in the four months he had been hooked up to all these strange-looking machines. He had been in a coma since the night of his terrible automobile accident. She remembered his last phone call so well. "Hi, honey, I'm still in Sun City. We should close this deal over supper tonight. I'm going to stay and drive home afterward. I'll be late, so don't wait up for me. I'll be okay."

Only Pete wasn't okay. The officers surmised someone sideswiped his car as he or she passed, causing him to lose control and ram into a tree. In that brief moment Betty's strong, virile husband became helpless and dependent upon the respirator for every breath he took. The doctors gave him no hope for recovery. According to all tests, there was no life in his brain, so that even if he regained consciousness he would need constant care for even his basic bodily functions.

Betty winced as she thought of what her strong, proud husband would have thought of that quality of life. Indeed, they had talked about such a possibility. He had always urged her, "Put me out of such misery if something ever happens."

Betty talked with her family, pastor and friends and prayed about what she should do. As she sat beside her husband, she thought back over their years together. They had been good years! It hurt to see her husband so helpless, yet she couldn't bear to think of giving up, of turning off the life-sustaining machines.

Months went by. Nothing changed. Pete continued to live only because of the machines to which he was attached. A few of Betty's friends began to suggest that maybe "enough was enough." Even Betty had doubts at times, especially during the middle of the night. Several times she dreamed of the good times she and Pete had enjoyed and then turned over with a start to rediscover that she was indeed alone.

The pastor and members of Betty's church prayed that whatever the outcome, God's will and comfort would be revealed. Then one night she received a call from the hospital. Pete had smiled at a nurse and asked for some water. When Betty arrived at the hospital, their doctor was already with Pete. "It's a miracle" was all the physician could say through his own tears and smile. Betty shook her head in agreement as her husband looked up at her with his first sign of recognition since the accident.

A doctor takes an oath to preserve and protect life. It is his duty to use any means possible to prolong it. Life is too precious a commodity to allow it to slip away without a fight. When the poet Dylan Thomas says, "Do not go gentle into that good night . . . ," he challenges the physician and the patient to fight for all the life there is.

Even when there is great pain and little hope for recovery, a patient and his or her family should not be allowed to terminate life. They are often the least objective about such a matter. Medical staff certainly should not encourage family members to consider euthanasia as a solution to their loved one's continuing pain or prolonged coma. There have been numerous cases of a comatose patient coming back to consciousness after many years for reasons we don't understand.

If the decision to turn off life-sustaining machines should become widespread, it would cheapen human life. The practice of euthanasia could creep into other areas of medicine, especially as the cost of caring for the terminally ill and mentally handicapped continues to escalate.

NO, using heroic means to prolong life should be eliminated in many cases. Patients should be allowed to die a "dignified" death.

Bob Smith found his parents and his brothers and sisters in the hall just outside his grandmother's hospital room. All were talking in hushed whispers. "The doctors are in with Gram now," his dad told him. "They say she has no chance of coming out of this coma. There's been too much brain damage. But her heart is so strong she could hold on for another week or even months.''

Bob had overheard some of his relatives' conversations ever since Gram went into the coma three weeks ago. Her long hospitalization had used up most of her benefits from Medicare and the insurance company. Several family members, including Bob's parents and his aunts and uncles, had already dipped into their savings that had been earmarked for their kids' college funds. And it looked as though they would have to reach in again.

Bob hated to think of money when it came to his Gram, yet he knew the family had to discuss the situation. The doctor had already said Gram would die unless she continued on the life-support system. But what kind of life were they supporting? Would his Gram, that proud, attractive woman he knew and loved, appreciate this slow, torturous descent into death? He recalled the struggle and tears of his Uncle Phil when he said: "The doctor told us Gram will never be the same again. We all know how she felt about her independence. I think we should tell the hospital to turn off the machines and let her die in peace." A sob welled up in Bob as he thought of all this. "God in heaven, what should we do?"

The cancer patient who must be heavily sedated so that he or she is seldom conscious and who begs to die when awake; the victim of an automobile accident who shows no sign of brain activity on the monitoring devices; and the elderly patient whose kidneys, liver or other vital organs have ceased to function yet who is kept alive by machines. All these people would have died a few years ago. They should be allowed to choose death now, especially if they request it. Family members know their loved ones better than the medical professionals who care only for their bodies. Families should have the right to choose a dignified death for their loved ones, rather than watch them linger and deteriorate with no hope for recovery.

Human life has to be measured in more than quantitative terms. There is the matter of quality, the ability to live relatively free of pain, to communicate, to make one's own decisions and to control one's own destiny. Every person should have the right to choose a dignified death rather than a continued existence, a loss of life rather than perpetuation by machines or heavy sedation.

The decision to die well (the meaning of euthanasia) must be a shared decision to guard against its abuse. The patient, family, medical staff and possibly the family's informed pastor should be part of this decision. Since a patient may not be conscious at the time this decision needs to be made, families should discuss this issue in advance and agree to abide by the patient's decision.

There are times when the body cries for death, and for release from pain and trauma. Death was once a natural part of the scheme of life. The heroic measures that merely prolong the *physical* existence of a terminally ill patient actually interfere with the natural process of dying. We should interfere with this natural process *only* when there is a chance that the patient can continue to live with dignity. Heroic measures should not become a punishment for those forced to exist as human vegetables. There are times when we should accept death as God's attempt to release one of his children from suffering.

Programming Ideas for Issue 11

Preparation—Because young people already have many questions about this subject, include your teenagers as you plan this session. Have the group members list what they would like to know about this issue.

Gather newsprint, markers, magazines, scissors and glue; and, for each participant, a large piece of white construction paper (approximately 11 x 17) and a Bible. You will also need a long table with sheets and a blanket. Make copies of the vignettes in the Yes and No sections of this issue and include the directions for role plays from the Program section. Make several copies of Chart 7.

Arrange sheets and blankets on a table to make it look like a bed. Ask a group member to come early and lie in the bed, pretending he or she is in a coma.

Opening—After the group has arrived, instruct everyone to gather about the table. Ask the group members to imagine that their best friend is terminally ill. His or her pain has been excruciating during the last few weeks. The doctor has put him or her on life-support systems because this was the only way life could continue. Pain medication was prescribed, but every time the friend wakes up, he or she begs to die.

Ask the kids to talk about how they would feel and what they would want to do for their friend. Conclude this experience by asking two questions: "Which of you would keep your friend on life-support systems until he or she died? Which of you would allow your friend to choose death if that is what he or she wanted?"

Program—Ask the group members and the patient to number off into two groups to read the vignettes at the beginning of the Yes and No sections and present them as role plays.

Group One should read the story of Betty and Pete. The group should try to use all of its members to play family, friends, Betty's minister and other people they may want to include. Ask them to talk as individuals and small groups about what should be done for Pete. Some people should urge Betty to discontinue the life-support measures. Others should argue against this. Betty doesn't have to be included in all the discussions. Conclude the role play as it was written.

Group Two will read through the story of Gram. Ask individuals to play the parts of Gram, Bob Smith, his mom, dad, uncles, aunts, cousins, and the nurses, the minister and the doctor. Have the group meet with the doctor as he explains there is no hope for Gram. The doctor should reassure the family that he will continue to use every means possible to keep Gram alive, unless the family intervenes and says no. Ask the family members to talk over this decision, recalling incidents from the past and looking at all the emotional, financial and ethical aspects they can think of.

Allow about 20 minutes for the groups to prepare their role plays, with five minutes for each presentation.

Response—When the role plays are finished, unite the groups around some large tables with a large piece of white construction paper at each place. Provide magazines, scissors, glue and markers for each table.

Ask group members to create a feeling collage by going through the magazines and cutting or tearing out words or pictures that express how they feel about this issue. Have

---

Chart 7
Death With Dignity

1. Would you want a relative diagnosed as having a terminal illness to be kept alive with tubes and machines? Why or why not?

2. Would *you* want to be kept alive with life-support machines? Why or why not?

3. What does the concept "death with dignity" mean to you? Can this idea be a cover-up for legalizing murder? Explain your answer.

4. Which would cheapen life more for you: to let your loved one suffer continuously until the body finally wears out, or to disconnect your loved one from the life-support machines? Explain your reasoning.

5. Why is this issue more of a problem today than in Moses' or Jesus' time?

6. How does our increased medical knowledge alter or affect our ethics?

7. Read Romans 8:18-39 and 1 Corinthians 15. How do these passages relate to this issue?

them glue these items on their construction paper. After 15 or 20 minutes ask everyone to come together and share his or her collage with the rest of the group. Be prepared for all kinds of feelings to surface with this activity.

After the sharing, divide into small groups to discuss the questions in Chart 7.

Remind the group that a deep and important issue like this cannot be fully resolved in one session. Have the group join hands to form a circle. Ask the kids to close their eyes and feel the life in the grip of the people next to them. After a few moments of silence, thank God for the precious gift of life. Close with a brief prayer, centering on the hope Christians have in the Resurrection of Christ.

Celebrate the life we have at this moment by singing "I Am the Resurrection" or "You Are Free to Live This Day" from *Songs* (Songs and Creations).

Options:

1. If your teenagers' questions are primarily medical- or equipment-oriented, arrange for an on-site visit to the intensive care unit at your local hospital. Ask a doctor or a nurse and the hospital chaplain to be present when you attend. Share the questions your young people have asked ahead of time so your guide can be as prepared as possible.

Ask the doctor or nurse to show the group some of the equipment and explain how it is used to "prolong life." Ask about the emotional and spiritual effects these kinds of decisions have on the patients and their loved ones. Remember to include questions about financial costs and who's responsible.

Make arrangements at least one month in advance and reconfirm your plans during the week before your actual visit. Be prepared for last-minute changes since hospitals have no way to control the influx into their intensive care units.

2. Invite various medical experts including an emergency room physician, a surgeon, a family doctor, a nurse in an intensive care unit and a hospital chaplain to speak on

this issue. Have the young people suggest some of the questions they would like the speakers to cover.

ISSUE 12

Does God punish people by afflicting them with AIDS or other diseases?

YES, God punishes some people by afflicting them with diseases that are the result of their sins.

The little cemetery was quiet as the pastor stood by the coffin and read the words for the burial service. Jane sobbed silently as she thought of her father. If only he had listened to his family's pleas to give up smoking.

After the service Jane shook hands and listened to people's comments and concerns. Most individuals shared words of comfort and offers of help. But she overheard one woman's conversation with a mutual friend: "This should teach you that you don't fool around with God and his commands. If you keep breaking rules, he'll get you one way or another."

Both the Old and New Testaments make it clear that God punishes the wicked. In Deuteronomy 27—28, Moses leads the people of Israel through a series of blessings and curses. Within this scripture Moses promises blessings upon these people and their land if they keep God's covenant, but curses if they depart from it. Moses said, "The Lord will plague you with diseases until he has destroyed you from the land you are entering to possess" (Deuteronomy 28:21). In the New Testament Paul tells the Corinthians that many of them are ". . . weak and ill, and some have died" (1 Corinthians 11:30) because they were profaning the Lord's Supper.

Our modern society has overstressed the love of God. We often forget he is also Judge. We have turned love into a wishy-washy emotion that says: "Evil doesn't matter; don't worry about sin. God will forgive you." But our sin *does* matter. It offends both the law and the Lawgiver. Our violation of God's laws brings his judgment upon us.

The doctrine of God's judgment is not contradictory to the teachings about God's love. Punishment actually is *part* of God's love. In the Old Testament parents were expected to punish their erring children; it was an important part of their children's discipline. The writer of Proverbs points out: "Do not withhold discipline from a child; if you punish him with the rod, he will not die. Punish him with the rod and save his soul from death" (Proverbs 23:13-14). Earlier he said, "He who spares the rod hates his son, but he who loves him is careful to discipline him" (Proverbs 13:24).

Based on the teachings of Deuteronomy, the prophets proclaimed that the various calamities overtaking Israel resulted from God punishing Israel and Judah for violating the covenant. In Hosea, the prophet sees love and punishment as inseparable. This spiritual leader tries to explain that God loves Israel like a husband loves his wife and a father cherishes his son. Yet he must subject the nation to judgment because its people have been unfaithful to their covenant. Not to do so would cheapen the meaning of the covenant.

We can definitely attribute some diseases to a particular sin. The terrible punishment of AIDS is borne primarily by individuals who are promiscuous in their sexual relationships. Smokers often develop lung cancer. Alcoholics eventually destroy their liver, and drug addicts die of overdoses or disease transmitted by infected needles. Paul's warning to the Galatians is still true today. "Do not be deceived: God cannot be mocked. A man reaps what he sows" (Galatians 6:7).

NO, God does not afflict people with disease as punishment for their sins.

Jeff was still full of anger when his friend left. With his Bible in his hand, George had marched into Jeff's hospital room and started talking to Jeff about his soul. He read several scripture passages that left no doubt that God was punishing Jeff for some terrible deed in his past.

Jeff seethed! He knew he wasn't perfect, but he

couldn't think of anything he had done to deserve a broken back and a crushed leg. He hadn't even been driving. The other driver had veered into their lane and smashed into them. What was all this talk from George about sin and punishment? In what kind of God did George believe? Jeff wasn't sure he wanted to have anything to do with the punitive type of God George was talking about.

To suggest that diseases, plagues and misfortunes are God's punishment for people's specific sins is a judgmental stance we cannot afford to make. Even though this is sometimes said in the Bible, we have no way of knowing why or how people contract these terrible diseases. *Some* promiscuous individuals, especially homosexuals, do contract AIDS, but many do not. Numerous "straight" adults and children also have AIDS. Some have contracted the disease from infected blood while others find the cause difficult to trace. If God directly afflicts individuals with AIDS, then God is very capricious. Many who are guilty of promiscuous sex, including homosexuality, are left "spared" while many innocent victims, including children, struggle with the insidious effects of this disease.

To try to label sinners by pointing to their diseases and afflictions is to deny the mystery of life and faith. The comforters of Job tried to help him identify some foul sin in his past so they could understand and explain his affliction. The disciples were also searching for an explanation when they asked Jesus about the man born blind. "Rabbi, who sinned, this man or his parents, that he was born blind?" (John 9:2). In both instances the scripture rejects the idea of sin causing physical affliction.

In fact, some biblical writers expressed consternation that the wicked seemed to grow stronger in their sin while the righteous perished. This evidence directly contradicted the theology that you could identify the wicked as those who suffered and the righteous as those who prospered. The psalmist confessed, "For I envied the arrogant when I saw the prosperity of the wicked" (Psalm 73:3). The prophet Habakkuk impatiently cried, "How long, O Lord, must I call for help, but you do not listen? . . . " (Habakkuk 1:2).

These other scripture passages illustrate the tension between those who applied the blessings and curses of Deuteronomy to all individuals and those whose sensitivity recognized the intense suffering and death of the innocent while the wicked prospered and lived to enjoy old age. The sensitive writers realized you cannot easily identify the wicked and the righteous by their outward prosperity or their afflictions. Life is a mystery that can be experienced only by faith. As the Lord declared to Habakkuk:

For the revelation awaits an appointed time;
   it speaks of the end
   and will not prove false.
Though it linger, wait for it;
   it will certainly come and will not delay.
See, he is puffed up;
   his desires are not upright—
   but the righteous will live by his faith (Habakkuk 2:3-4).

The blessings and curses of Deuteronomy were applied to the nation, not directly to individuals. The text is written in a plural sense, not singular. The author recognizes we are members of a community; and as a community, we will either prosper or die according to our collective sins. Abraham Lincoln used this same argument in his second inaugural address. He explained that the Civil War was God's just punishment upon our nation for the wickedness of slavery, even though not all Americans practiced or condoned slavery. God did not so much cause that terrible war, but he allowed the consequence of our ancestors' sin to unfold, catching the guilty and innocent in all of its terror.

There *are* times when an affliction is the direct result of carelessness, bad habits or outright wickedness. God has established physical laws which we violate only to experience a direct consequence. But this is a different concept than saying that God directly causes the sad outcome. Too many automobile wrecks caused by a drunk driver either injure or kill the innocent while the drunk walks away unscathed.

No, we cannot point our fingers at the victims of diseases or misfortunes and say God is punishing them. This self-righteous theology diminishes our natural sympathy for innocent victims and makes us glory in our own prosperity.

Programming Ideas for Issue 12

Preparation—This important issue will test your group members' faith throughout their lives. The great success of the book *When Bad Things Happen to Good People* (Schocken Books) testifies to how many people struggle with this issue and look for answers.

Gather newsprint, markers, masking tape, scissors and a Bible for each participant.

Prepare copies of the vignettes from both the Yes and No sections of this issue, and include these with the role-play suggestions listed in the Program section of this issue. Also, prepare several copies of Chart 8.

Save newspapers for three or four weeks. Keep each day's paper intact, with all its sections.

Opening—Open your meeting by describing a current accident or a calamity. Ask the group members if they are familiar with the story. Say: "This session will go beyond the headline and facts of such stories to raise the more basic question: Why? Is tragedy a form of God's punishment?"

Program—Divide the group in two. Designate one small group as the Yes position and the other small group as the No position. Ask one teenager in each group to read the example from his or her section, concluding with the following suggestions for discussion.

Yes position: At the cemetery Jane tells her two best friends about the lady's remark. One friend agrees with it, the other doesn't. Pretend you are one of these friends. What would you say to Jane and the other friend to support your position and still convey care and concern for the relationships? Be sure you discuss both positions.

No position: Jeff calls George and asks him to return to his hospital room. He presses George to explain what he means. Jeff wants to know what "sin" he is being punished for, especially since another person was at fault for the accident. Talk through this conversation between Jeff and George, remembering they are good friends. What would each person say? How could both people convey their concern for each other in the midst of their disagreement?

Ask the groups to summarize their thoughts on a piece of newsprint and share these with the other group. Meet as

---

Chart 8
Bad News

1. Identify the kind of bad news this is:
- A crime involving human passion, greed, etc.
- A human-made disruption such as a war, riot, etc.
- A large-scale social disruption like an economic recession or widespread unemployment.
- An accident due to human failure or machinery malfunction.
- A natural disaster such as an earthquake, storm, etc.
- Any combination of the above.

2. Who has been hurt? just the ones directly involved? others related to the victims? individuals not involved?

3. Can bad news be blamed on specific people? If so, are these people the *only* ones being "punished"? Are the guilty caught in some way or made to atone for what they have done?

4. Several countries suffer earthquakes every few years. Does this mean the people in those countries are more wicked than others who do not endure such calamities?

5. Choose three or four biblical passages from the following list. Interpret your news stories in light of the passages.

Genesis 45:4-8	Psalm 58:10-11
Job 5:17-27	Psalm 73
Psalm 10	Psalm 94:1-19
Psalm 49:5-20	Isaiah 53

a total group and share these summaries.

Response—Pass out a day's newspaper to each participant and divide into small groups by the days of the week. For example, everyone who got a Tuesday paper will be in one group. Ask your young people to look for stories of sorrow and woe. They won't have any trouble finding them since bad news seems to grab more headlines than good news. Remind them to look beyond the front-page calamities to the little stories buried in the back sections.

While everyone is looking through the newspaper, distribute one copy of Chart 8 to each small group. Ask each person to select a sample of bad news that touches him or her, cut it out and then read that selection to the rest of the small group. Ask each group to talk about the newspaper articles using the questions in Chart 8.

Listen to the discussions among your young people. Help them clarify various points of scripture or theology. Have them take notes of the main points and questions raised in their group and deal with them in the closing session.

Ask the groups to summarize their discussions and present any questions that came up during this session. Answer any questions you can, and ask your minister to answer those of which you are unsure. Remind your young people that they will face the question of God's intervention throughout their lives. Ask one of your young people to prepare to read Romans 8:31-39. Introduce his or her reading by saying: "One of the greatest theologians in the early church came up with this answer for the heart and soul of the believer. Notice that Paul does not attempt to answer the question, 'Why?' " Close by saying the Lord's Prayer together.

Options:

1. The Yes and No position sections present a lot of material that could be investigated more thoroughly and presented as an introductory stimulus to the Bible study.

2. The material in the Yes and No statements could be

the starting point for further study, resulting in an educational debate later. Your teenagers will need time to study and develop their cases, so be sure you assign the debate ahead of time.

3. Rent the video *Tender Mercies*. This academy award winner raises the question of God's "tender mercies" in a world of unexpected death and unfulfilled dreams. Play back then discuss the last scene in which Robert Duvall questions the "why" of sudden death and yet still affirms the future.

ISSUE 13
Should Christians support capital punishment?

YES, Christians should support capital punishment.

Michael was arrested in 1970 for child molestation. He was convicted but was put on probation for two years and ordered to undergo psychiatric treatment. During the next two years he was arrested several more times for drug dealing, armed robbery and several sex-related incidents. Although two of the arrests resulted in convictions, Michael never spent much time in prison thanks to shrewd lawyers.

In 1983, he kidnapped a young mother, raped her and then brutally murdered her in front of her 5-year-old daughter. He was just about to kill the child when the police caught up with him. For this crime he was convicted, but he did not receive the death penalty. The defense attorney painted a sad picture of the defendant as the victim of a terrible home.

Michael went to prison for life, but recently broke out. He killed two guards during his escape and has since killed several people for their cars or money. Editorials in the papers insist that Michael should get the electric chair when he is caught and convicted. They point out that had he been sentenced to death after his first murder, several innocent people would be alive today.

There are some crimes so loathsome that the death penalty is the only suitable punishment. A torture-slaying of a young child, the beating deaths of an elderly couple by thugs out for a thrill, the killing of a police officer, the repeated drug and Mafia executions carried out by hit men who kill for a price and the assassination of a U.S. president. All of these crimes are directed at individuals who are innocent victims of anger inside the perpetrator.

Crime has continued to increase for many years. Violent crimes have grown in number. Criminals get off with light sentences. In many states professional criminals think little of killing someone since they know they won't have to face the death penalty if they are caught. Often the worst punishment they will receive is a 10- to 15-year sentence, with time off for good behavior.

Therefore, society's demand for return of the death penalty continues to grow. Although Christians are against bloodshed, they should join in the effort to reinstitute this deterrent to violent crime. People need to learn once more that terrible deeds bring terrible consequences. The time for going soft on criminals out of a misguided sense of love is over.

The use of capital punishment has a long history in the Bible and among Christians. The Sixth Commandment says, "You shall not murder." The Law of Moses actually prescribes death for a number of crimes: adultery, murder, having sex with animals and rebellion against the king. These are just a few of the crimes for which people were put to death. The prophet Elijah even stood by and encouraged those who slayed the Baal priests on Mount Carmel.

The death penalty will make people think more about the consequences of their violent acts. When our society decides to use the death penalty, it will actually enhance the value of life. When the state holds life so sacred that the ultimate crime is to destroy another's life, that crime must be met with the ultimate penalty, the taking of the murderer's life. This severest punishment must be used with extreme caution and equally on all murderers, whether they are white or black, rich or poor. But with capital punishment as a weapon in the arsenal of justice, our police and courts can make significant progress in the ever-continuing battle against lawlessness and violence.

NO, Christians should not support capital punishment.

Two groups held vigils outside the tall stone walls of the state prison. One group carried posters and banners that proclaimed such sentiments as "Fry the rat," "Death is too good for such scum" and "God wills the death penalty." The other group carried lighted candles and a few posters like "The death penalty is wrong" and "No one has the right to kill."

Inside the prison Willy spent a restless night. He talked and prayed briefly with the chaplain at 5 a.m., ate an egg and toast and then walked with his guards to the execution chamber. He protested his sentence for the last time, claiming again that he was a victim of mistaken identity. He admitted he had committed many lesser crimes, but never murder.

At 6:03 a.m., the announcement was made to the world that Willy was dead. He had paid the full penalty for the terrible crime of murder. One of the groups cheered, while the other knelt and offered a brief prayer on behalf of Willy, other victims of the death penalty and the other residents of death row within this nation.

Later that morning the prosecutor told the press that justice was finally satisfied. Across town the defense attorney stated that Willy would still be alive if he had been white. He claimed Willy had been the victim of the city's zealous search to find anyone guilty of the serial rape-murders of young white women in the community.

Less than a year later, another young woman was raped and murdered. This time the killer was careless and left a clue that led to his arrest. He confessed not only to this murder, but to the others as well. It became clear that Willy had been telling the truth after all. When asked by the press to comment, the prosecutor said: "Mistakes occasionally happen. It's too bad. But most of the time, the system works fine." When Willy's defense attorney was told of the prosecutor's remarks, his response was unprintable!

Capital punishment is the answer of a society that has given up on an erring individual. It is a sign of the system's failure to deal with the root causes of crime. It is evidence of humanity's attempt to maintain law and order by fear.

Jesus commanded his followers to go beyond the Old Testament law of "an eye for an eye and a tooth for a tooth." Christians believed in Jesus' commandment to "love your enemy" so much that for the first 300 years of the church's existence they refused to serve in the army or as government magistrates. These positions required the shedding of blood upon the battlefield and within the courts and the prisons. Only when the church became officially accepted and began to adapt to the ways of the world did its leaders accept capital punishment.

Over the years since the 16th century, more and more Christians have developed a keen social conscience based on love. Slavery was finally abolished, as was child labor and the subservient position of women. Christians also fought against the cruel mishandling of the insane and the mistreatment of animals, along with many other inhumane practices once routinely accepted. Capital punishment belongs among these practices relegated to the scrapheap of history.

The execution of a prisoner, innocent or guilty, cannot be undone. Since the courts have made mistakes, innocent people convicted by prejudice, passion or an overzealous prosecutor have needlessly lost their lives. We must not allow this injustice to happen again.

Capital punishment is not an effective deterrent. Studies of societies that use capital punishment do not show any decline in the number of murders. Most murders are not planned, but are the result of an emotional explosion during a family quarrel or a barroom fight. In most cases the murderer never intended to kill the victim, and he or she would never commit another murder. But carried away by a flood of emotion, the killer wreaked vengeance with no thought of the consequences. Capital punishment is unjust because it is almost always inflicted on the black and the poor, the people who cannot afford the expensive lawyers who would work to get them tried on lesser charges or acquitted for lack of evidence.

Capital punishment is also wrong because it makes the state a murderer. Killing someone at an appointed time in front of witnesses is far more cruel than the original crime. If killing is wrong, then it is just as wrong for the state as it is for the individual. Christians should have no part in capital punishment. Instead they should do everything they can to oppose it—to bring about a humane criminal-justice system that will attempt to change the heart and mind of the criminal and not just avenge another death.

Programming Ideas for Issue 13

Preparation—At least one month before your meeting, ask various people to make a four- or five-person panel to present this issue to your group. Try to include the following professionals: a judge, an attorney, a law enforcement officer, a jail chaplain, a member of a peace and justice group, a criminal social worker, a theologian and a pastor.

Tell each panel member you would like him or her to speak for five to seven minutes on the issue of capital punishment from the perspective of his or her profession. Let the speakers know that after the panel's presentations, you will open the floor to questions from the audience. Since this presentation has the potential to be quite an evening, the group members might choose to open it to their parents or the rest of the congregation. They might also invite other youth groups. Take care, however, to limit your audience so your young people are the primary participants.

For the week before this meeting, have the group collect newspaper articles about violent crimes and murder trials. Ask them to bring their collection to this meeting.

Gather markers, newsprint and Bibles. Make the following signs on large sheets of newsprint:
- The murder of a policeman
- The rape and murder of a mother
- The assassination of a U.S. president

- A bank robber who kills and has been convicted twice before
  - A kidnapper who murders his victim
  - A terrorist whose bomb destroys a plane full of people
  - A mass murderer
  - A traitor who has sold secret plans to the enemy
  - A Mafia hit man
  - A drug dealer whose drugs have caused the death of a young teenager
  - (Others you may want to use).

Set up your room so everyone can see and hear the members of the panel. In the room you want to use for the Response, tape the signs onto the wall just before the meeting begins. Set up the number of chairs you want for each group under each sign. Place a Bible on each chair.

Opening—Remind the group that Jesus himself was an executed prisoner, a victim of capital punishment. Therefore, it's appropriate that we find out more about the current state of capital punishment and the attitudes people have about it. Ask your group to share some of the crime and trial stories they found in current news publications.

After a few minutes of sharing, talk about how the different cases were handled. How many different crimes were mentioned? What forms of punishment were administered? How many times was capital punishment used or recommended?

Program—Introduce your panel members by name and professional position. Explain how the panelists will offer their presentations, and remind the audience there will be questions at the end.

Allow 30 to 45 minutes for the panel's presentations and questions from the audience, depending upon how many people your group has invited. Thank your panelists for their time and sharing. Arrange for an informal time at this point so adults and panel members may leave gracefully. Meet in the youth room for the final part of the session.

Response—Once the young people have congregated,

ask them to look around the room at the signs you have posted. Ask them to choose one of the situations that bothers them the most and sit in one of the chairs under that sign. If all the chairs are filled, they should choose another group.

Ask the participants each to pretend they are the judge at a trial in which the person described on the sign has been found guilty. They have to impose the sentence on this individual. Ask them to share the sentence they would present and give reasons for their choice. (The group does not have to agree.)

Ask two individuals in each group to read Romans 12:9-19 and Romans 13:1-5 aloud. Ask the groups to talk about these scripture passages. Ask the group, "Do these verses make any difference in how we should look upon or treat a murderer? Explain your answer."

Ask another young person to read Jesus' words in Matthew 5:43-48. Tell all the groups: "Some say these words were intended for guidance in how we should relate to each other in the church, not as laws for our society. They say our society must defend itself against those who break its laws. What do you think? Discuss this issue within your small groups."

To close the session, ask the groups to bring their chairs together in a large circle and summarize the main points people have raised within each small group.

Ask everyone to look at the signs around the room. Talk about who would need our prayers in each situation. Ask the group how they could offer sentence prayers for each of these individuals. Ask for strength and guidance in learning how to pray for those who are injured and those who perpetrate the injury. Then pray for deeper understanding and love for everyone in the group. Close by singing "Make Me a Channel of Your Peace" from *Songs* (Songs and Creations).

Options:

1. Arrange for a visit to the local jail. Ask ahead of time to meet with an official or a chaplain who will agree to talk

about the justice system. Ask him or her to speak to the issue of how capital punishment does or does not fit as a punishment within the judicial system.

2. If there is a lawyer in your church, arrange for your group to meet in his or her office. Perhaps he or she could arrange to talk with your group in a courtroom at the local courthouse. Ask the lawyer to share specific information on the arguments for and against capital punishment and how these points fit into his or her Christian faith

3. A corollary to this issue that stirs the emotions of many is concern for victims' rights. Capital punishment usually reflects a reaction to a horrendous crime, one that involves the death or disability of another human being. Society cannot ignore the pain and anguish of family members who remain, but must be responsible for easing that trauma. But there must also be concern in these situations to be sure emotions do not override reason or doubt. Use the scripture passages suggested in the Response section to help the group struggle with how we can minister to those who have lost loved ones and struggle with their very real feelings.

CHURCH ISSUES

The church is God's own people (1 Peter 2:9). We are the body of Christ (1 Corinthians 12:27), yet we are also human. Within the fellowship of the church, young people experience Christ and are challenged to be his men and women. For better or for worse, the local church represents the church universal for teenagers involved in its fellowship.

Because church members don't always live up to their high calling, teenagers may become disillusioned with the church. They may be surprised that issues which trouble and divide society also trouble and divide the church—issues like divorce, homosexuality, sexism, wealth, the importance we place on things and how we accept authority.

The sessions in this chapter can help young people and adults deal with these issues in a faith context. Because these issues deal with the close relationships within the fellowship of believers, the conflicts can be painful, especially when friends in Christ find themselves on opposite sides of an issue. But Christians should continually remind each other that they are "brothers and sisters in Christ"; therefore, they are bound by a unity that no difference of opinion can destroy.

ISSUE 14
Should church leaders always be obeyed?

YES, church leaders should *always* be obeyed.

"Boy, Toby, Pastor Grayson really attacked the smokers yesterday! Even my dad was talking about giving up the habit."

"I suppose so, but the way I see it, he's just stating his own opinion."

"Oh? Even when he's preaching from the pulpit and basing his ideas on the Bible?"

"Sure. After all, he's just a man. He can make mistakes like everyone else. And besides, the Bible doesn't say anything about smoking."

"But Pastor Grayson showed how the scripture talks about our bodies as temples of the Holy Spirit and also how we shouldn't be slaves to anything. No, I'll go along with the pastor when he says not to smoke or do anything that would pollute our bodies or spirits. I think he knows what he's talking about."

Church members should always obey their church leaders. Leaders are appointed or elected because they have studied and prepared themselves for leadership. The church would be in chaos if the members did whatever they desired and paid no attention to their leaders.

Most churches have two kinds of leadership: professional and lay. Both are important for the health and effectiveness of the church. The professional or full-time leadership position requires that individuals spend a great amount of time studying the Bible, theology, the history of the church and many other aspects of leadership. Thus, when pastors or Christian educators speak on a topic, they communicate more than just their own opinion. Their thoughts and ideas have been shaped by the Word of God and many hours of reading, attending lectures, studying and thinking. Anyone who opposes their opinion should have a good reason to do so.

Most churches teach that only those called by God can be ordained pastors. This call comes in various ways, depending upon an individual's denominational teachings. Hierarchical churches believe that the Holy Spirit works through bishops whose training and understanding guide them in the selection process. Other churches teach that the Holy Spirit works through church councils or boards who prayerfully evaluate and select their leaders. The "free" churches (Baptist, Disciples of Christ, etc.) believe the call must come from a vote of the congregation. No matter how the call comes, this call constitutes God's approval for an individual's ministry. Therefore, people who oppose the pastor should do so carefully, lest they find themselves opposing God's will.

Persons elected by their congregations to lay offices also deserve respect and obedience. These people are not setting themselves up in authority, but are responding to God's call to serve their congregation. Even if we do not always like these individuals personally or agree with their decisions, we must respect their office and, out of respect for the office, obey them. God didn't create the church for confusion and chaos but for service. The only way the church can move forward in service is for the people to follow its chosen leaders.

NO, church members should not feel compelled to *always* obey their church leaders.

"So what are you going to do, Terry?"

"I don't know, except that I know I'm not going to give Meg up, no matter what my parents or Pastor Cleery say!"

"But he's the minister. You heard what he said about mixing the races. He even pointed out *why* you shouldn't think of going with her. What if you felt you should marry?"

"Maybe we will; maybe we won't. But whether we do or don't, her being white and me being black isn't the issue. The important thing is what we believe and how we feel about each other. I'm not that concerned about what the minister says."

"But he's studied the Bible more than we have!"

"Well, I think he's studied the wrong part. He's obviously overlooked the part about loving one another! And doesn't it say somewhere, 'He has made of one blood all men and nations'?"

Many ordination services ask the members of the congregation to follow their new leader as they see him or her following Jesus Christ. The authority of the church leader does not arise from his or her personality or ordination, but from personal obedience to Jesus Christ.

Ordained pastors deserve the respect and support of their congregations, but they are not infallible just because they have been ordained. They can make mistakes, sometimes in judgment and sometimes in interpreting scripture. This is why Protestants insist on an individual's right to read the scripture. Then guided by the Holy Spirit, the individual can arrive at his or her *own* interpretation. The individual still respects the opinion of his or her trained pastor, but only when the pastor agrees with scripture.

Churches often build into their constitutions provisions for dissent within the church, including protection for the rights of the minority. These churches recognize the fallibility of their leaders and reserve the right to correct them if they are wrong. If a leader teaches or orders something contrary to the scripture as a whole, it is the duty of those under his or her care and guidance to correct the error or misunderstanding. This should be done in humility, love and patience. In all matters the leader, as well as the church members, must obey Christ as he is revealed in scripture.

Programming Ideas for Issue 14

Preparation—Prepare copies of Chart 9 for each small group to compare church authority among denominations. Also prepare a large copy of this chart on newsprint or make a transparency and use an overhead projector.

Gather copies of the rule books or constitutions from several denominations such as The Discipline (United Methodist), The Book of Order (Presbyterian Church, USA) and so on. For an independent church, use the bylaws or covenant of the congregation. Collect the list of rules your congregation follows.

Go to a paint store and ask for multiple copies of four or five different paint strips.

Opening—Pass out the paint strips and tell each person that he or she should find the rest of the people who have the same paint strip. Once everyone has found his or her group, ask the groups to choose one color on the paint strip they would use to paint the youth room. After each group has selected a color, ask all the groups to meet together and argue for the one color. In most groups you will have a lot of different opinions with the first part and even more opinions when the other colors are introduced. Encourage the group members to discuss *why* the room should be painted the color selected by their small group.

When discussion is at a peak, stop it and ask who has

Chart 9
Authority in the Church

Denomination: _____

    (Who) governs the church?

    Pastor has **(how much)** authority?

    Decisions pastor can make

    Decisions board can make

    Decisions that require **both** pastor and board.

    Pastor called/dismissed **(how)?**

    Disagreements are handled **(how)?**

    Appeal process

    Ordination service

        Purpose of ordination

        Pastor's vows

        People's vows

the authority to choose the color for the youth room. Point out how difficult it is to make decisions when everyone wants input into every decision made.

Talk about some of the decisions that must be made in the church. How can anyone know who is responsible for what decisions?

Discuss how denominations operate differently. Give an example of how some pastors have total control and how some must take into consideration every whim of their congregation.

Program—Ask the small groups to meet again and give each group a copy of Chart 9, a Bible and a copy of an official church document for one of the various denominations. Tell the groups to skim through the denominational information for the part that describes the duties and authority of the pastor. Ask the groups each to record the information they discover on their comparison chart. After all groups have answered the questions for their denomination, have everyone meet together to share their information. Write the information on the large form or overhead transparency you prepared ahead of time.

Response—After the group has examined the authority of church leaders within the various denominations, ask group members to respond to the following situations. Tell them: "If you believe you should obey the church leader or pastor in this area, hold your thumb up. If you believe the church leader or pastor has no authority over you in this area, turn your thumb down. If you are not sure about the authority of the leader or pastor in this area, shrug your shoulders." Read the following statements and wait for the young people to respond after each situation.

The church leader or pastor should have the authority to:

1. Tell you not to listen to rock music or to dance.

2. Tell you what races or ethnic groups can and cannot belong to your church or youth group.

3. Order you to make four visits a month to inactive members.

4. Command you to tithe your income or allowance.

5. Order you not to play cards.

6. Forbid your youth group to invite a speaker from another denomination to your meeting.

7. Order all group members not to attend R-rated movies.

8. Tell church members to vote for a specific political candidate.

9. Tell you how to do your wedding in the church.

10. (Add your own.)

Ask participants to share their responses to each situation presented and give reasons for their responses. Are any of the reasons scriptural? Are their responses based on their church's official teachings?

Tell the group that the model for a church leader's or pastor's use of authority must be, as in everything, Jesus Christ himself. Ask two people to read John 13:1-17. Have one read the narrative, while the other reads the words of Jesus. Remind the group that Jesus' authority comes from being the servant of all. Close with a prayer like this one:

"O God, we call your Son 'Lord,' yet he took the form of a servant, even dying on the cross for us. May we seek to be servants rather than attempt to control. May we see the servanthood of Christ within our pastor so we can follow his (or her) example. Remind us to seek not our own will but yours. In the name of Jesus we pray, Amen."

Options:

1. Invite a panel of clergy members to present the role and authority of the clergy within their denominations. Include your own pastor along with a Catholic or Episcopal priest; a member of a free church, such as Baptist or Congregational; a United Methodist; and possibly a Lutheran or a United Church of Christ pastor. Be sure to provide them each with a list of specific questions you would like answered during their presentations.

2. Ask your pastor to explain what your denomination teaches about the topic of authority.

3. Lead a Bible study of scripture passages that describe the qualities necessary for a good church leader. In 1 Timothy 3:1-13, the writer talks about a bishop in verses 1-7, an office that corresponds more to today's "pastor" than to the modern bishop. The Greek word "episcopos," translated here as bishop, means "overseer." Acts 14:23 uses the term "presbuteros" as "elder" when referring to the pastoral office in some parts of the Roman Empire. In other places within the scripture, there seems to have been both offices, with the bishop overseeing the elders. Compare the Timothy passage with Titus 1:5-9 and 1 Corinthians 3—4.

Divide into three groups and assign the scripture passages: 1 Timothy 3:1-13, Titus 1:5-9 and 1 Corinthians 3—4.

Ask each small group to list the qualities of leadership in the passage. Use the following questions for discussion in each group.

● Did the scripture talk about the *source* of a pastor's authority? On what source does this authority depend?

● Are there limits to a pastor's authority? If so, what limits are described?

● How do you see this authority operating in your church? Read the sections of your denominational documents that describe the role and authority of pastors.

ISSUE 15
Should divorced pastors continue to lead their congregations?

YES, divorced pastors should be allowed to continue leading their congregations.

"Midge, did you hear about the pastor and his wife?"

"No, what do you mean?"

"Well, you're not going to believe this, but they're getting a divorce!"

"A divorce? You can't be right! Why, our group was at the parsonage just two weeks ago, and everything seemed fine."

"It's not fine now. Evidently their problems have been brewing for a long time. You must have noticed that she's missed church a lot the past few months."

"Oh, I wonder what they will do? How can he be our pastor if they go through with this divorce?"

Asking a divorced pastor to remain and serve the congregation is an excellent way for the church to show that it is a place of grace, love and forgiveness, not harsh judgment and punishment. Of course, the congregation's decision should be based on the circumstances surrounding the pastor's divorce. If the divorce were due to a pastor's adultery, he or she shouldn't be allowed to serve as pastor anywhere, until sincere repentance and renewal occurs. And even if the pastor were the "innocent party," he or she should receive counseling from a qualified professional who can help him or her learn from the experience and repent of any personal blame that led to the divorce.

Pastors are human beings like everyone else in the congregation. They are subject to the same temptations and mistakes other Christians go through. Their position in the congregation can even add extra strain to their personal lives. The long hours spent in church activities often lead to a spouse's resentment and can be instrumental in destroying a marriage.

Prayers and support from the congregation are vital to the pastor, whether or not he or she intends to stay after the breakup. Too many congregations have turned their backs on the divorced pastor and treated him or her as a moral outcast. If ever God's grace and understanding were needed from his people, this is one of those times. Churches that have stood by their pastor and spouse report a deepened awareness of the riches of God's mercy and love. They realize that Christian love can even support their leaders as they struggle over the rough, hard places of life.

Yes, a divorced pastor should continue to lead his or her congregation. If there is enough love, understanding and forgiveness so that the congregation is not torn apart or disrupted, it is probably best for the pastor to remain with the congregation he or she is presently serving. If this is not possible, however, a new congregation can serve its new leader through prayers and personal support. Although a pastor's divorce, like anyone else's, represents the failure of two individuals to maintain their relationship as husband and wife, it can also be an opportunity for a congregation's expression of God's love and grace.

NO, divorced pastors should not be allowed to lead congregations.

"I'm not going back there no matter what you say."

"Just because the pastor got a divorce?"

"I don't expect a pastor to be perfect, but I do expect him to stand for something, to uphold the morals and ideals of the church. His getting a divorce goes against everything I've been taught in the church all my life!"

"What do you mean?"

"The Bible and marriage ceremony talk about marriage as a lifetime commitment—the two shall become one until death do they part. How can I think about God when the person giving the sermon is someone who has obviously flouted God's law?"

There are enough problems in the church without sanctioning divorce. When the church allows a divorced pastor to continue to serve a congregation, it says to all that divorce is okay. If the pastor or spiritual leader is divorced and is still allowed to lead the church, his or her presence says: "Don't worry. Divorce is no big deal."

A divorced pastor is a case of the blind leading the blind. Although in some cases Jesus was very liberal, he informed the Pharisees that Moses wrote this commandment to permit divorce only because their hearts were hard (Mark 10:5). Marriage joins two people in a close, intimate relationship. This relationship takes priority over all other human relationships, even that of parent and child. In marriage, the two people become one. Jesus then told his disciples that whoever divorces a spouse and remarries another is committing adultery (Matthew 5:31-32).

That's a hard statement, but it shows in what high regard the Lord held marriage. It should not be entered into lightly, and in the eyes of God it cannot be dissolved. The liturgy of the marriage ceremony really means "for better or for worse" and "for richer and for poorer, as long as we both shall live." Pastors, above all, should know and accept this.

Thus, if a pastor is divorced, he or she should give up the calling and seek other employment. The pastor's life can no longer be a witness to the gospel; it is too compromised for him or her to be effective after a divorce.

Programming Ideas for Issue 15

Preparation—Gather newsprint, 3×5 cards and at least 10 Bibles. Tape each of the situations from Chart 10 onto a separate 3×5 card.

Check periodicals (or your denominational office) for current statistics about divorce. Try to find the following pieces of information:

_____percent of marriages in our country currently end in divorce.

_____percent of marriages between pastors and spouses end in divorce.

_____percent of pastors continue to serve once they have been divorced.

Write these statistics on a sheet of newsprint for all to share.

Opening—Point out that most families in North America have been touched by divorce. Share the statistics you found. Let the group know that in some parts of the country, half the marriages end in divorce. Tell everyone: "Since church pastors are human, they too have experienced trouble in their marriages. At one time pastors would not have resorted to the divorce courts, but today many do. This decision has disturbed church members and often left them perplexed as to what they should do about divorced pastors. In this session we will look at the problem and how each of us feels and believes about this."

Program—Divide the group into teams of two or three people. Each team will receive one of the situation cards. Ask the teams each to read their card and talk about the situation presented. Then each team should prepare a scenario by filling in details and coming up with an ending that shows what they believe the congregation should do about the situation. Let them know they will have 20 minutes to work on this activity and will then share their stories with the other teams.

Chart 10
Ten Situations

1. The pastor commits adultery.

2. The pastor's spouse commits adultery.

3. The pastor switched careers over the objections of his wife, and she has decided she is not fit to be a pastor's wife.

4. The pastor, a workaholic, is never home with her husband or children. Fed up, the husband leaves her.

5. The pastor and wife drift apart and decide to separate.

6. The pastor and her husband argue vehemently over theology. Unable to agree, they decide to divorce.

7. The pastor decides to leave the ministry and the church. His wife doesn't understand the decision and refuses to leave with him.

8. The pastor's husband, brain-damaged in a car accident, exists in a deep coma in an institution. There is no chance for recovery. After several years the pastor meets a special gentleman and falls in love. She seeks a divorce so she can remarry.

9. While in seminary, the young pastor fell in love with a non-Christian. Against the advice of everyone, they were married. The first few years were fine, even though the wife took no part in church. Slowly they began to drift apart and decided to separate. Now the pastor has met a special Christian woman in his church.

10. The pastor's wife has become an alcoholic and refuses to admit she needs help. Her illness is beginning to affect their three children. After several years things are so bad that the pastor feels he must protect the children. She refuses to get help, and he seeks a divorce.

After each team presents its story, invite comments from the others. Do they agree with the group's conclusion for the story? If not, how would they end it? Which solutions seem to emphasize "law"? Which ones emphasize "grace"?

Post a sheet of newsprint at the front of the room. Point out that this issue involves two important principles which often conflict—the pastor as an example of one who lives in the kingdom of God and the pastor as a fallible human being. Ask the group members what they expect from their pastors. List these ideas on the newsprint. Take another look at the list. Star those expectations which show that the pastor is an example for the people in his or her congregation. Circle those examples that recognize the pastor's humanity and fallibility. Ask the group members if they can recognize any expectations that may be unrealistic or need to be altered.

Response—Have the teenagers imagine that their pastor has just been divorced. Divide into small groups, and have each group write two letters, one to their pastor and one to his or her spouse. After 15 minutes meet together as a large group and share the letters. Examine each letter for concerns about the standards of conduct in the church and statements about grace and forgiveness. Close with the following prayer:

"God, you have called the church to be your people, yet sometimes we fail to live up to your standards. Even our leaders stumble at times. Yet you are the God of grace, of second chances. You changed Jacob from a heel to a saint, Peter from a fearful failure to a bold booster for your kingdom. Continue to visit us with your Spirit, forgive us and renew both us and our pastors, that we might be molded into the likeness of your Son, even Jesus Christ, our Lord. Amen."

Options:
1. Borrow the pastor's handbooks or liturgical guides for several different denominations. Assign two or three

people to each book and have the group compare the wedding services or liturgies. What do the services say about "hard times"? What view of marriage do the different denominations hold? (Many have official documents that spell out their position.) Talk about how the church can communicate both grace and forgiveness to its members while it maintains strict standards of conduct for its ministers and members. Can the young people see a tension here? On the one hand, the church needs to maintain rules and standards of behavior or chaos will break out. Yet the church wants to avoid harsh and unfeeling attitudes that can lead to legalism.

2. Ask your pastor to speak to the group concerning what your denomination teaches about divorce. How does the church approach the scripture passages in Mark 10:2-12, Matthew 5:31-32 and Deuteronomy 24:1-4? How can the differences be explained? On which passage does your denomination base its teachings?

3. Invite several local pastors to serve as a panel to talk about this issue. Prepare a list of questions you and your group have about this issue and present a copy to each panel member ahead of time.

ISSUE 16
Should homosexuals be pastors or other church leaders?

YES, homosexuals should be accepted in the church on an equal basis with others, including the right to become church leaders.

"Are you absolutely sure, Carl?"

"Pastor, I've fought this for all my adult life. I've been to a psychiatrist and two sex therapists. Mary has tried to help me, but she now realizes that I can't change. Like it or not, I'm gay. We've prayed and prayed about this, but I still don't know what to do—about my marriage to Mary and about my nomination as trustee for the church board.

"What do you think? I've been in the church all my life. I've taught Sunday school, served on most of the committees, helped remodel the Christian education wing, and yet I often feel completely worthless. Can God possibly love or use a person like me?"

The church needs to stand beside homosexuals, the group of people today's society has designated as the new lepers, the outcasts for others to look down on. In the past the church has too often *joined* in the persecution of this misunderstood minority. This persecution by the church has resulted from centuries of misunderstanding of both scripture and the nature of homosexuality. Several scripture passages used to condemn homosexuals don't actually deal with the homosexual expressions heard about today. For instance, the story in Genesis 19 condemns the men of Sodom for their attempt to seize and gang rape the two men (angels) who were visiting Lot. This behavior actually violated the sacred custom of hospitality to strangers, and thus was not concerned with homosexuality.

Paul's statements about homosexuals not being able to enter the kingdom of God was directed at those who freely *chose* to reverse their sexual roles. Since the custom at many pagan feasts called for guests to indulge in sexual orgies, the diners would choose the role—male or female— they wished to play at the feast. Many who were bored or tired of ordinary sex would *choose* to have sex with members of the same gender.

The dilemma of most homosexuals today is that they do *not* choose their sexual preference. Time after time gay individuals describe how they gradually became aware that they were different, how they realized they were attracted to members of the same sex and how they fight against that preference. Some even marry members of the opposite sex, hoping their preferences will change. Many pray and undergo intensive therapy in an attempt to change. Until recently, virtually all homosexuals kept their secret to themselves out of fear.

In 1973, the American Psychiatric Association dropped homosexuality from its list of illnesses or disorders. The or-

ganization took this action because there was no scientific
evidence that homosexuality was indeed a disorder. Studies
could produce no conclusive evidence that a person's environment would produce a homosexual, especially when
identical circumstances often resulted in one person becoming a homosexual and another, a heterosexual person. Just
why a person becomes a homosexual is still a mystery;
some scientists even claim that a person is born this way.
Studies of the attempts to get homosexuals to change their
sexual preference were also unfruitful. Even those individuals
who *claimed* to change experienced a great deal of anguish
and sometimes pretended to change to gain acceptance
from those around them.

The subject of homosexuality stirs the emotions of
many people, especially those uncertain of their own sexual
nature. As a result, many myths feed the misunderstandings
and fears of this condition. People are shocked when a big,
burly football player turns out to be a homosexual because
they expect effeminate mannerisms in homosexual men and
masculine mannerisms in homosexual women. Even though
some statistics indicate that most child molesters are sick
heterosexuals and are usually members of victims' families,
society has great difficulty trusting homosexuals around
children.

Because of the stirred-up passions, it may be wise that
a homosexual should not hold an office in a particular
church, but this decision should be made out of concern
for the peace and unity of the church, not because the person
is a homosexual. In Jesus' day the lepers and the Samaritans
were despised and treated as outcasts, yet Jesus welcomed
them. Today the homosexual has taken their place in society. A great many homosexual church members fear they
will be rejected by the very people with whom they worship. They are afraid that they will be rejected even by
those who follow the compassionate Christ, if others learn
that they are by nature homosexual. Many have lived for
years with their mate of the same gender as faithfully committed as any man and woman in a regular marital relationship.

The church should not make a person's sexual preference the basis for being a leader in the church.

NO, homosexuals should not be allowed leadership within the church.

"Hi, Ben. Congratulations on being elected delegate to the church's national assembly."

"Thanks, Mark. It should be quite an experience."

"Yes, it seems there are quite a few important issues coming up. I would like to talk with you about one of them."

"I'll bet I know which one it is, too. The ordination of homosexual candidates?"

"Well, yes, but how did . . . ?"

"Because you're about the 10th person to have brought up the subject. Don't worry, I plan to vote against it."

"Good! I'd hate to see our church torn apart over this."

"So would I."

Homosexuality has been condemned as a sin since Old Testament times. No matter what the American Psychiatric Association says, the church should continue to oppose this sexual practice. The name of a sin may change according to society's whims, but sin remains sin.

Genesis tells us that God made two kinds of human beings, not three: "So God created man in his own image, in the image of God he created him; male and female he created them. God blessed them and said to them, 'Be fruitful and increase in number . . . ' " (Genesis 1:27-28). In order to perpetuate the human race, God made the two sexes. This is a part of the natural-created order. When a person gives in to his or her own lust for an individual of the same sex, he or she is rejecting the order established by God.

The Apostle Paul describes humanity's rebellion against God and its terrible consequences. "Because of this, God gave them over to shameful lusts. Even their women exchanged natural relations for unnatural ones. In the same way the men also abandoned natural relations with women who were inflamed with lust for one another. Men committed indecent acts with other men, and received in themselves the due penalty for their perversion" (Romans 1:26-27).

Paul continues this scripture passage with a description of how these unnatural passions led to other kinds of sin. The people became so corrupted they not only committed evil themselves, but they approved of others doing so. Thus, the scripture clearly condemns homosexuality as an abominable practice.

It is true that Christians sometimes allow their own fear and hatred to dictate their behavior as they struggle against this evil, but that does not make homosexuality right. We should follow Jesus' example of treating sinners with kindness and understanding, but this does not mean approving the sin! When Jesus confronted the woman caught in the act of adultery, he was kind and refused to condemn her to the terrible penalty of the law, death by stoning. But he did not accept her behavior; instead he told her, "Go now and leave your life of sin" (John 8:11). This is the way we should approach homosexuals—with the love and acceptance of Christ, but with a firm command to end the sinning.

There are Christian therapists who have treated homosexuals successfully. Curing people with homosexual tendencies is indeed difficult, and some people do not respond to treatment. But many do and move forward to lead normal lives. The church should accept homosexuals in love on the same basis as former embezzlers, adulterers or others who have gone astray, but all should be urged to "sin no more." If homosexuals cannot respond to treatment but are willing to give up their homosexual activities, they should be allowed to hold office in the church. They must, however, repent their past misdeeds and state their intention to honor and support the heterosexual lifestyle as the one upheld by the Bible.

Programming Ideas for Issue 16

Preparation—Prepare nine signs out of posterboard or newsprint. On each sign write one of the statements in Chart 11. Tape the signs in order on a continuum along one wall. Have Bibles on hand.

Opening—Ask, "What do you think of when you hear someone refer to a 'queer,' 'gay,' 'fruit,' or 'homo'?" Pause for the nervous laughter or limp-wristed gestures you will probably experience. Suggest that homosexuality is one of the most controversial topics of our day and also one of the most misunderstood. Remind the group that it is unlikely they will clear up all of their misconceptions in this session, but everyone will try to look at the underlying issues in a Christian manner.

Program—Tell the group to read the statements along the wall and move to the one with which they agree the most.

After everyone has taken a position on the continuum, have each person look around and find someone who chose a different position. Ask the kids to go to each other and try to convince each other of the truth of their position. Allow five minutes for this first encounter, after which individuals will return to the sign with which they agree. Then have them select another person and spend five minutes trying to convince that person. Tell them to return again to the sign with which they agree and then choose a third person to convince.

Some young people will return to the same sign over and over; others, however, may change their opinions and their positions. Ask everyone to look at the signs again and choose their final position. Encourage the group members to talk about their experiences. Ask them: "How do you feel about your experiences? Did you have a difficult time selecting *one* position? If so, what other position would you have chosen and why? Is this an 'either/or' topic, or do you have ambivalent feelings about this issue?

"What arguments did you use to back up your position? Did you convince anyone to change? Did you find

Chart 11
Homosexuality

1. Homosexuality should be outlawed, and all homosexuals that refuse to change should be arrested.

2. Homosexuals should be segregated from the rest of society.

3. Homosexuals should not be allowed to join the church, but may attend services.

4. Homosexuals should be able to join the church and have most civil rights, but not teach children or young people or work in health care facilities.

5. Homosexuals may teach adults or adolescents, but not young children. They may work in hospitals and nursing homes as long as there is no physical contact with patients.

6. Homosexuals may join the church and participate fully as teachers or leaders with any age group, but may not serve as officers or pastors. They may work in the medical community as long as they identify themselves to the staff so that their interaction with others can be regulated.

7. Homosexuals may be church officers, but not pastors; teachers, but not principals. They may serve in the medical community as nurses and support staff, but not as physicians.

8. Homosexuals should be accepted equally in the church, including the right to be pastors. They should also have the right to be physicians, even surgeons, and aspire to any level in the field of education.

9. Homosexuals should have all the rights of other citizens, even though I do not approve of their lifestyle.

that your position hardened the more you talked? Did you listen to the other persons during the five-minute exchanges, or did you tend to do most of the talking?''

Response—Divide into small groups to read and discuss some of the Bible passages that deal with this controversy. Ask each group to take one passage, discuss it and then report back to the group.

● Genesis 19 (Is the sin of the Sodomites homosexuality, gang rape or refusal to honor hospitality? See Luke 10:10-12 and Ezekiel 16:49-50 for ways this incident was interpreted elsewhere in the Bible.)

● Leviticus 18:23 and 20:13

- Romans 1:26-27
- 1 Corinthians 6:9-10
- 1 Timothy 1:9-10

After the small groups have shared their findings, tell the young people: "The term 'homophobia' has risen from the hateful reaction of some Christians to homosexuals. What do you think of this attitude? Is it possible to disapprove of homosexuality and still love the homosexuals? How? Some call homosexuals the 'new lepers' of our society. What do you think? Do Christians sometimes react in unchristian ways to the evils they deplore? How should the church treat homosexuals?"

Continue: "No matter how strongly you may feel about the issue, the Christian message is one of grace, not law. In the eyes of God, all of us come to Christ as sinners who need reconciliation by his cross. Our view may or may not be right, but the final judgment is God's. Therefore, we should witness to the truth as we best understand it, but always with humility and love."

Close with prayer:

"God our creator, we come seeking your love and guidance. Some of us are sure we know the answer to this tragic issue; some of us are not so certain. But no matter where we stand, we know that we need your love and grace. Some of your children are experiencing terrible pain because of this issue. Enfold them in your love as the mother eagle covers her little ones with her wings. Forgive us for any harsh thoughts or unkind remarks we have directed toward others who are so different from us. We ask this in the name of him who welcomed the leper and the Samaritan, Jesus Christ our Lord, Amen."

Options:

1. Invite a panel of pastors, doctors, psychiatrists or counselors to make a presentation of this subject. Prepare a list of questions ahead of time to guide the panelists in preparation for their presentations.

2. Read the two passages from the following books and

ask the group to comment on them:

● The letter by a homosexual Christian, *Is the Homosexual My Neighbor? Another Christian View* (Harper & Row), pp. 6-7.

● The last three paragraphs of the Preface, *When You Are Concerned With Homosexuality* (Abbey Press), pp. 7-8.

ISSUE 17

Should the church spend money on elaborate buildings, furnishings or celebrations?

YES, the church should spend money on elaborate buildings, furnishings or celebrations.

The building committee of Faith Church met to discuss the kinds of windows their new sanctuary should have.

"I think the windows should be plain, clear ones," Sam started off, "clean and simple like those in a New England chapel. It would also save a lot of money."

"But how can you have a church without stained-glass windows?" Judy asked. "They're so beautiful, and they add so much to the mood of worship."

"Not only that," Stu joined in, "but stained-glass windows can also be great teaching devices." Everyone smiled at this statement because almost everyone had experienced Stu's enthusiasm for teaching. "Some churches are a treasure of great symbols of faith and pictures from the Bible. I would hope that *our* sanctuary could be this way, too. I've also heard our pastor express the same idea. Right, Bob?"

The pastor nodded. "Yes, artisans have expressed many of the great teachings of the church in stained glass. Besides, if the sermon gets boring at times, the people can still be inspired by the windows."

Although spending money on buildings and beautiful furnishings can be a selfish practice, this isn't always so. There are times when expense should not be the issue. The Lord deserves the best of what we have—our time, our talents and even our material goods. Although a congregation can go overboard, the church building should appear beautiful and clean. An attractive and well-kempt structure says, "Here are people who choose to give their best to God." When designed creatively, the building and furnishings, including stained-glass windows, can teach valuable lessons to those who gather for worship.

When Solomon built the temple, he imported the costliest materials and the best artisans so that God's house would be a place of beauty. When the scripture says, "Worship the Lord in the beauty of holiness," it refers to more than just the spiritual attitude of the worshippers; it refers to the worship setting also. A beautiful sanctuary can actually lift the spirits of worshippers to behold the beauty of God. Lovely furnishings and ornaments like stained glass can move our minds to recognize God's presence. And a worship service, supported by a pipe organ and a robed choir, can lead worshippers to the "heights of heaven," if even for a few moments.

Congregations with older buildings frequently fight the battle of what to do with their physical buildings. Should a steeple be pulled down, or should it be repaired? Should a sanctuary be remodeled, or should another one be built? Which choices would be more faithful to a witness for Christ?

The cost of removing a steeple and capping the tower may appear high at first. Some may argue that when this expense is figured over a long period of time and compared with continual repairs, taking down the steeple would be best. Others may counter this argument by describing the impact a steeple has on its community. Many times the steeple is the first thing people see when they enter a town or village. Pointing heavenward, the steeple declares to all that God's people worship in this building. When it is maintained, the steeple says that these people care about their church and the beauty of their community. And in some deteriorating neighborhoods, this Christian symbol says, "These people choose not to abandon their mission to the people of the area." This witness may seem less tangible than sending money to missions, but it can be just as important.

The people of God do not *need* fancy buildings or elaborate furnishings to worship their Lord. This group of believers once worshipped in the catacombs, the underground burial place for the dead. But buildings and furnishings can enhance ministry. Our physical beings need a place to gather out of the elements, but our spiritual beings long for beauty in objects like stained-glass windows, paintings and carvings. These things can facilitate our worship and aid in our spiritual education. If we can avoid worshipping these objects, they can point beyond themselves to the Creator of truth and beauty.

There are times when the people of God need to celebrate great spiritual events and other special occasions. These times call for items that might be extravagant if they were used every Sunday. But church members should recognize these unique opportunities for using celebrative paraphernalia like balloons, special music and banners. Remember, even Jesus was alert to those special moments of celebration. He even chastised his disciples when they objected to the woman anointing his feet with costly ointment (Mark 14:3-9).

Christians should spend as much on mission and outreach as they do on themselves, but this should not prevent them from creating beautiful buildings and furnishings.

NO, Christians should not use church money for elaborate buildings, furnishings or celebrations.

"Sorry, kids, but we can't meet in the church parlor when our guest speaker comes next Sunday," Tom informed the group.

"But why not?" Derek asked. "It would make everything so much more special."

The president of the youth fellowship looked totally dismayed.

"The Women's Association just bought carpet and furniture for the parlor. The church board is concerned about keeping it new and shiny, so they've adopted a policy of no food and no kids.

"And that's not all," Tom continued. "The board also said we don't need to make an Easter banner for the sanctuary this year."

"But why not?" piped up Cathy, the talented senior who had headed the banner work group for the past three years. "Our group has been making the Easter banner for 10 years! It's something we look forward to."

"The worship and building committees decided banners don't fit the decor of the sanctuary since it's been redecorated. We've become a bit too fancy, I guess."

We live in a world of acute needs, daily starvation and mass misery. Christians should spend as much as they can on the needs of "the least of these," not on themselves. Impressive buildings and fancy furnishings are out of place in today's world.

During the first part of their history, the Israelites worshipped in a tent or tabernacle to emphasize the mobility of God. They believed God was a traveling God, not tied down to a particular place or building. When the temple was built, the people began to develop a superstitious awe and trust toward the building, rather than toward the God to whom the temple was dedicated. Even though Solomon had cautioned the people to retain the image of God over all, this tendency to limit God's presence to the temple became so great that Jeremiah finally called the temple "a den of thieves" and prophesied it would soon be destroyed. Too often the same thing happens to those who build elaborate, costly church buildings. Fear that something will be damaged or stolen limits the building's use, promotes a false sense of value in things and eliminates many from church fellowship.

Congregations saddled with older buildings and dwindling numbers of people find themselves spending more and more money on the upkeep and heating of their buildings and less and less on missions. Some churches even split into "steeple-people" and "mission-minded" factions, especially at budget-making time.

Churches challenge their people to be good stewards of their time, talent and money. They urge them to weigh carefully how they spend their money and not waste any of it. The church should also do this with its own money. Simple buildings and furnishings should be selected over costly and elaborate ones. The money the church spends on people and on its missions near and far should be far greater than what it spends on itself. Neither Jesus nor his disciples rode around on expensive animals or wore fancy clothing. They were too busy serving the needs of others to worry about themselves. Jesus set the example. We should follow in his footsteps of simplicity and service.

Programming Ideas for Issue 17

Preparation—Make copies of Chart 12 for all participants. Gather church furnishings and educational supply catalogs, copies of the church budget, Bibles, pencils, paper, a marker and cups for drinks. Prepare lemonade or punch or purchase soft drinks in large containers for the group.

Set aside enough cups for the number of people you think will attend this session. Divide the cups into four groups and mark the bottom of each cup with one of the following letters: T, M, E or O. For example, if you think you will have 24 people at the session, count out 24 cups. Divide the cups into four groups of six cups. Turn the cups over. On the bottom of the six cups in the first group, write T. On the bottom of the six cups in the second group, write M, and so on. After the cups are labeled, turn them over and use them to serve the drinks you have prepared.

Prepare four large signs with T, M, E and O and place these in four different parts of the room. Place a Bible, paper and pencils at each location along with a description of the group's assignment.

Opening—As your young people arrive, encourage them to take something to drink and hang on to their cups.

Ask the group: "How many think *most* church buildings or sanctuaries are too fancy? How many think your church building is too fancy? just about right? not fancy enough?" Ask if the expense of the building or its furnishings bothers anyone when he or she reads about or sees on television the stories of homeless and hungry people. Let the kids know that Christians have debated this issue since they came out of the catacombs and started worshipping in their own buildings.

Ask the kids to check the bottom of their cups, look for the same letter on the wall and go to that small group. The T's will represent the trustees and talk about the budget and money from a strictly financial perspective and what would be best for the church from a business point of view. The M's will represent the mission people. These individuals will deal with all church matters by considering how actions affect ministry to others. The Christian education folk, represented by the E's, will concern themselves

---

Chart 12
Suggested Ideas

1. Give it all to the mission program of our church or denomination.
2. Set up a scholarship fund for students of the congregation and area minority students.
3. Set up a neighborhood ministry—a food kitchen, a shelter or another facility needed within the community.
4. Remodel the sanctuary and the Christian education wing of the building.
5. Invest the money and use only the interest for continuing projects around the church.
6. Use half of it to remodel the building, and send the other half to missions.
7. Use the money to balance the budget.
8. Give the pastor and other staff members a raise or bonus and use the rest to beautify the building.

primarily with the church family and how things will affect them. The O's will represent the feeling individuals within the church community and will be most concerned about how the worship and music will be affected.

Program—After everyone has found his or her group and understands the position the group should take, make the following announcement:

"A wealthy member has died and left the church $100,000 with no strings attached. This board must come up with a plan for how to use the money. Using the budget, catalogs and personality descriptions for your small group, decide on a plan of action for how your group would want to spend that money. Designate one individual from the group to maintain that position throughout *all* discussions."

After all groups have formulated their plans on how they think the money should be spent, meet as a large group and share these plans. Pass out the list of suggested ideas and open the discussion for input from all.

Response—After 15 minutes of brainstorming, ask the kids to react to what they have just experienced by discussing questions such as these:

1. What seemed to be the basis for your group's plan? Did anyone bring in scripture? What might Jesus have you do?

2. What does your plan say about your group's understanding of the church's mission? Is your group's plan building-centered or people-centered?

3. Look at the budget of your own church. What does it say about how your congregation views its mission?

4. Since budgets don't tell the whole story, look at your church newsletter and Sunday bulletin. Check the church calendar to see what else might be going on in your church building. What groups hold their meetings in your church building? How many of these groups are set up to run the church? How many reach out to groups outside your membership?

Ask the group to sit in a circle and play the children's

finger game, "Here's the church, and here's the steeple, open the doors, and see all the people." Suggest that this may be a child's activity, but nonetheless it says something about the importance of the church building. "The people are the church; they are joined to Christ by the Holy Spirit. People are definitely more important than buildings. But buildings can be a great aid in local mission and witness."

Close with the following prayer:

"God of heaven and earth, thank you for the love and goodness you have offered us. Help us keep our priorities straight. Remind us to love people more than things, to realize that our church building is nothing more than a means whereby we can worship and serve you. Thank you for the beauty of our churches, but thank you even more for the witness and love of the people who worship within. Send us out as your scattered people, in the name of Jesus Christ our Lord, Amen."

Option:

1. Talk about the basic concept of stewardship, how to use one's personal resources wisely for serving the Lord. What part do young people have in the stewardship program of your church? (If your denomination publishes youth stewardship materials, pass around some of these pamphlets for study and comment.)

Are young people encouraged to make pledges? On what basis are young people instructed how to allocate part of their allowances and other funds to the church? How does this allocation compare with what they spend on records, movies and refreshments? Are we as careful in our own stewardship as we think the church should be in its stewardship of resources?

Check with the young people and youth leaders from other congregations. How do they deal with this issue? Or do they? What do their buildings and furnishings say about their stewardship? Are they more concerned with themselves or others? Does the appearance of the church building reflect what is happening with the actual budget figures? For

example, is the large, ornate church spending as much on
its mission projects as it is on itself? This is something you
may not know if you cannot see the actual budget figures.

ISSUE 18

Should the Bible, hymns and other Christian works be changed to get rid of sexist language?

YES, sexist language should be purged from the Bible
and other Christian works as much as possible.

"Rise up, O men of God, have done with lesser
things . . . "

"Faith of our fathers living still, in spite of . . . "

"Men and children everywhere, with sweet music . . . "

"Good Christian men, rejoice . . . "

"And so in conclusion, my brothers in Christ, we must
never give up or lose heart as we work for peace and
brotherhood. Christ our brother needs each man of good
will to give his all for the kingdom!"

"When I look around and see that over half the church
is women, I am struck by the fact that we are usually left
out of the hymns and sermons."

"Oh come on, Shirley. You know you aren't being left
out. The words 'men' and 'brother' include you, too."

"How would you like it if we changed everything to
'women' and 'sister' and never used the words 'men' or
'brother'?"

Over half the church's membership is female, yet most
of the language members hear is male-oriented. Men created
many of the ancient prayers and hymns, and several versions of the Bible were translated by a patriarchal society in
which women were considered chattel. Language is powerful, and biblical language clearly indicates that the power in
the church belonged to men, not women.

A few places in the Bible reflect women in a different
light from the culture surrounding them. Men often quote
Genesis 2 to prove that women are subordinate since they
were created after man and from his rib. But the account of

creation in Genesis 1 states that women were equal creations, "male and female he created them." More importantly, Jesus' example showed a new appreciation for women in contrast to the way society regarded them. When Jesus gently rebukes Martha for wanting Mary to join her in the kitchen, he says, "Mary has chosen the good portion . . . " (Luke 10:42). He actually commends Mary for choosing the traditional male role as a learner at the feet of the teacher. This statement would have shocked everyone in the room, but it is part of the new liberation that Jesus came to proclaim (Luke 4:16-21).

Progress in race relations began when white people realized how their misuse of language perpetuated old prejudices and myths. Likewise, conscious attention to the sexist language within the church would raise the status of women in the church. Those who say the term "men" includes women should try using the opposite term for a while and see if they can accept using "women" everywhere for humanity, when it means both men and women.

The original languages of the Bible—Hebrew and Greek—did not always indicate the sex of the subject. The translators, who lived in a domineering patriarchal society, adopted the male form with little thought about what they were doing. Such passages can be changed to inclusive language without much difficulty. In other passages and in many hymns, neutral words can be used to include both sexes. Contrary to what some claim, the call for inclusive language in the church is not a trivial matter but an important concern to more than half the church. Since we accept some as leaders and some as followers on the basis of our perceptions of one another, it is important to think about what alters our perceptions. Language definitely affects our perceptions of one another and can generate attitudes that may create second-class citizens if we are not consciously alert to what we say.

NO, we should not change our Bibles or hymnals to get rid of sexist language.

"I wish people would use more inclusive language in church. I don't understand why most biblical references talk about brotherhood, fathers or men of God when they mean all believers."

"We could probably be more sensitive, but don't you think some of the attempts to be inclusive sound rather ridiculous?"

"Maybe some are a little cumbersome at times, but I still think it's a good idea."

"Can you imagine how awkward it would be if the pastor always had to use 'his or her' whenever he spoke? Or what if we were forced to pray to God as 'Our Mother, who art in heaven'? You know we can't change the way the Bible refers to God."

"We wouldn't actually change the concept, but we could broaden it to include . . . "

"No, there's a good reason why biblical writers stayed away from female language in referring to God. They wanted to avoid any possibility of confusing God with the corrupt fertility religions that worshipped goddesses. We'd better leave the Bible and the hymns alone. Tampering with these expressions of our faith could lead to numerous other problems."

This issue is one of those "tempests-in-a-teapot" issues that feminists have stirred up in the past few years. All of the patriarchs and the apostles were men, and the leadership in the New Testament was male. Paul obviously supported this position when he instructed the wives in Ephesus to be subject and obedient to their husbands. In Corinth Paul urged the women to follow the men's leadership. He forbade women even to speak in church, for he believed it was unnatural for a man to be subject to the jurisdiction of a woman.

In recent years when women have sought the power of men within the church, the church has entered a period of serious decline. Members have been diverted from sharing the gospel with those outside the church because they have been preoccupied with fights within the church, including disputes over the roles of women in the home, the church and today's society. There have been endless arguments over the language and how it has affected the church.

Just as the church has declined in influence, so has the home experienced a tremendous decline as women have left to enter the job market. Divorce has increased dramatically. Today almost half of all marriages end in divorce. As the home has become more and more unstable, so has society. While mothers work away from home, their children often receive little training in ethics, religion and just plain good manners and respect. The TV set, the schools, daycare personnel and peers have assumed more and more responsibility for what is taught and how it is transmitted.

Thus, the church should turn down those who want to alter its language. It should call upon those people to change their views and practices, to read what the Bible teaches and return to the way things should be.

Programming Ideas for Issue 18

Preparation—Gather newsprint, markers, paper and pencils, plus copies of your church hymnal, Bibles and several Bible concordances. Try to include several Bible commentaries on Corinthians and Ephesians.

Choose hymns that use "man" and "brother" and write the words on large sheets of newsprint. Tape the sheets around the room for all to see as they arrive. Have the tape recorder playing prerecorded hymns as the group comes in.

Opening—Ask the group members if they are bothered by the male-oriented language used in many churches. Discuss the male references in the hymns they heard as they arrived. How many noticed that the hymns contained male-oriented language? How many didn't notice?

Program—Divide the group into three smaller groups and pass out the Bible study materials.

Ask Group One to look through the hymnal and list the hymns that use "man" and "brother." Suggest that the group start with the index to see how many hymns begin this way.

Have Group Two look through the Psalms and Proverbs to list the places where "man" and "brother" are used to mean everyone.

Help Group Three use the concordances to locate and discuss the New Testament letters where women are thought to be subordinate to men.

After 20 minutes call the groups back together, and have each one report its findings. Discuss questions like the following:

1. Did you find many places where male nouns and pronouns are used to refer to everybody? How do you feel about this as a girl? as a guy?

2. Is this practice "sexist" or should male terminology be used to include everyone?

3. Have Group Three read its passages from the New Testament letters. Ask: "What do you think of Paul's view of women? Should women keep silent and submit to men both in the church and in marriage? Why or why not? How do today's scholars interpret some of these passages?" (If no one can answer this last question, take time for several volunteers to look up the passages in Bible commentaries.)

4. How did Jesus relate to or regard women? Have volunteers read Luke 10:38-42 and John 4:4-15, 27. In the story of Mary and Martha, which woman followed the traditional female role? Who assumed the male role? How? In the story of the woman at the well, why did the disciples marvel?

5. According to John's Gospel, who was the first witness to the Resurrection? Does Paul mention her in his famous Resurrection chapter (1 Corinthians 15)? What do you think was Paul's reason for this?

6. There are a few passages where feminine imagery is used for God:

Deuteronomy 32:11-12
Isaiah 66:13
Matthew 23:37

Why do you think these images are used in these situations?

7. Many theologians see this issue as more than a struggle over language. Some believe it is an issue of power in the church—who will hold it, and will it be shared equally between the sexes. Does your denomination allow women pastors? Which ones forbid this? If your church allows women to serve in this capacity, how do the people accept them? Do they have a difficult time securing pastorates? How many women do you know who are in charge of large congregations or who hold important denominational positions? Should they? Why or why not?

Response—Ask the kids, "From what we've discussed so far, what do you think about changing some of the nouns and pronouns of hymns and Bible passages?" Try changing nouns and pronouns in several of the hymns listed by Group One. Make a list of neutral nouns that could be substituted for male terms such as "folk" and "people" for "men," "God" and "God's" for "him" and "his." Say to the young people: "For some hymns, changing the words can be difficult. Some attempts may sound awkward and confusing. In such cases should we leave the hymn alone, sing it anyway or abandon it?"

Suggest that this issue will be around for a long time, just as it was when Paul was alive. Only in Christ will it finally be resolved. Read Galatians 3:28 and sing the first stanza of "Blest Be the Tie That Binds" from *Songs* (Songs and Creations). Lead the group in a prayer similar to the following:

"O God of Abraham and Sarah, Moses and Miriam, thank you for the good news in Jesus Christ that frees us from all forms of bondage. In Christ you unite us, regardless of our human condition. Continue to make us aware of your grace. Even though we may differ in the way we see things, keep us united in the love and acceptance brought about by the acceptance of your Holy Spirit. We pray this in the name of Jesus, Amen."

Options:

1. Show the film *Included Out* by Sharon Neufer-Emswiler (available from Mass Media Ministries, 2116 N. Charles St., Baltimore, MD 21218). Use the discussion guide that comes with it to talk about the way women have been "included out" in church and society.

Play Helen Reddy's song "I Am Woman" and discuss how it might apply to the place of women in the church. Is this song too strong or just about right? Ask individuals to explain their opinions.

2. Secure a copy of The Inclusive-Language Lectionary prepared by the National Council of Churches. Discuss some of the changes suggested in the readings. Which changes do you like? dislike? Which of these ideas seem acceptable? Which ones torture the language?

3. Invite your pastor and others, especially a female pastor, to speak to the group about this issue. Use this session to educate, not indoctrinate your young people, and allow them to ask questions and dispute decisions.

4. Rent and watch the video of Barbara Streisand's film *Yentl*. It describes a Jewish girl who wants to study the Torah in a Rabbinic school. The underlying principles could also apply to the church.

After viewing the film, ask the group what they think of Yentl's desire. Is she reaching for something that is not properly hers? Why isn't she content to accept her traditional female role?

THEOLOGICAL AND DOCTRINAL ISSUES

C onfronted by screaming headlines of war, crime, sex scandals and famine, any thoughtful teenager is bound to question how a loving God can figure into the scheme of things. Does God have a plan worked out for all of us? Or does everything happen, as many believe, merely by chance and free will?

While television evangelists preach that the end of the world is close at hand, how are young people supposed to plan for the future? How can they handle the Bible texts that give rise to such apocalyptic beliefs? Even more basic, how should young people respond to the Bible itself, since it has been interpreted in so many different ways? One of the great denominations of our time continues to be wracked with a power struggle between those who would interpret the Bible literally and those who believe in a more liberal approach.

The popularity of Eastern religions is also growing and will continue as celebrities become attracted to and promote their beliefs. Some Hollywood stars have spread the doctrine of reincarnation through their books and interviews on talk shows. How does this belief relate to Christian teachings? And, looking way ahead, what about heaven? Do believers who practice other religions have any chance of getting in?

Teenagers today are besieged by stories from the news media and from their peers that raise faith questions. No longer can the church expect young people to simply accept its teachings without question. Teenagers want and need opportunities to examine and test their beliefs. What better place for them to do this than in the youth fellowship where they have adults and friends who love and accept them as they are.

ISSUE 19

Does God have a predetermined plan for our lives?

YES, God has a predetermined plan for our lives.

"Dad, look at those headlines. What a mess the world's in! Sometimes I wonder where in the world God is!"

"I'm sure we all do at times, Chuck. That's when we need to look at the big picture."

"The big picture?"

"Sure, history, the universe, all of creation. When we look back, we can see how God worked things out."

"What things?"

"Big events, like Jesus' birth. If Jesus had been born a century earlier, there would have been no Roman peace and unity for the gospel to spread so quickly. The Romans had been fighting some bloody civil wars that made travel and communication all but impossible. And if Jesus had been born a century later, Mithraism, Christianity's chief rival for the hearts of the people, might have gotten too much of a head start."

"I didn't realize how important timing was in this process."

"And then there was the Protestant Reformation. At this time the church was corrupt and people longed for a purer faith. Coinciding with a rise in nationalism, the invention of the printing press and the spread of new ideas in

science and world exploration, Martin Luther and John Calvin came along at just the right time. Or I should say God
raised them up at just the right moment in history."

"Your explanations help, Dad, although I'm not sure
what the big picture is developing into now."

"People seldom do. Luther certainly never thought he
was starting a new church or was part of a new era. We're
just too close to the events when they happen. But I'm sure
everything that happens is part of God's plan. We need to
keep searching to see how we fit in."

God is the all-wise Creator who sees the future as well
as the past and the present. The Lord made us for fellowship with him and with one another. Even though our sin
disrupted the original harmony of the universe, God's intentions were not overturned. The Almighty has a plan whereby
the world will be restored. Sin will be put down, and peace
and justice will prevail.

God set this plan in motion when he called Abram to
leave his home and venture forth in faith to a land that God
would show him. God's plan, as it unfolds in the Bible, was
to call a special people and covenant with them to minister
to a fallen world. The prophets saw that Israel was to be
" . . . a covenant for the people and a light for the Gentiles"
(Isaiah 42:6). After preparing the Israelites and the ancient
world, God carried out his plan in " . . . the fullness of
time" (Ephesians 1:10) to bring salvation through his Son.

God's plan doesn't stop with Jesus, but continues
through the apostles, the church and down to the present
time. And the plan includes each of us. The Psalmist declares God's plan for us begins before our birth, that in the
womb God knew us: "My frame was not hidden from you
when I was made in the secret place. When I was woven
together in the depths of the earth, your eyes saw my un-
formed body. All the days ordained for me were written in
your book before one of them came to be" (Psalm 139:15-16).

Theologians such as St. Augustine and John Calvin
based their teachings for predestination on this and many

other scripture passages, especially those in Ephesians and Romans. In these letters, Paul stresses the omnipotence and omniscience of God to the point that no person can boast about his or her own power or find any way to save himself or herself from sin. Only the gracious power of God can rescue humanity from the consequences of sin. Thus, even our acceptance of Christ is a gift from God, not our own doing. As Christ put it, "You did not choose me, but I chose you . . . " (John 15:16). This is not to deny that we have a choice, but even our choices are a part of God's choosing for us. To recognize God as sovereign in the universe, we must recognize ourselves as tiny helpless creatures. To boast "I am the master of my fate, I am the captain of my soul" is foolish denial of our God's sovereignty.

NO, God does not determine everything that happens to us; our lives do not have a predetermined plan.

"Hey, watch out, Aaron! That truck almost hit us!"

"Don't worry about traffic, Kelly. There's no real danger when the Lord is with us."

"Well, the other drivers might not know that, especially the guys driving those big 18-wheelers!"

"The way I figure it, when your number's up, that's it, no matter what you do."

"You said the same thing when the doctor suggested you give up smoking."

"Sure. The Bible says we can't add an inch to our height or a moment to our lives by worrying."

"Yeah, but I thought the Bible also says something about being responsible, about taking charge of our lives, and also about not tempting God. I think I'd rather ride with a careful atheist than a reckless Christian any day!"

God is the sovereign ruler of the universe he has created. In Genesis, however, we see that he has chosen to share that sovereignty with humanity. "God blessed them and said to them, 'Be fruitful and increase in number; fill the earth and subdue it. Rule over the fish of the sea and the birds of the air and over every living creature that moves on the ground" (Genesis 1:28).

In the second creation story in Genesis 2—3, God also gives humanity the ability to choose between obeying or not obeying him. To offer this free will was risky, but God realized we must have this ability to choose if we are truly created in his image. We cannot be puppets, pulled by a string to perform this way or that; sovereign creatures must make up their *own* minds. Unfortunately, we often make the wrong choices, and the ancient story of the Fall is repeated all over again, but God is willing to take this risk. Out of his great love and desire to communicate with his creation, our Lord has chosen to share his sovereignty.

Those who say that God determines everything forget how important and necessary it is to have free will and the responsibility that goes with it. We cannot blame God for our sins or for the ills that befall us, the way small children can. Those Christians who refuse to make any plans or decisions unless "the Lord directs them to do so" not only exasperate their friends, but fail to act responsibly by taking charge of their own lives.

In many places the Bible upholds the teaching that we are creatures of free will, able to make choices. Moses says, " . . . Now choose life, so that you and your children may live" (Deuteronomy 30:19).

Joshua also supports this freedom of choice when he says: " . . . choose for yourselves this day whom you will serve . . . But as for me and my household, we will serve the Lord" (Joshua 24:15).

Even Jesus supports this teaching when he congratulates Mary for choosing the good portion (Luke 10:42).

God may have a plan for us, but he does not dictate our every action or thought. If this were so, there would be no free will. We have to *choose* to accept his will for our lives. In God's sovereignty he gives us the freedom to choose—we can accept him or reject him. That is why the Psalmist could say that God has made us a little lower than the angels (Psalm 8).

Programming Ideas for Issue 19

Preparation—The week before this session, ask for volunteers to look over and present two skits for the Program section. Gather three sawhorses, a long heavy plank, string, two lightweight sticks (36 inches long) to make a control for the puppet master, 3×5 cards, a pen, newsprint, markers and several Bible concordances. In a book of poetry collections, look up William Ernest Henley's *Invictus*.

For the first skit, rig a group member with strings like a marionette and attach these to a control to demonstrate the kind of control God has over us. To prepare the control for the puppet master, cut one of the lightweight sticks in half. Place the shorter pieces across the longer stick about 12 inches from both ends and attach with nails or masking tape. Cut pieces of string long enough to tie to the young person's ankles and wrists and reach about 3 feet above the person's head. Attach a fifth string to the person's head or neck. To avoid tangling the strings, tie the young person first and then tie the strings to the control. Set up three sawhorses with a long plank lying across them. The puppet master will stand on the plank, and use the control to put the puppet (young person) through his or her paces. Have the group write a short vignette that shows how the puppet master controls the puppet as he or she goes to school or participates in some other typical teenage activity. Close the skit by asking another young person to read Romans 8:28-30.

For the second skit, write the following questions on 3×5 cards:

"What do you want to eat for your birthday?"

"What career have you decided on?"

"Come on, why not take just one drink? It won't hurt you."

"Who are you taking to the prom?"

"Will you marry me?"

"Do you plan to join that club?"

"Why did you *choose* that color of coat?"

"Do you promise to follow Jesus Christ and be his disciple?"

Ask someone to read Henley's famous poem on in-
dividualism called *Invictus*. Have another young person
mime the emotions or feelings from the poem as it is read.

"It matters not how straight the gate/How charged with
punishment the scroll/I am the master of my fate/I am the
captain of my soul."

Immediately after the reading ends, have individuals
scattered throughout the audience call out the questions on
the 3×5 cards. Have the mime react to each of the questions.

Ask another young person to close the skit by reading
Joshua 24:14-15.

Opening—The ancient issue of God's predetermination
once was a primary factor in dividing the followers of John
Wesley and John Calvin. Tell the teenagers they are going
to see two skits that deal with the issue, and then they'll
have a chance to respond to their experiences by talking
about what *they* think.

Program—Ask both groups to present both skits.

Response—Post sheets of newsprint at the front of the
room and have markers available. Use questions like the following to help your kids evaluate what they have just seen:

1. List the choices you have made today or this past
week. What choices were involved in the skits?

2. In what areas of your life do you believe you have
little choice or control? Why?

3. What is the view of God in both skits? of humanity?
Which skit seems closest to the truth for you? Why?

Divide the large group into smaller study groups. Pass
out Bible concordances to each small group and assign
words like called, choose, chosen, elect, destined, plan, and
predestined.

After a period of study, have each small group report
back to the larger group. Do the passages agree or do they
seem to fall into two categories, "free will" and "predestination"? Are the ideas mutually exclusive, or is there a way
to affirm both thoughts? Point out that the Presbyterians
amended their basic teaching on this issue many years ago
to include both, since scriptural support could be found for

each position. (See their *Book of Confessions*, "The West-minster Confession of Faith," Declaratory Note on Chapter 3.)

Some theologians talk about the paradox of the gospel, how we choose yet we are chosen, how our God is in charge yet limits his sovereignty to allow us free will. Read Romans 8:28 in the Revised Standard Version. This passage should be helpful to everyone. It assures us that we work with God in "everything," while it continues in verses 29 and 30 to affirm the absolute sovereignty of God.

Ask the group to form two concentric circles. Play music and have the kids walk in opposite directions. When the music stops, the kids will be partners with the person across from them. The leader will ask a question about predestination or read a scripture concerning it; then the kids will discuss in pairs. After a few minutes start the music again and have the kids select a new partner. The leader will ask a new question and the kids will discuss it with their new partner. Do this as many times as you want.

Close by playing the music one last time. When the kids pair off, make sure everyone knows who his or her partner is and give the following instructions for the Trust Fall. "Those of you in the outer circle will catch those in the inner circle as they relax and fall straight back into the arms of your partners. If you feel uncomfortable as a catcher for someone who is much larger than you, do not hesitate to ask for assistance. If you feel uncomfortable as a faller, remember you can help the catcher by not sitting down but falling straight back and relaxing once you are caught. Remember we will reverse the process in a moment, so be careful with your partner."

After the Trust Fall, tell the group, "When we believe in the sovereignty of God, we believe that God will support us like we supported each other in the Trust Fall, even when we don't always understand what is going on. Just as you trusted that your partner would be behind you even when you could not see, you also trust that God will be there no matter what. Form a large circle with everyone holding hands. Close with a prayer of trust and a plea for guidance in making choices:

"O God, you are our creator and sustainer. You have fashioned this mystery we call life. Help us understand as much as we need to know and where our understanding stops to trust you and your ways. Because we are neither as free as we sometimes think, nor as bound as we often assume, may *all* of our choices, even our wrong ones, somehow fit into your wondrous plan. In Jesus' name we pray, Amen."

Options:

1. This issue would make an excellent debate subject. Using the scripture passages and research suggested in the Programming Ideas, students could divide into teams to present both sides of the issue. One week could be used for research and planning with the debate scheduled for the next meeting.

2. The story of Joseph (Genesis 37—50) is a good introduction to the topic of God's providence and our free will. Use one of the filmstrip or film versions available to present the story to the group. Focus on Joseph's theology in Genesis 45:4-8.

ISSUE 20
Should the Bible be interpreted literally? liberally? skeptically? moderately?
(Because of the scope of this issue, the format has been enlarged to include all four positions in the introductory material.)

"Come and join us, Terry."

"Thanks. The place seems extra crowded today," Terry said as he sat down with his tray of food. "Bet you guys were talking about Freeman's science lecture on evolution and the Bible."

"Yeah, Phil didn't care much for what he said."

"I sure didn't. How can anyone say that you can believe the Bible and also believe what Darwin says about evolution? My church teaches us to believe in the Bible alone, and the Bible says that the world was created in six days, not in a billion years."

"But Phil," Terry replied, "maybe Mr. Freeman's right. We do have to look to the Bible for knowledge about our faith, but science has the information about our physical world. After all, the Bible was written a long time ago. Science came later as man began to understand more and more about his surroundings."

"That doesn't matter. The Bible is the Word of God, and that's timeless."

"Maybe it does matter," piped in Mary. Everyone turned to look at the new speaker. "In my youth group we recently studied the Apostle Paul. Our adviser pointed out that Paul was raised in a male society where women had little place, and that was why he put women down so much in some of his letters. Our church doesn't go along with what he says about women; we think women can be good leaders. We also believe if Paul were alive and writing today, he would think so, too."

"What's that got to do with evolution and creation?" Phil asked.

"Well, both are matters of how you approach and interpret the Bible," Mary replied. "Either literally, as you do, or in a way that recognizes the history and ideas of the time when the Bible was written."

"Whew, this is getting a little deep for lunch time," Terry joked. "What do you think about all this, Hank? Seems a bit much while you're trying to munch on this stuff they call food."

"What do I think? You guys know my family doesn't go to church. There's just too much feudin' and fightin' for me. Personally, I don't think it matters much what the Bible says. It's such an outdated conglomeration of fairy tales. It's always talking about a bloodthirsty God who orders the people to go to war and destroy all their enemies, even the women and children. I think we have to grow beyond such primitive ideas!"

"Wow!" Mary exclaimed. "I'll bet there's at least one point where Phil and I will agree."

"What's that?" Phil smiled as if he knew what Mary

was going to say.

"That Hank is our resident cynic. We're going to have to work on you, Hank. We may not convert you into a Bible-totin' believer, but I would like to see you a little more open-minded concerning the Bible and God."

The clanging of the bell to end lunch time drowned out Hank's reply.

The Bible should be interpreted literally.

The Bible is the Word of God. Paul wrote, "All Scripture is God-breathed and is useful for teaching, for rebuking, correcting and training in righteousness" (2 Timothy 3:16). Therefore, we must accept the Bible's every word.

Too many people in today's church have given in to attacks from the secular humanists who ridicule the Bible as an outmoded collection of myths and fables. Such Christians try to make the Bible fit the teachings of science, rather than see the world through the eyes of the biblical writers. They water down the Bible and its teachings in the vain hope that scoffers will come to accept it and its laws as reasonable, rather than as commands from God himself.

A literal interpretation of the Bible does raise problems for the unsaved intellectual. But believers willingly accept the Bible and its God on trust. Any problems are resolved as simply works of the Holy Spirit.

Thus, when Genesis 1 says that God created the world in six days, we must accept this statement as fact and not try to twist it to fit some scientific theory. This doesn't mean that it was a 24-hour day; a day in God's eyes could have been much longer. But we do have to stick with the basic truth of the chapter—that God created everything there is in a definite time period divided into six "days," and on the seventh day, he rested. There is no room in the Genesis creation story for such theories as evolution.

The same goes for the numerous miracle accounts in the Old and New Testaments. Some scholars try to explain these away until there's very little left of the Bible. Thomas Jefferson, a well-known skeptic, once published his own version of the New Testament in which he deleted all the miracle stories and references to the divinity of Christ. His version included only an abbreviated Gospel of Luke and a few of the historical letters.

As we read earlier, Paul wrote that all scripture is inspired by God. This means the Holy Spirit entered the writers so they would not err when they wrote the scripture. Today that same Spirit helps the reader interpret the text accurately and arrive at the correct answers to life's problems.

The Bible should be interpreted liberally.

The Bible is a collection of ancient writings that reflect the values and views of the people who lived thousands of years ago. It contains an array of beautiful poetry and stories and offers numerous examples of high ethical choices. These writings are mixed in with degrading tales of bloody wars supposedly sanctioned by a militaristic God who ordered his people to unmercifully kill their enemies, including the women, children and elderly. To accept all of the content literally with no question or evaluation would say that we worship a tyrannical God who demands even the slaying of non-combatants, a code of battle that is against every rule of so-called civilized warfare. It is also in direct contradiction with Jesus' later teachings.

As a collection, the Bible includes primitive ethics and laws as well as the exalted teachings of Isaiah and Jesus. We must go beyond the primitive portions and adhere only to those that teach the law of love as laid down by the great prophets and Jesus. The rest is of interest and help only to historians.

To interpret the Bible literally is to ignore the different levels of worth and value of its writings. For example, it is far better to follow the New Testament teaching to "love your enemies" than perform animal sacrifices according to the various commandments in Leviticus and Deuteronomy. And what literalist follows the Old Testament commandment prohibiting us from wearing two different kinds of cloth? (See Leviticus 19:19.)

Even a literalist has to admit that some of the Bible needs to be interpreted metaphorically. Does anyone actually believe that when Jesus said "I am the door" that he looked like a flat rectangle with a doorknob sticking out of his bellybutton? or that when he said "I am the vine," leafy, grape-laden branches sprouted from his ears and nose? The debate really concerns itself with *which* parts of the Bible we shall interpret liberally or metaphorically. Jesus said: "If your right eye causes you to sin, gouge it out . . . And if your right hand causes you to sin, cut it off . . ." (Matthew 5:29-30). The consistent literalist would unnecessarily limit his own ability to serve if he were blind and had no hands, but the liberal could see that Jesus was talking about the seriousness of one's sin and its consequences.

Unlike the literalist, the liberal finds no real problem with modern science and the Bible. The two stories of the creation account in Genesis merely reflect the ancient people's understanding of the universe. This primitive view suggested that a flat earth floated on subterranean waters and below those waters was the realm of the dead. Above the earth was a firm bowl or hemisphere that protected the earth from the waters of the firmament and heaven was above those waters. Today few people accept this ancient view, but literalists fought for centuries against visionaries who sought to introduce new scientific evidence about the universe.

The literalists have argued against almost every advance in knowledge during the past few hundred years, from the study of anatomy to that of the stars. They have opposed the study of biological science and the use of anesthesia, the abolition of slavery, the emancipation of women, the civil rights for blacks, and the freedom of the poet and the novelist to express their personal views within their own writing. For freedom to advance, a liberal approach to the Bible is a must. It is no coincidence that those who would censor our books and magazines and purge our libraries of unwanted books are fundamentalists who believe in a literal interpretation of the Bible. Had our ancestors listened to them, we would still be living in the Dark Ages.

The Bible should be interpreted skeptically.

The Bible is an ancient, outmoded book that should be put on the shelf with the great classics of the past that people admire but never read. The Bible has caused so much pain and anguish that it doesn't deserve anyone's admiration. The human race has grown up. It no longer needs childish superstitions; so, in the words of one of the biblical writers, society should "put away childish things."

The Bible teaches that the earth is flat and covered by a bowl, which Genesis calls a "firmament." Biblical writers often refer to the four corners of the earth and speak of the wind and rain as natural phenomena directed by God. No one really believes those concepts today; even fundamentalists tune in to the weather reports.

The God of the Bible is pictured as a fiery potentate who leads his people into battle and commands them to slay all of his enemies, including women and children. He commands people to obey impossible laws and then condemns them to hell for their failure. Millions of people, from the time of the Crusades through the wars of the Reformation and down to the skirmishes of the Irish civil war, have been slaughtered when their leaders have declared, "This is God's will!"

The commandment, "Do not allow a sorceress to live" (Exodus 22:18), resulted in the death, disfigurement and imprisonment of hundreds of women because good Christians interpreted this verse literally. These committed individuals transformed their communities into living hells for those who acted a bit differently and therefore were suspected of working evil spells.

More good Christians enslaved millions of Africans, shipped them to the colonies, sold them like cattle and worked them without mercy in the fields and the plantation homes. All of these actions were justified by the literal interpretation of passages like Paul's command, "Slaves, obey your earthly masters . . . " (Colossians 3:22).

So much evil has been perpetrated and justified by the Bible that it would be best if people simply ignored this book. Rather than worrying about how to interpret it, either literally or liberally, it would be best to disregard the book completely.

The Bible should be interpreted moderately.

The Bible should be taken seriously, but not literally. Too often tyrants have misused this book to justify their injustices. For example, while the slave masters used it to justify their continued oppression of a whole people, the Bible also inspired those slaves to dream of freedom, to believe that the God of the Exodus was still with the oppressed and would soon help them throw off their taskmasters' yoke. Some have misused changing language patterns to try to keep humanity ignorant of the truth, but others have recognized God as the author of truth and have grown and stretched their faith as they sought to preserve the meaning more than the words.

Educated people agree that it is best to use as many sources as possible to interpret the meaning of scripture. It is far better to use the insights of archaeologists and historians to interpret the Bible than to take every statement literally. When the Jewish historian wrote about Joshua's conquest of Palestine, he could think only in terms of his nation and what that victory meant to the Jews. So he interpreted the actions, which included the wholesale slaughter of innocent people, as sanctioned by God.

If we look at the scripture as a whole, we can see a pattern of progressive revelation. This means that God revealed himself in stages as people were ready to understand, much the way a teacher introduces a child to the ABCs, helps him or her learn to read simple stories, and then encourages the child to move on to books that he or she can understand. No teacher would try to have first-graders read *Hamlet*, for these children could not understand what was happening, nor could they understand the language.

The Hebrews had to learn their ABCs of faith, that God had called them to be his special people. Abraham learned this when God covenanted with him and promised that he would be the father of many nations. Since Abraham had no understanding of a God of love, it did not surprise him when God later demanded the life of his firstborn son, Isaac. After all, the gods of his neighbors made the same kind of demands. Sacrificing the first fruits of the field, of livestock, and of the family was customary to ensure the gods' blessings for future fruitfulness.

Later, through Moses, the Hebrews learned that there is only *one* God, the God who saved them from oppression. After they received his commandments, they learned that this God did not allow murder. This new understanding led to a prohibition against sacrificing children to idols.

The Lord led his people beyond the basic commandments to understand that he wanted to create a very different kind of nation. He sought a society in which the poor and unfortunate would be cared for and the greed of the rich would be curbed. When the people chose to follow the evil ways of their neighbors, God sent the prophets to call the people to repentance. And later, when the people refused to listen, God instructed the prophets to pronounce a judgment of doom.

The prophets, especially Amos, Micah and Isaiah, led the people to a deeper understanding of God's call to justice. Hosea helped the people understand the unique covenant relationship between God and Israel as based on love when he compared this relationship to one between a man and his unfaithful wife and that between a loving father and his rebellious son.

This insight into God's deeper, redeeming love was carried even further in Isaiah, beginning with Chapter 40. This section of scripture includes a series of so-called servant poems that describe the servant whom God will send to bring justice and liberation to the captive people. For by now the nation of Israel had fallen and Judah's people were living as captives in Babylon. In the last poem, the servant is described as a suffering servant, one who gives his life so that the guilty can be healed. (See Isaiah 53:4-12.)

The author never identifies this servant specifically. Some scholars think it might be the nation of Israel, while others believe it is an individual. For Christians the mystery of the suffering servant's identity is revealed in the life, death and Resurrection of Jesus Christ. In him is the full revelation of God. The process that began 1,900 years earlier when God called Abraham to become the "father of many nations" is completed in Jesus' ministry as the suffering servant. He is the humble carpenter who washes the feet of his followers and shows that he and those who follow him must become servants, not masters. Jesus also teaches a new ethic in his Sermon on the Mount. This ethic is based on the Law of Moses, but goes further in a loving concern for one's neighbor. Beyond this it even demands loving one's enemies and dying for them.

The progressive revelation of God leads from the dawning knowledge of his nature as revealed to Abraham to the full revelation of himself as the loving father who willingly sacrificed his only Son. This process of expanding revelation continues in the New Testament with followers like Paul. Raised as a male chauvinist, Paul at first accepts the mores of his male-dominated world. In his Corinthian letters, he tells women to be silent in church and submissive to their husbands. Later, however, in his correspondence with the Galatians, he states that in Christ "there is . . . neither male nor female . . . " (Galatians 3:28). This position is more in keeping with Jesus' example when he broke the social taboos by inviting women to choose "the good portion" (Luke 10:42). Like everyone else, this great apostle to the Gentiles, who dared to declare that Gentile Christian converts did not have to follow the law by submitting to circumcision, continued to grow in his understanding of God's will and nature.

Scripture passages cannot be read as if every section has the same authority; there is a progression of understanding from a lower to a higher level. Each section must

---

Chart 13
Bible Interpretations

Literal—The Bible says exactly what it means.

Liberal—The Bible is a collection of valuable ancient writings that reflect the values and views of the culture and time during which it was written. Aside from the law of love presented by many of the great prophets and Jesus, the rest is merely interesting history.

Skeptical—The Bible is a book of myths and fairy tales. It should be set aside as just another classical piece of literature.

Moderate—The Bible is a serious book of faith. Its purpose was to record the revelation of God to his people, not to spell out every detail of how and when things happened.

---

be read in light of Jesus Christ's life and message. Some have concluded that the Bible contradicts itself, or that there is no connection between the Old and New Testaments since they picture God so differently. When we realize that a loving God slowly revealed only as much of himself as each generation could grasp, we can recognize the fundamental unity of the scripture.

Christians should take the Bible seriously; we have learned this from our conservative brothers and sisters. We must not explain away its difficult demands, especially those that call us to "take up our cross" and "love our enemies," even as Christ did. But we must also approach the Bible with our minds as we seek to understand the will of God. This means that we must accept the discoveries of those who have based their studies on the history and archaeology of the Middle East. We must accept the fact that biblical writers were influenced by primitive science, mythology, social order and customs of their day. Since the Bible was written as a book of faith, not of science, much of its content was based on metaphor and poetry. We must take scripture seriously, but not always literally.

Programming Ideas for Issue 20

Preparation—Ask a person who does mime to prepare a short two- to three-minute presentation for the beginning of this session.

Gather Bibles, 3×5 cards, paper and markers. On separate 3×5 cards, tape each of the cards found in Chart 14. Skim through several religious art collections in your church and local libraries for pictures of the Crucifixion of Jesus and bring these to the meeting. On four sheets of paper, make signs that say "Literal," "Liberal," "Skeptical" and "Moderate." Make copies of the introductory material that explains these four positions.

Make at least four copies of Chart 13.

Make a copy of a picture of Jesus and cut it into four pieces. Label the back of each piece with the four positions—Literal, Liberal, Moderate and Skeptical.

Opening—Introduce the mime and ask the kids to watch his or her presentation carefully. When the act is complete, ask the mime to leave the room and have the group talk about what they saw. As they pick up on more and more detail they will probably begin to disagree, and discussions may begin to become arguments. After a few minutes, have the mime return and go through his or her routine exactly as before. Talk about what they saw this time and let the mime answer or clarify any comments. Talk with the group about how many different ideas there were about what had happened. Tell the group, "Just as we all saw something different in the mime's presentation, so did people see and interpret things differently during Jesus' day."

Program—Divide into four small groups and pass out Bibles, newsprint and a marker to each group. Assign each group one of the following scripture passages: Matthew 28:1-20; Mark 16:1-8; Luke 24:1-53; and John 20—21:14. Ask the groups to read their scripture passages and the details reported on this event. When everyone has finished, share the findings and point out how even biblical writers disagreed. Show the paintings of the Crucifixion from different artists to support the idea of different interpretations. Keep the same small groups and tell everyone: "One reason we have difficulty understanding scripture is due to the different ways we interpret the Bible. Today we're going to look at four of those ways and see where we might fit in."

Assign each group one of the position statements from the introduction material of this issue. Ask each group to read its position and explain all scripture from that viewpoint.

After the groups understand the position from which they should operate, pass out Card 1. Ask each group to read these scripture passages and explain them from their groups' assigned positions. After all four groups have explained their positions, evaluate how well they stuck to their assigned roles.

Pass out Cards 2, 3, 4 and 5, one to a group. Hand each group a copy of Chart 13, which summarizes four types of Bible interpretation. Have each group choose one scripture passage from its card, read it, and discuss how it should be interpreted. Tell the groups: "Talk about what it meant to the first readers. What does it mean to you now? Ask the groups to share their discussions and decision with the other groups."

Response—Meet as a total group to discuss the following questions: What problems did you have understanding or interpreting the passage? Would knowing the historical context have helped? Would it have helped to read the passages before and after your scripture passage? Is all of scripture on the same level? Why or why not? Support your answer.

Post signs around the room labeled "Literal," "Liberal," "Skeptical" and "Moderate." Read each of the following scripture passages and ask your young people to stand by the interpretation they prefer for each scripture.

Exodus 21:24
Matthew 5:38-42
John 6:36, 8:12; 10:7, 11; 14:6; 15:1

When this part is over, ask individuals if they varied

their interpretation at all. Ask: "How many stayed at one sign throughout the activity? How many had more than two interpretations? How many used each position at least once?"

Ask the group to form a square around a table on which you have placed the four-piece picture of Jesus Christ face down. Appoint someone from each side of the square to turn over that section of the picture when you name the position.

Tell the group: "There are at least four ways of interpreting the Bible: 'literally,' 'liberally,' 'skeptically' and 'moderately.' No matter how we interpret the Bible, the purpose of the Bible remains the same—to present Jesus Christ to the reader. Take a few seconds to think about the fact that all four of these interpretations add to the picture we get of Jesus Christ." Offer a prayer thanking God for

---

Chart 14
Scripture Cards

Card 1: Genesis 1—2 Exodus 20:8-11	Card 4: Mark 9:2-8 Mark 10:1-16 1 Corinthians 11:2-16
Card 2: Leviticus 19:19; 26-27 Joshua 6:15-21 2 Samuel 24:1-14 1 Chronicles 21:1-13	Card 5: Ephesians 5:22-24 Revelation 6
Card 3: Matthew 1:18-25 Matthew 5:38-42 Matthew 15:32-38	

scripture and asking for guidance in understanding and the courage to follow what we understand.

Option:

1. Show the film or read the play *Inherit the Wind.* This experience will require at least two sessions or possibly a retreat setting. Authors Jerome Lawrence and Robert E. Lee based their story on the famous 1925 Scopes trial in which a science teacher was tried for violating the Tennessee law that prohibited teaching the evolution theory in public schools.

The play is available in paperback and at public libraries. Secure enough copies so there is one for every two or three people. Assign parts and have a play-reading session. Discuss the various characters and the biblical views they represent. Then talk about the issues that were raised.

ISSUE 21
Is the end of the world near?

YES, many signs of our time indicate that the end of the world is near.

"I never thought much about the end of the world."

"You should. The Bible teaches that Christ will come again. Many religious creeds say he will come again 'to judge the living and the dead.' The promise of Christ's Second Coming makes us take seriously what we do each day of our lives."

"Maybe so, but I don't worry about that. It's such a long way off."

"Are you sure? Today there are so many signs of the end times, just like the Bible says there will be."

"Aw, come on!"

"No, seriously! If you knew that tomorrow you would die and meet your maker, wouldn't you spend today differently?"

"Well, I guess so. But since I won't, I . . . "

"How do you know you won't? Wouldn't it be better to believe that you will be meeting God soon so you can keep your life in order? I really think we're living in the end times!"

A great many people believe we are living in the end times and are preparing for it. Books such as Hal Lindsey's *The Late Great Planet Earth* reflect how he and other church leaders are looking for the end to come soon and are following in the tradition of such ancient prophets as Daniel and Joel.

The Bible teaches that history is not a forever occurrence. It has its beginning and end in God. Jesus also taught this and left his apostles with the promise that they would see him return in glory to put down evil and vindicate the faithful. Three of the Gospels, Matthew (Chapter 24), Mark (Chapter 13) and Luke (Chapter 21) include large blocks of Jesus' teachings about the end of the world. He speaks of great tribulation and wars. "Nation will rise against nation, and kingdom against kingdom. There will be great earthquakes, famines and pestilences in various places, and fearful events and great signs from heaven" (Luke 21:10-11).

Many students of the Bible believe that the great cataclysmic events of our time are signs of the last times. There have been tremendous upheavals in nature like the earthquakes shaking Mexico and Nicaragua. Long-silent volcanos have erupted, and changes in the weather patterns have produced massive storms. There is a continual threat of nuclear destruction plus outbreaks of conventional war in many places like Africa, the Middle East, Latin America and Asia. In our own country morality has broken down with people flaunting and ridiculing the moral laws of God. Some even see the church itself as infected with the evil spirit of secularism and falling away from the Word of God. Christians are being persecuted not only in other countries but even here in the United States. Our government promotes laws that allow abortion and forbid the teaching of creationism. In several states, government agents have either closed Christian schools or threatened them with legal action if they did not teach those things that the government requires.

When Israel was re-established as a nation in 1948, after almost 2,000 years, the belief that the end times were not far away was refueled. When the Israelis recaptured Jerusalem a few years later many felt this was a sign the ancient temple would soon be rebuilt. And many believe the reconstruction of the temple will occur not long before the ancient prophecies about the return of Jesus are fulfilled.

Everything seems to point to the imminent return of Christ. It is time for Christians to prepare and get their lives in order so they will be ready when the Son of God returns in his glory. And as good neighbors, we must tell others and urge them to get right with God so that they will be ready also.

NO, the end of the world is not near, at least not on the time schedule that many would-be prophets so confidently predict.

"Our pastor says that we should get ready for Christ's return, probably before the year is over."

"Then I suppose you've stopped shopping for clothes and given your clothing allowance to others?"

"I hadn't thought about it."

"Well, you should. Think of all the good you might still be able to do if you gave all that money to the church mission program. I presume your church won't be completing construction on its new sanctuary, either."

"Well, we did sign a contract with the builder. Why do you ask?"

"What will you need a building for if you're going to be in heaven so soon? Do you plan to take it with you?"

God will end things when he chooses, not when we decide. Virtually all Christians believe in the return of Christ. This is certainly part of Jesus' teaching. This statement of faith has been incorporated into the great creeds of the Christian faith such as the Nicene Creed and Apostles' Creed, and many accept these statements as authority that Christ shall come again "to judge the living and the dead . . . " (1 Peter 4:5).

But the time schedule belongs to God, not humanity. Jesus and the apostles thought it would be during their time. In this respect Jesus was limited by his own humanity, taking our form at birth and thus accepting our limitations to knowledge about such things. Jesus also said, "No one knows about that day or hour, not even the angels in heaven, nor the Son, but only the Father" (Mark 13:32). If Jesus didn't claim to have such knowledge, then how can we believe the individuals and groups today who say they are so certain?

Many groups and individuals in the past have claimed to know the exact time and date for the end times. Some people predicted that the end of the world would come in A.D. 1000. In the 19th century Joseph Miller stirred up numbers of people who gathered on hilltops to await the coming of Christ. The night came and went, and Christ didn't return. The Jehovah's Witnesses were certain the end would be in 1917, but we're still here and they're still producing and selling their tracts and magazines. In the 1960s several "prophets" boldly predicted that the Second Coming would take place in the '70s or '80s.

Those who look to the great cataclysms of nature and mankind for signs of the Second Coming ignore the teachings of scripture as well as the lessons of history. When Jesus was on his way to Jerusalem for his showdown with the forces of darkness, some Pharisees asked him when the kingdom of God was coming. Jesus answered them, "The kingdom of God does not come with your careful observation, nor will people say, 'Here it is,' or 'There it is' because the kingdom of God is within you" (Luke 17:20-22). This passage corresponds with Paul's teaching that Jesus' coming will be like a thief in the night (1 Thessalonians 5:2).

Jesus does not satisfy our curiosity about when his kingdom is coming. In fact, in Luke 21:7-10 he warned us against false teachers who will come in his name and announce that the time is at hand. We are not to follow these individuals, but we must remain faithful. We must be confident that whenever he does return we need not be afraid.

Jesus told several parables about watching and waiting, stories that seem to say we should go about our daily lives, living in faith according to the gospel. It is a misuse of scripture to pore through it for some secret code that will unravel the mystery of the end of the world. The Bible was written so we might know what is necessary for salvation and for right living. It was not written to satisfy our curiosity about things even Jesus admitted belong exclusively to our Creator. The end of the world could come today or tomorrow or in a thousand years or in a million years. But it will come in God's time, not ours.

Programming Ideas for Issue 21

Preparation—Plan a trip back in time to the days of the early Christians. Choose a secret meeting place, or "catacomb," like a garage or an unfinished basement. Pass the word of your meeting place in secretive ways like whispers and notes at school. Ask everyone to bring foods typical of biblical times to share with everyone else—bread, fruit, cheese, and fruit juices to represent the wine that was common with most meals. Gather cups, napkins, candles, candleholders and Bibles and schedule your meeting for after dark.

Opening—Have one candle lighted as your young people arrive. Ask each person to light another candle from the original and place it somewhere in the room. Sing familiar hymns and have individuals tell stories about how they got to the meeting place without anyone seeing them.

Program—Once most people have arrived, ask them to share their personal concerns. What worries them? Of what are they afraid? How do they feel about the future?

Pass out Bibles and have different kids read these scripture passages: Matthew 24; Mark 13; and Luke 21. Discuss what these passages might have meant to first century Christians. Ask these questions: What were the main points? Does Jesus think the end will come soon or in the future? Explain. Is there a definite time given or is there any reference to time? What messages might people get from these scripture passages today? What questions do you have about the end times?

Discuss possible reasons why God gives "signs" of the end times like earthquakes, wars and famines. Take turns reading the following scripture passages: Daniel 7:13-14; Matthew 25:1-13; 1 Corinthians 7:29-31; 1 Corinthians 15:51-57; 1 Thessalonians 5:1-24; 2 Thessalonians 1:5—2:12; 1 Peter 4; Revelation 1—4; and Revelation 6—9. Ask these questions: "What seems to be the most important point made—the time, how to behave or the information on what will happen? Does it matter *when* the end comes? What is really important according to the passages? Do Christians need to worry or be fearful about the end? Explain.

Point out that one of the treasured passages of the Gospels deals with both our behavior now and our place in heaven, with no mention of chronology. Whether Christ is returning in our lifetime, we cannot say, but we *can* say what we should be doing in the meantime. Read Matthew 25:31-46.

Response—Invite the kids to form a circle and place their food offerings in the center. Offer sentence prayers and say the Lord's Prayer together. Close by sharing one another's food offerings.

Options:

1. Have someone read Hal Lindsey's book *The Late Great Planet Earth* (Bantam) and Everett Carver's book *When Jesus Comes Again* (Presbyterian & Reformed). Ask that individual to give a comparative book review. Discuss how the authors approach or regard the Bible—literally, liberally, skeptically or moderately. What are their views of prophecy, as concerned with justice or with predicting the future?

2. Ask two different people to read the books suggested in Option 1. Have them prepare a dialogue comparing the two books issue by issue. Another variation of this particular choice would use those who read the books as radio

talk show hosts. Tell the kids they can ask any questions they would like.

3. Simulate the end times. Plan a regular fun night. Have the lights suddenly go out with an explosion from a sound-effects record. Have the group find candles, light them and talk about end times. Discuss how the kids feel and use the Bible verses in the Program section to help answer any questions they might have.

ISSUE 22

Is there hope for non-Christians to go to heaven?

YES, it is possible for non-Christians to go to heaven.

"Tell me, why do you, a Christian, wish to study at our monastery?" The saffron-robed monk seemed very surprised at the request of the fair-skinned Westerner.

"I've come from a country where we have forgotten many of the ancient disciplines of prayer and meditation. My church has become so engrossed with *doing* good things that we are in danger of losing touch with the source of our faith. A number of years ago a wise man from my country—Thomas Merton—came here to inquire into your ways, but he died early in his quest. I wish to resume his journey of faith."

The monk smiled slightly. "Then you do not come here to convert us to your faith?"

"No, I come to learn. Though in my learning there may be things of my faith that I can share, for I believe that my master is indeed 'Lord.' "

"We shall see. You may stay, and perhaps we shall find that our paths converge at times along the journey."

"I've only studied your faith from books and from conversations with students and professors from your country who came to my university. But from these experiences I've come to believe that God is the source of all religion, that he has not left any people without some clue to his existence."

Salvation is more than the result of belonging to a

church or saying certain words about believing in Jesus Christ. Salvation is not ours to earn or to claim as a right, even if we have been lifelong Christians. Salvation is a gift. John declares, ". . . Salvation belongs to our God, who sits on the throne, and to the Lamb" (Revelation 7:10).

For those of us who have heard the gospel, salvation comes through conscious acknowledgment of Jesus Christ as Lord and Savior. We have his commandment to go and tell others, and we cannot escape this obligation. But those who know him as Lord and Savior talk with others not out of a sense of superiority, but simply because they are faithful to their Lord's will. Sri Lankan theologian D.T. Niles effectively described both evangelism and the evangelist when he said, "Evangelism is one beggar telling another beggar where to find bread."

But all people have not heard the Good News of Jesus Christ. There are vast expanses of Asia and other continents where the name of Christ is unknown. Even in our own country there are large numbers of people who have never heard the real message of the gospel. Sometimes their lack of experience is due to Christians' terrible examples and their failure to live up to the ethic of love. One vivid example of this lack of love and acceptance was when Christians cursed Madalyn Murray O'Hare and threatened to beat up her and her children. Incidents like this one promote a false witness from believers and prevent others from hearing the gospel's message.

It may well be that God, in his great mercy, will excuse persons who live according to their best insights. Other religions should not be written off as totally false or evil, for they contain much beauty and truth. Most, for example, contain some version of the golden rule and are concerned with man's relationship to the poor and the weak. If God is the source of all beauty and truth, then he must have revealed himself in other religions, too, even though that revelation may be confused or distorted.

Paul allows for this possibility when he writes: "Indeed, when Gentiles, who do not have the law, do by nature things required by the law, they are a law for themselves, even though they do not have the law, since they show that the requirements of the law are written on their hearts . . . " (Romans 2:14-15).

Note that Paul says judgment will be based on Jesus Christ. The same would be true for any revelation God has made through other religions. Jesus' statement that "I am the way and the truth and the life" means that even though men might not recognize him, any truth about God comes through him and only through him. He is, as John's Gospel says, "the Word."

One of the best examples of this obedience to the law of the heart is the great Hindu leader Mohandas Gandhi. Partly because of the racial bigotry he saw in the whites who ruled his country, and even more, because of the complicated and conflicting theologies they professed about Jesus and personal salvation, he could not accept their Christian religion. Yet he accepted and practiced the way of Christ, taking to heart Jesus' command to "turn the other cheek" and to "love your enemies and pray for those who persecute you." By the life he chose to live, Gandhi brought Christians to a new awareness of their gospel's powerful love. By adapting and using the teachings of Christ in his non-violent revolution against the British, millions of lives were saved in the Indian revolution. He was more faithful to "the Word" than many pious Christians who would damn the soul of such an "unbeliever" to the fires of eternity. Gandhi, therefore, may be one of those whom Jesus said would enter the kingdom before those who claimed to be righteous.

In the final analysis, we must add that it is God's place to judge who will and who will not go to heaven. We must be comforted by the words of the old hymn:

> There's a wideness in God's mercy
> Like the wideness of the sea
> There's a kindness in his justice,
> Which is more than liberty.
> There's no place where earth's sorrows

Are more felt than up in heaven;
There is no place where earth's failings
Have such kindly judgment given.

NO, there is no hope for non-Christians to go to heaven.

"Why do you want to invite Joe to church? He seems like the last guy in the world who'd be interested."

"That's just the reason. He doesn't go anywhere now, and he needs to hear and believe in the gospel."

"But Joe must be one of the most moral people in our class. Even though he doesn't go to church, he doesn't drink or smoke pot. I never even heard him cuss."

"That's fine, but getting into heaven isn't just a matter of doing good. It's a matter of faith—faith in Jesus. If going to heaven depended upon our good works, then Jesus wouldn't have needed to die on the cross."

"What do you mean by that?"

"Well, if we could earn our way into heaven by doing good things for others, all we would have to do is prepare a list of ways to earn salvation and do them. But Jesus changed all that. His life reflected his acceptance of others just the way they are. But his death demanded faith from his followers, faith that they would recognize his unique relationship to God and faith that God could take even the worst of circumstances—death—and create good from this. Because Jesus died for our sins, it is no longer necessary for us to offer a sacrifice for those things we have done wrong like they did in the Old Testament. Jesus was that sacrifice for all who believe in him. But we must believe in him as Savior in order for the sacrifice to be effective for us."

"I guess I just never heard it explained that way before. Now I can see why it is important to be a Christian. Look, there's Joe now—let's go over and invite him to youth fellowship."

The Bible is very explicit at this point. "I am the way and the truth and the life. No one comes to the Father except through me" (John 14:6). "I am the true vine, and my

Father is the gardener. He cuts off every branch in me that bears no fruit . . . You are already clean because of the word I have spoken to you. Remain in me, and I will remain in you. No branch can bear fruit by itself; it must remain in the vine. Neither can you bear fruit unless you remain in me" (John 15:1-4).

The early church also believed this. Peter declared to religious leaders in Jerusalem, "Salvation is found in no one else, for there is no other name under heaven given to men by which we must be saved" (Acts 4:12). After his meeting with Nicodemus, Jesus states: "For God so loved the world that he gave his one and only Son, that whoever believes in him shall not perish but have eternal life . . . Whoever believes in him is not condemned, but whoever does not believe stands condemned already because he has not believed in the name of God's one and only Son" (John 3:16, 18). Paul devoted his whole life to preaching "the gospel of salvation," declaring that the law was not enough, that only in Jesus Christ could salvation be found.

Today it is not popular to seem so intolerant and to insist upon belief in Jesus Christ as necessary for salvation. Some people, in the name of tolerance and good will, want to water down the gospel and say that all religions are good, that we shouldn't send missionaries overseas to convert people to the way of Christ. This logic opposes the teachings of Christ, whose last commandment was, ". . . go and make disciples of all nations, baptizing them in the name of the Father and of the Son and of the Holy Spirit" (Matthew 28:19). If Jesus Christ is not necessary for salvation, then he was either a crazy egomaniac or a liar to make the claims that he did. Or he was telling the truth, a truth we dare not water down or deny.

Programming Ideas for Issue 22

Preparation—The week before this session, announce that everyone should wear older clothes since they will be sitting on the floor during the meeting. Prepare a list of clues to guide your group to different places around the building. Write these clues on one side of a file card and on the other side print the scripture references and discussion questions listed in Chart 15. Prepare a master list of where you are to go so you can help your kids search for the cards. Use your ingenuity, both in hiding the cards in unusual places and in wording the clues. You might want to use a rhyme as a clue like the following: "You're doing great! Our leader would shout! Where the children sing, you're bound to find out." (Did you look on the director's stand in the children's choir room?)

Scriptural questions also make good clues. For example: "Read Matthew 26:26-29. Where do we celebrate this event in Jesus' life?" (The communion table would add significance

---

Chart 15
Scriptures and Questions

1. Genesis 17:1-8
Why are Abraham and Sarah unlikely candidates to start a new people? Would you choose such "senior citizens" for this purpose? What does this reveal about God? Who can tell us more about what happened to the couple? (See Genesis.)

2. Genesis 25:21-34
Was Jacob a nice person? Would you buy a used car (or more likely, a used donkey or a used camel) from him? Yet he forms an important link in the long chain of believers that make up God's people. What does this reveal about God? Does anyone know what happened to Jacob? (See Genesis.)

3. Isaiah 42:6
Who is being addressed here? What does it mean that Israel has been given as a "covenant" and a "light to the nations"? Did the Israelites like Gentiles or want them to be saved? Would this passage be surprising to those who first heard it?

4. John 8:1-11
What did the Law of Moses say should be done to the woman? Why did the scribes and Pharisees bring this situation to Jesus? What did they think he would do?

Can you think of other times when Jesus surprised the people by the way he treated those regarded as sinners or undesirables? Remember the tax collectors, especially Zacchaeus and Matthew; the woman who anointed Jesus' feet; the lepers;

to the scriptural references in Isaiah or Romans.)

Plan your last stop for the music room or the sanctuary where there are hymnals. Provide Bibles for each person for the spiritual journey.

Gather art supplies including different kinds of paper and paint, markers, crayons, watercolors, finger paints and colored chalk.

Opening—Ask for a show of hands of how many believe there is hope for non-Christians to go to heaven. How many think there is no hope for non-Christians?

Tell the group: "We're going to take a journey through scripture and look at some of the surprising ways of God. By following numerous clues, we will actually travel around

---

the Samaritan woman at the well; the Roman soldier whose servant was ill; and the thief on the cross. What do these stories reveal about God?

5. Matthew 25:31-46 and 7:21-23

Why are the "sheep" in Matthew 25 surprised? What does Jesus indicate is true faith: correct doctrine or loving acts? Is it possible, then, for Muslims or Hindus to do the will of God? How is their situation different from a Christian doing the same acts? Or is it the same?

6. Romans 2:12-16

What does Paul mean here? Are there some who do God's will without fully knowing the law or Christ and thus are welcomed into heaven by God? How does the apostle's teaching fit with John 14:6? Some think that since Jesus Christ is "the truth," any truth found in other religions is also from him, even though it may be hidden or unrecognized. What do you think of this idea?

7. Matthew 28:18-20

If there is truth in other religions, then why do we send missionaries to other countries? Is it so we can lord our religion over the "heathen," or do we merely wish to share Christ and help others recognize how he has already come to them in their own religion and culture? How should we approach and relate to members of other religions? As far as heaven goes, can *we* decide who's going to be there? To whom does this task belong? How can recognizing this fact keep us a little more humble?

our church building where cards with scripture passages have been hidden. So pick up a Bible and listen carefully to this first clue.''

Program—Ask a person to read the clue, and then as a group decide where everyone is going. If the kids misunderstand the clue, allow them to make a mistake and then help them rethink what they should do. Go with your young people and keep them together. When they find the scripture card, have them sit down and read the passage together. After discussing the scripture passage, ask another young person to read the clue for finding the next scripture card.

Response—Go back to the youth room where various art supplies are prepared. Ask each person to take a sheet of paper and create two pictures—one of heaven and one of hell. Play background music and instruct the group not to talk. After 15 to 30 minutes, ask individuals to share their creations.

After everyone has shared, join hands with only four of the young people in your group. Tell everyone, "When *we* decide who will be saved, we almost always make the circle too small." Instruct the four young people to drop hands and each one reach out to include one other person in the circle. Join hands again and tell the group: "This exclusive selection process was true in biblical days when the Jews wanted to keep out the Gentiles. Even the disciples excluded sinners, women, lepers and children." Drop hands again and ask the people in the circle to reach out and bring everyone else into the group. Tell everyone: "This means we must not take lightly God's judgment upon our sin. There are some so blinded by their sin that they are lost. But heaven will include surprises for all of us." Pass out hymnals and sing or read the hymn, "There's a Wideness in God's Mercy." Close with a prayer similar to the following:

"O God, our creator, sustainer and redeemer, thank you for your great mercy in sending us your son, Jesus, to show us how to live and to save us by his death on the cross. We would too readily shut out some whom you would choose to include. We would also include those whom you might choose to cast out. You alone know the hearts of humanity, and you alone can save and call into your kingdom those whom you desire. Keep us faithful to our calling so that when we stand before you, we will recognize you as the Father of our Savior, Jesus Christ our Lord. Amen.''

Options:

1. This issue lends itself to debate quite well. Try having a short debate at the beginning that allows the kids to speak from their own feelings and knowledge without Bible study or research. Have the kids vote on the question after the debate. Then have a study session using the scripture cards and discussion questions. Have the kids vote again. If any people have changed their minds ask them to explain why.

2. Have small groups work with Bibles and concordances to look up words like "judgment," "heaven," "hell," "Gentile," "Christian," "faith" and "Law of Moses." Close the session with the art activities and closing circle ideas suggested in the Response section.

3. Invite your pastor to speak on this topic, sharing both sides of the issue and presenting the rationale for the stand taken by your particular church.

ISSUE 23

Can Christians believe in reincarnation?

YES, Christians can believe in reincarnation.

"Did you see the last issue of the National Tattler with the article about reincarnation?"

"No, I don't read those things."

"Well, you should have read this one. There are a lot of people, some of them movie stars, who can remember having lived other lives."

"That seems a bit dramatic and far-fetched to me."

"Well, I thought so too until I read the article. It was

amazing how they could recall even insignificant details which no one would find in typical reading. But when these facts were checked with historians who were experts on that time period, they were not only accurate but helped to clarify some of the confusion created by the language barrier.

"You know, a short time ago people laughed at the idea of nuclear fission, yet today our world teaches this as a basic scientific concept. Every day we discover more and more new things about our universe as we probe its mysteries. Why couldn't reincarnation be another of those new, astounding discoveries?"

Reincarnation, meaning that we have lived other lives in the past, is a real part of many cultures around the world. Too many people can recall past lives for this theory to be written off as just another hoax.

Many individuals, including film stars like Shirley Mac-Lain, have remembered, often in dreams, the names and places of past incidents. When these recollections have been checked with historical records, the dreams and remembrances are sometimes found to be accurate. These people actually lived, and there were incidents that occurred just as they were pictured in the dreams.

Reality is even greater than the biblical writers realized. When we die, our soul does continue to exist. It passes into the mysterious spirit world, from which it returns through the birth of another body at a later time. Most people do not recall their past experiences, but for some reason others have instances of vivid recall. Since our present consciousness dominates our minds during our waking hours, it is usually when we are sleeping that the dimmer images from our pre-existence can be recalled.

Some open-minded Christians have begun to study reincarnation just because so many people have testified to how real it is for them. They are finding that this belief does not need to conflict with the Bible. Many believe this concept can be added to Christians' understanding of the world and how our Creator works within it.

NO, Christians cannot accept any belief in reincarnation.

"Look at this, Sarah. Here's another article about Cheryl McDermott's new book. It says she remembers at least a dozen other lives."

"I saw her on Bill Bradley's talk show yesterday. She's really gone off the deep end, if you ask me."

"But look at all the details she can remember about growing up in the Pharaoh's court—wearing the gold gowns and jewels she can describe almost perfectly, being waited on by hundreds of slaves . . . "

"But don't you think it's interesting that these people always remember being kings and queens, not slaves or servants?"

"Here it says she remembers being Marie Antoinette."

"Sure, Angie, and I'll bet she gets a pain in her neck every Bastille Day. I think she's been watching too many old movies and reading too many historical novels!"

Reincarnation is a belief basic to Hinduism, not to Christianity. Although both religions have doctrines about the soul, Christianity teaches that the soul or essence of an individual is unique. It belongs to God and finds its meaning as the human being recognizes his or her relationship to the Creator. The soul remains unique even after death. Hinduism teaches that the soul migrates from one body to another following death. If the person has been good, he or she will pass to a higher plane of existence until he or she eventually achieves nirvana, the total immersion in the universal soul. If the person has been bad, the individual's soul may migrate to a lowly animal like an insect or a spider. The whole caste system of India is based on this belief. Each person's status in society depends on one's karma, the result of the thoughts and deeds in a previous life. Therefore, a person should not try to change one's social position in this life, but accept it as one's karma. If the individual behaves well in this life, he or she will be born into a higher caste the next time around.

This is a long way from Christian teaching. The concept of time in the Bible is linear, not cyclical—that is, that there is a beginning and an ending point in life, not a series of repetitions. In Christianity a person is born, lives and dies. During this one lifetime he or she has numerous chances to accept the grace of God. At death the person dies and awaits resurrection to life or eternal death. An individual is not part of a universal, indestructible soul; he or she *is* a unique creation.

There have been countless claims of people "remembering" past lives and incidents. Some of these have been sincere claims while others like the Bridey Murphy case in the '50s have been hoaxes. Usually, there is an explanation other than reincarnation. For example, the person may have read or heard about the past, consciously forgotten it and then dreamed about past experiences while sleeping.

Thinking Christians should reject reincarnation for numerous reasons. It encourages the terrible Indian caste system, it undermines a person's chances to better himself or herself and it promotes the attitude that nothing can be done to make the present life more valuable or worthwhile.

Programming Ideas for Issue 23

Preparation—Locate a library book on the religions of humanity and read the chapter on Hinduism.

Duplicate Charts 16—19. If you wish to use the Karma Cards several times, cut them, attach them to a sheet of posterboard with rubber cement, laminate them and cut them out again, leaving at least a 1/8-inch margin on all sides.

Learn the rules of the game, and be prepared to share these with the group. If there are too many group members for one game, prepare duplicate game materials, or ask the young people to double up as partners.

Gather one die for each game and use coins, beans or sunflower seeds for game pieces, or provide materials for the kids to create their own markers. You also will need Bibles and concordances.

Opening—Ask people to share what they know about reincarnation. Some may have heard movie stars speak about it or they might have seen articles about it in publications like The Star and National Enquirer. Point out the fact that many Americans accept the idea of reincarnation without realizing that it is an integral part of one of the world's largest religious sects. To understand reincarnation, it is important to know something about Hinduism. The game Karma was created to introduce people to the beliefs and concepts of this religion.

Program—Say: "Karma is designed to acquaint you with a few basic concepts of Hinduism that underlie the belief or doctrine of reincarnation. Millions of people believe that when you die your soul passes immediately into another body that is being born. When you live ethically, you are born again into a higher station. In India, you would move into a higher caste. If your current life is bad, then your next life would include a form of punishment like being placed in a lower caste or migrating into the body of some lowly animal. Reincarnation refers to the process in which the soul passes from one human body into another human body; the larger doctrine of transmigration of souls teaches that a soul living a series of bad lives can descend to the form of animals. Likewise, the soul of an animal that lives a good life can pass into the higher forms of life, including human beings. This rebirth continues in an almost infinite series of cycles until the soul, after purging itself of all desires while living as a holy man, finally is merged with the Brahma-Atman, the universal or cosmic soul of which all life is a part."

Have each person choose a marker and place it in the Start square. Tell the group: "These markers represent your atman, or individual soul which is a part of the Brahma-Atman (the great universal or world soul). The goal of the game is for you to return your individual atman to the Brahma-Atman, to be swallowed up or blended into the universal soul. This is a difficult task and may require that you live millions of lives full of pain and suffering. Each space on the game board represents another life through which you must pass on your way to moksha, which is the final release from the grinding series of lives you must live. When you finally reach the Brahma-Atman and are beyond all desires, you will lose yourself into the universal soul and achieve nirvana." (Note: To save time and space, only three cycles, which represent the three higher castes, are used in this game. It is assumed that all players have been members of the Sudra caste, the peasants and serfs, in their previous lives and that their ethical living earned them good karma so that they can now enter the Vaisya caste, which includes the farmers and merchants.)

"Throw the die to determine who will begin. The one

Chart 16
Karma Cards—Vaisya Caste

Place cards inside the circle labeled Vaisya Caste (Merchants and Farmers).

You helped someone. Go forward 3 spaces.	You made a pilgrimage to a shrine. Advance 2 spaces.
You were selfish today. Go back 3 spaces.	You read part of the Upanishads today. Advance 3 spaces.
It's been discovered that you are an Untouchable. Go back to Start and miss the next turn.	You withstood the temptation to eat meat. Advance 3 spaces.

who gets the lowest number throws the die first. All players will advance their markers around the cycles of life according to the number on their die. When you land on a space labeled Karma Card, take one of the cards from the appropriate stack, read it aloud and follow its directions. Replace the card on the bottom of the stack.

"In order to enter a higher caste and live this series of lives, you must roll the *exact* number and land on the 'Enter Higher Caste' space. If you approach this space and roll a higher number, you must continue around the circle and try again. Failure to land on this exit/entrance space is due to bad karma.

"To end the cycle of lives, your atman, or marker,

You tried to enhance your status by mingling socially with someone of a higher caste. Go back 3 spaces.	You made a trip to bathe in the Ganges. Advance 4 spaces.
You ate beef today. Go back 2 spaces.	Your new child is a boy. Advance 2 spaces.
You fed a sacred cow today. Advance 2 spaces.	Your new child is a girl. Go back 2 spaces.
You allowed an Untouchable to come into your home. Go back 3 spaces.	You died while bathing in the Ganges. Go directly to the "Prepare for Moksha" space.

must land on the 'Prepare for Moksha' space. (Moksha means 'release.') If you overshoot this space, you must continue around the circle until you achieve good karma and roll the exact number to land on the space. After entering

---

Chart 17
Karma Cards—Kshatriya Caste

Place cards inside the circle labeled Kshatriya Caste (Rulers and Warriors).

Your new child is a son. Advance 3 spaces.	You died after living an evil life. Thus your karma dictates that you be born into a lower caste.
Your new child is a daughter. Go back 2 spaces.	Go back to the exit/entrance space of the lower caste. You must throw a 5 on the die in order to enter the Kshatriya Caste.
You arranged a marriage of your daughter with a family in a slightly higher subcaste. Advance 2 spaces.	When you dined in the market, you ate soup made with beef in it. You should have checked this. Go back 3 spaces.
Your son, accepting new ideas at the university, has married someone from a lower caste. Go back 3 spaces.	You completed a three-day fast. Advance 4 spaces.
You came too close to an Untouchable. Go back 3 spaces.	You retired today to devote yourself to the study of the holy books. Advance 5 spaces.

the 'Prepare for Moksha' space and as your atman approaches the Brahma-Atman (or the universal soul), you must roll the exact number to reach nirvana. If the number rolled is too high, the atman stays on the same space until

You chose a guru today. Advance 3 spaces.	You practiced ahimsa, or nonviolence, when insulted. Advance 4 spaces.
You adopted the Yoga of Action today. Advance 4 spaces.	You disciplined your body by lashing it. Advance 3 spaces.
You touched an Untouchable. Go back 4 spaces.	You brought a food offering for a cobra. Advance 3 spaces.
You bathed in the Ganges. Advance 3 spaces.	You gave away all your property and vowed to become a holy man. Advance 6 spaces.
You protected a sacred cow today. Advance 3 spaces.	You are 12 today and received the sacred thread. Advance 3 spaces.
Today you died; however, you were a very good person and thus have earned good karma. You are reborn into a higher caste. Advance to the "Enter Higher Caste" space.	

your next turn. When you roll the exact number, move to the Brahma-Atman area. You have reached your goal; you have achieved nirvana and have blended with the universal soul.''

Response—Play the game long enough for some kids

Chart 18
Karma Cards—Brahman Caste

Place cards inside the circle labeled Brahman Caste (Priests and Scholars).

You have become a priest at a temple. Advance 5 spaces.	You are a woman. Lose your next turn.
You are a priest, but you thought about a woman. Go back 3 spaces.	You have left public life to enter a monastery. Advance 5 spaces.
You craved meat. Go back 2 spaces.	You were in a trance but allowed a beggar's entreaties to call you back. Go back 2 spaces.
You have fasted for a week. Advance 4 spaces.	You stepped on an insect during a night walk. Go back 2 spaces.
You are a man. Advance 5 spaces.	You traveled a great distance to bathe in the Ganges. Advance 3 spaces.

to succeed and some to become frustrated. Stop the game after 20 or 30 minutes and use the following questions to facilitate discussion. Post a sheet of newsprint on which you can record things you want to remember or reinforce. Use the following questions to stimulate discussion:

You died while bathing in the Ganges. Go straight to nirvana.	You have memorized a holy book. Advance 4 spaces.
You died after living an evil life. Return to Start at the Vaisya Caste.	You have learned 10,000 names of the gods (only 32,990,000 more to go!). Advance 5 spaces.
You are a holy man, and have suppressed all desires today. Advance 5 spaces.	You have become another man's guru. Advance 5 spaces.
You are a holy man, and you gave in to your desires. Go back 4 spaces.	You neglected a holy day. Go back 2 spaces.
You practiced ahimsa, or nonviolence, when attacked. Advance 4 spaces.	You strongly chastised your son who wanted to marry a girl of a lower caste. Advance 3 spaces.

Chart 19

KARMA
GAME BOARD

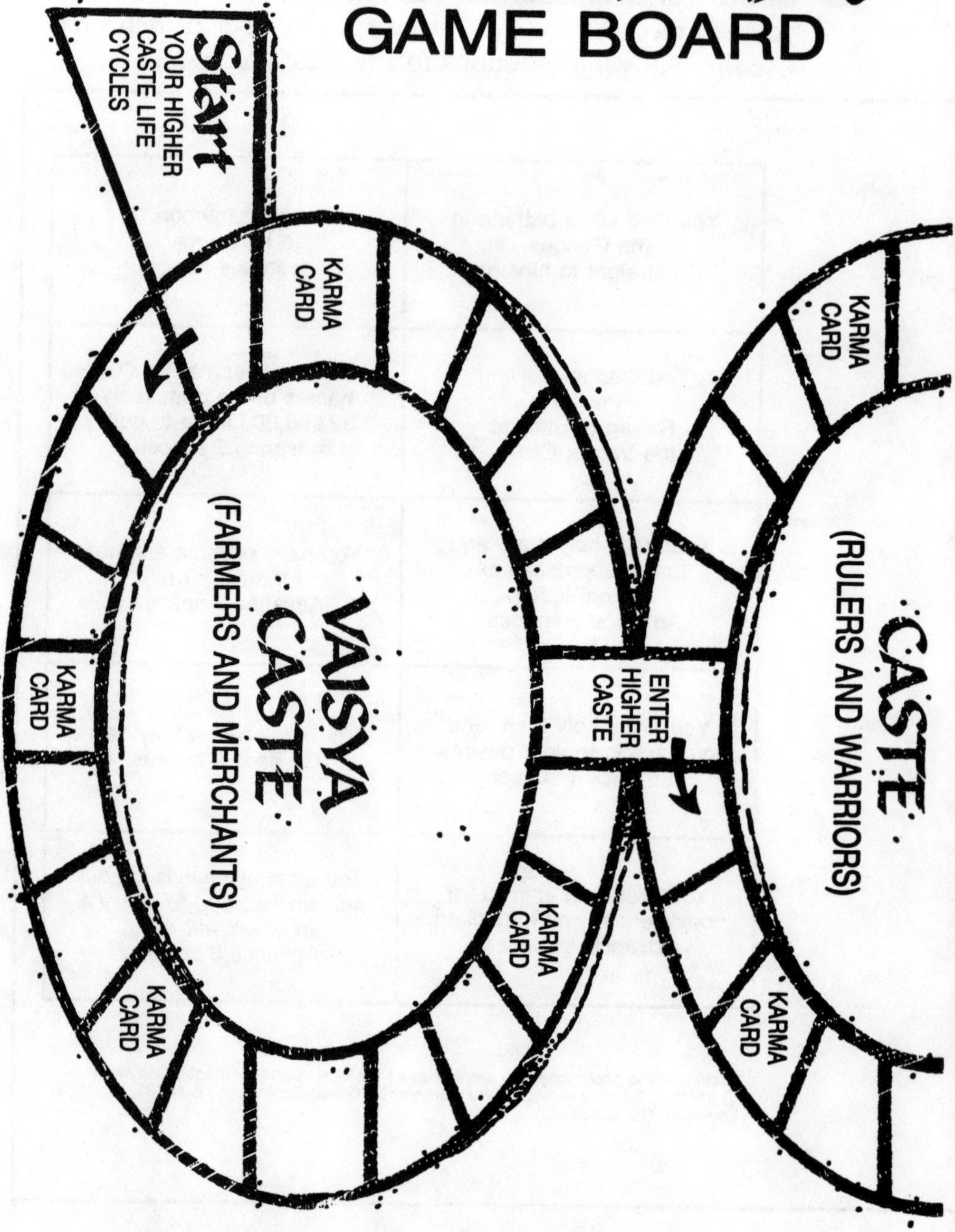

Start
YOUR HIGHER CASTE LIFE CYCLES

KARMA CARD

VAISYA CASTE
(FARMERS AND MERCHANTS)

ENTER HIGHER CASTE

CASTE
(RULERS AND WARRIORS)

KARMA CARD

KARMA CARD

KARMA CARD

KARMA CARD

KARMA CARD

KARMA CARD

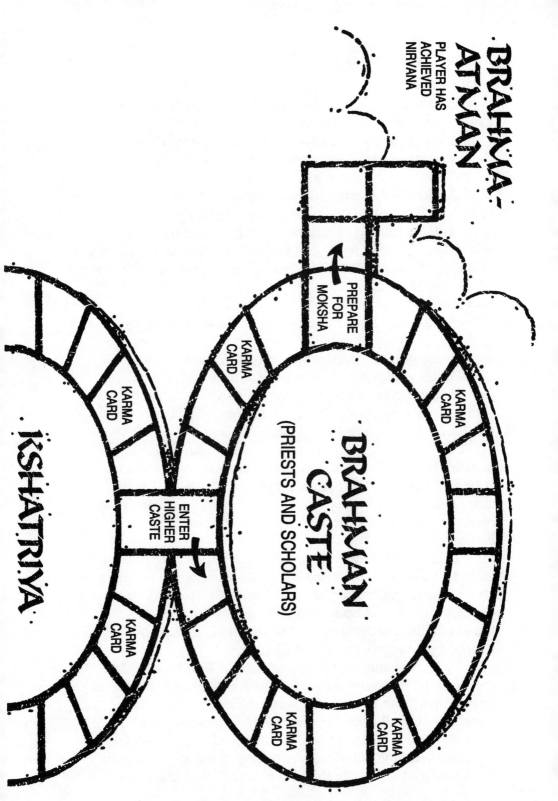

BRAHMA-ATMAN

PLAYER HAS ACHIEVED NIRVANA

PREPARE FOR MOKSHA

KARMA CARD

KARMA CARD

BRAHMAN CASTE
(PRIESTS AND SCHOLARS)

KARMA CARD

ENTER HIGHER CASTE

KSHATRIYA

KARMA CARD

KARMA CARD

KARMA CARD

1. What similarities do you see between Hinduism and Christianity? What are the major differences?

2. What is the Hindu religion's concept of God? How do intellectual Hindus explain their people's belief in 33,000,000 gods? their use of statues?

3. How is the game Karma similar to Paul's statement in Galatians 6:7? How is it different? Define karma.

4. How do the two faiths view time and history? Which one views time as circular and which one views time as linear? Which faith has no beginning or end? Read Revelation 1:8. How does this statement compare with the Hindu viewpoint?

5. How does the Hindu view of the soul compare with the Christian view? How can either of these ideas be used to support the concept of reincarnation?

(Hindu viewpoint: The atman (soul) is imperishable, a part of the universal soul to which it finally returns. The soul is the string upon which the innumerable lives of a person are strung like a long, beaded necklace.

Christian viewpoint: Each person is a unique creation of God; he or she is not part of a universal soul. A person is born, lives one life, makes choices while he or she is alive, and then dies. Anything beyond this experience is the result of the choices the individual made during his or her lifetime.)

6. Read the following scripture passages: Genesis 2:7, John 3:16 and 1 Corinthians 15:35-57. How is the teaching about "perishing" different from Hinduism? How is Paul's concept of spiritual body and resurrection different from the Hindu atman? How does the Christian concept of heaven compare to the Hindu nirvana?

7. How is the concept of heaven in Revelation different from the Hindu nirvana? In which religion do we blend into the godhead as drops of water blend into the sea, thereby losing all sense of identity and consciousness?

8. Have the group look up the word "soul" in their concordances and Bibles to see how it is used. (In Hebrew the word soul is "nephesh" and in Greek "psuche"; these

are very different concepts from Hindu philosophy!)
Explain.

9. How does the caste system and the concept of karma fit in with reincarnation? How do these concepts justify "what is"? Some see this as an early form of social control, a way of the elite and comfortable saying to those at the bottom of society: "Don't try to change anything. Be good and obedient, and you'll get your reward in the next life." Do you agree? Why or why not? Has Christianity ever been used in this way? When or how?

10. Since nirvana is based on our karma (our living and knowing rightly), would you say that this concept is based on righteousness through good works? Why? What does Christianity say about the basis of our salvation? Is salvation something Christians "achieve" by good works or is it a matter of grace?

11. How do you account for those people who claim they "remember" former lives? Do you agree that reincarnation is part of a belief system and therefore cannot be "proven"? What Christian teachings fall into this category?

Have the group sit in a circle in the lotus position (legs crossed, hands together in a prayerlike position, heads bowed). Ask the group members to think about their concept of God. After a couple of minutes of silent meditation, read Revelation 1:4-8. Celebrate the concept of God as one who reaches out to others by asking all participants to put their legs out in front of them, lay down on their backs and open their eyes. Ask the group members to join hands at their sides and to raise their arms together over their heads. Tell the group: "Just as our feet are located on a central point, so is our Christian faith based on the central concept of salvation by grace through Jesus Christ. But our faith directs us beyond this point; it demands that we open our eyes and reach out to those whose lives we touch. We cannot afford to be satisfied. Because we have received the gift of salvation, we are called to share it with others to enhance their lives."

Close this session by singing "We Are the Family of

God" from *Songs* (Songs and Creations). Sing the first verse as everyone is on his or her back. Ask the group to stand and face out of a circle to sing the last two verses.

Options:

1. Ask two to four of your young people to research Hinduism in books at their school, church and public libraries and present a report on how reincarnation is an outgrowth of that religion. Use scripture passages and discussion questions from the Program and Response sections to facilitate discussion.

2. Check the public and school libraries for films on Hinduism. Preview these and see if they are appropriate for your group to watch and discuss. Use scripture passages and discussion questions from the Program and Response sections to facilitate discussion.

3. If you live in a large city or near a college or university, there are probably believers in Hinduism who would speak to your group. If you locate someone who is willing to talk with your group, prepare and send a list of questions ahead of time so he or she can have some idea of your group's areas of interest.

Chapter 7 ▶ ▶ ▶ ▶ ▶ ▶ ▶ ▶ ▶ ▶ ▶ ▶ ▶ ▶ ▶ ▶

SCIENCE ISSUES

I n the days when people considered theology the queen of sciences, there was no conflict between it and the natural sciences. Since the 16th century, however, when science emerged as an independent field, there have been numerous conflicts. First, the infant science of astronomy separated itself from astrology and bumped into the church's teaching that the earth was the center of the universe. Then biological science began to probe the intricacies of the human body and use anesthesia to eliminate the suffering many believed was caused by sin. After that, geology presented theories about the age of the earth and anthropology questioned the origin of human beings. When psychology began to question the reasons for human actions and attempted to manipulate behavior, the church had to examine several of its ingrained tenets of faith.

Since the natural sciences have had such an impact on our age, it's important for young Christians to examine some of the science and faith issues. The apparent conflict between evolution and Genesis, the possibility of life on other planets, genetic engineering, ecology—all have had an impact on people's faith. For some, science has become their faith. Our young people need to examine the whole picture and realize that they need not be afraid of these new and different ideas. As long as their faith continues to grow along with their minds and their experiences in the scientific community, they will operate as mature Christians.

ISSUE 24
Is evolution really "evilution"?

YES, evolution can accurately be described as "evilution."

"Wow, that was some school board meeting!"

"Yes it was! I'd never been to one before; but if they're all like this one, they're sure not boring. Did you ever see Reverend Getz so worked up?"

"Oh yes, you should see him on Sunday mornings. He gets pretty passionate about things he feels are wrong."

"He must! When he called Darwin's theory 'Evilution,' I thought it was a bit much."

"But that's the way he feels! Especially when the school board refused to allow the creationist theory to be taught along with Darwin's."

"Maybe so, but his attitude still seems strong. It certainly won't win him many friends here at school."

"He's not out to win friends; he appeared here to defend the Word of God. You must admit that the scientific theory of evolution does seem to be part of our country's slide toward decadence. Reverend Getz says that all of our country's problems—the breakdown of the family, the high divorce rate, disrespect for law and order, free sex, drugs, political corruption, child pornography and secularism—stem from a loss of faith in the Bible as God's Word. And it all goes back to when our society was taken in by Darwin's theory of evolution."

Evolution, the result of a humanistic attempt to explain the origin of life without God, has led many to doubt and reject the scripture as the divinely inspired Word of God. Science has become the new religion for many people today, with Charles Darwin as the prophet and his *Origin of Species* as the holy book.

Until Darwin came along, people accepted the biblical account of creation in Genesis as the way the world began. In this account God created the universe in six days, and on the seventh day he rested. This description of an orderly progression from the stars and planets, to the mountains and seas, to plant and animal life, and finally to humanity was evidence of God's intentional planning. The account did not reflect some shapeless, impersonal force called evolution.

Then came Darwin, who suggested a theory that everything in the universe came about by a random process of chance. Life somehow evolved out of primordial ooze and first appeared as one-celled organisms. Then over millions of years, more complex creatures evolved. The various animals of the sea arose as the highest forms of life, then some creatures began to spend time on land as well as in the sea. Bit by bit the descendants of these creatures adapted to life out of the water. The small crawling creatures became larger, and dinosaurs appeared. When the dinosaurs eventually disappeared, warm-blooded animals adapted to the changing climactic conditions and dominated the earth. After hundreds of millions of years, the primates appeared, splitting into two groups—the family of apes and human beings.

All of this process is supposed to have happened over billions of years without any guidance or planning, just chance, with the "law of the survival of the fittest" shaping what we see today. This theory directly contradicts the Bible, which states that God was involved and was making decisions from the beginning. Christians should oppose this theory not only for what it says, but for what it doesn't say.

Today, human beings continue to repeat the old tower of Babel story (Genesis 11:1-9). According to this ancient story, men wanted to make a name for themselves, so they tried to build a huge tower in an attempt to climb to heaven. With their technology, they planned to take God's place. Of course, God didn't just sit back and let the people reach their goal. The Creator confused the language of those who worked on the tower and scattered them abroad.

Today, human beings still think they can get along without God. They believe technology will protect them from the cradle to the grave, and will eventually push back or even eliminate death as a concern. The theory of evolution—and that's all it is, a theory—removes God from the creative process and attempts to displace him from all of life. Thus, it is not an exaggeration at all to call this concept the theory of "evilution."

Modern society has so entrenched this theory of evolution that it is accepted without question by magazines, newspapers, television writers, school teachers, some ministers and numerous scientists. This group howls with derision at Christians who dare to suggest that creationism, the Bible-based belief that God is the Creator of life, should be taught in the schools, and not just the theory of evolution. What started out in the 19th century as just a theory has now become undisputed dogma.

Today, we see two belief systems in conflict—the humanists who teach that the universe exists without the aid or presence of God versus the Christians who believe that God created, redeems and sustains life in this universe. The argument that the "days" of Genesis were longer than our 24-hour period still would not support the theory that life evolved by chance over billions of years. The Bible teaches that human beings are " . . . a little lower than the heavenly beings" (Psalm 8:5), the ultimate creation of a loving, involved God. They are not the result of some blind force that evolved from prehistoric slime and ooze. Human beings have a God-given dignity that imparts worth to each individual. Evolution, as part of the humanist faith, reduces human beings to mere thinking animals. With no God to impart dignity and worth, these beings become merely part of the masses. With no God-given value, humans exist only for the state and can be eliminated if they get in the way of "progress." Because of the numerous problems which lead back to the theory of evolution, it should be rejected and opposed by every Christian.

NO, evolution is not "evilution."

"Hey, Damon, are you going to picket the school, too?"

"I don't know, Kevin. I feel sort of weird doing this.

But after our pastor spoke, the youth group voted to join the protest."

"I don't get it. Just because we're reading that play in our English class? I think *Inherit the Wind* is neat, even if there aren't any good fights in it."

"But this play reinforces the humanist theories we're taught in biology. It's one of the most godless plays they could've found."

"You sound just like your pastor! Have you started reading it yet?"

"No, and I don't intend to. I don't have to eat poison to know that it's deadly."

"Now you really sound like your preacher. Read the play for yourself and make up your own mind."

"No way. It puts down God and those who believe in him!"

"No it doesn't! It puts down blind fear and people's refusals to look at the facts and think for themselves."

"Now *you* sound like Miss Coleridge."

"Maybe so, but that's exactly what the play does. It depicts a man who can't accept some of the ideas of his old-time religion, yet who believes in God. My own minister talked with our youth group last week about the significance of the lawyer's last act. When he holds Darwin's book in one hand and the Bible in the other and then slaps them together and puts them in his briefcase side by side he lets the reader know that these writings can exist side by side. It isn't necessary for one to be right and one to be wrong."

Calling Darwin's theory "evilution" would be a disservice both to science and to Christianity. The theory of evolution grew out of a new way of looking at the world that emerged about 400 years ago. Before that time, everyone looked at the world through the eyes of Aristotle and the writers of Genesis. They had been the authorities for centuries, and the people merely accepted their ideas. The knowledgeable men of the Middle Ages were historians more than anything else; they filled their minds with studies of the Bible and the ancient philosophers.

As people began to travel and encounter more of the world and different cultures, they began to ask questions that the old authorities could not answer. Men like da Vinci, Copernicus and Galileo sought to see the world for themselves. The idea of experimentation led to the scientific method that we use today. Its basic rule was never accept anything just on someone's authority; experiment and test the results with observable and repeatable procedures. Then share the theory based on the procedures used. When new, conflicting facts come to light, modify or throw out the theory and come up with a new one. From this scientific method has come many of the marvels of modern society.

Charles Darwin had no intention of opposing the Bible with his theory of evolution. Nor do millions of today's Christians who support his theory. Darwin did not oppose the Bible; he merely questioned the theory of creation as it was written in biblical times. The huge numbers of fossils in the various strata of the earth indicate that the earth and its life forms are far older than a literal reading of Genesis would account for. Creating the earth in six days just doesn't fit the facts.

Although some scientists who accept the theory of evolution are atheists, many are Christians who see no basic conflict between Darwin and the writers of Genesis. These scientists realize there are two valid ways to approach the creation of the world—the way of science and the way of faith. Each approach asks different questions.

Scientists want to understand *how* the world was formed. For this they look carefully at the world itself. They use the best instruments available to enhance their understandings—microscopes, telescopes, spectroscopes, scales, computers and processes like carbon-dating. When they have gathered all of this data, they use their minds to come up with the best theory that fits the evidence.

The Christian seeks to understand *why* the world was made, why it exists the way it is, and even questions, "Is that all?'' For answers to these questions, the seeker must look beyond the world to the Bible. The Bible is not a book of science; it is a book of faith. It records stories of people's encounters with God, some of which took place thousands of years ago. The Bible is the story of divine encounters, but its reports were written by human beings. These individuals accepted the worldview of their time—a three-story universe with a flat earth in the center between heaven and hell, a universe in which the stars and the sun revolved around the earth.

Writers of the Bible had no experience with laboratory or scientific methods; these methods of examination and thought process developed later. Their language was the language of the poet with metaphors and imagery, not the careful, precise language of the scientist. The great truth of Genesis is not dependent upon its scientific or historical accuracy because the authors weren't interested in proving ''facts.'' The biblical writers were more concerned with asserting their basic belief that God made ''all things . . . in heaven and on earth, visible and invisible . . . '' (Colossians 1:16).

How God created the universe really doesn't matter. Whether it was in six days, 4,000 years before Christ or over billions of years, God was still the one who started things off and who continues to watch over and work through his universe.

When we look closely at Genesis, we find two creation stories. In the first story (Genesis 1), each act of creation begins and closes with the same basic formula, ''And God said . . . And God saw that it was good.'' The author carefully affirms the goodness of God's creation over the other views that regard the universe as either evil or an illusion, something from which we must escape. Notice the distinctive cadence when you read this story out loud. The grandeur of this story is meant for worship and celebration, not as a basis for scientific study.

The second creation story (Genesis 2) is different. For example, it doesn't mention God's creation of human beings on the sixth day. In this version God merely creates a man while creating the rest of the world. When God can't find a companion fit for his creation among the lower animals, he draws a rib from the man's side and fashions it into a woman. This story is more like a folk tale. It pictures God as a huge man toiling in the dirt trying out this and that until at last everything is complete. In the temptation scene that follows, the biblical author portrays God as an Oriental landowner who loves to take evening walks in his garden. To take this story literally and worry about the conflicting details with the first story as well as with the scientific theory is to miss the point of the narrative. This author merely wants to bear witness to *God's* creation. He recognizes God's involvement in creating the world and its inhabitants and acknowledges God's gift of freedom to choose whether we will accept or deny him as Lord of our lives.

Numerous Christians read the Bible, love its message and adhere to its teachings about God and Christ. These same people also accept modified versions of Darwin's theory of evolution. Conflict need not exist between these two positions. Christians are people of both faith and knowledge. We need the Bible to tell us why and how we should live, and we need science to describe the world in which we live. Science is our map, but the Bible is our compass and gyroscope.

Programming Ideas for Issue 24

Preparation—Talk with school administrators in your community, or visit the library or your nearest college of education. Borrow current science texts from different companies and grade levels. Examine the material for different approaches to the subject of evolution, and note the appropriate pages for each text. Read through the content and be prepared to help your young people deal with this material.

Gather paper, a pencil and a Bible for each young person. Prepare several copies of Chart 20.

Opening—Ask: "How many believe God created the universe? How many believe in the theory of evolution?

How many see a conflict between the two?" State that Christians have been divided on this issue for years.

Program—Give a piece of paper, pencil and Bible to each young person. Divide the kids into three groups. Assign one group to read the creation story in Genesis 1. Have them rewrite the chapter as a worship liturgy or a responsive reading. For example, the leader could read a few verses and the people would respond with, "Behold, that was very good!"

Ask the second group to read Genesis 2 and rewrite it in modern-day language. The story might begin: "Once upon a time, there was God. God was very lonely, so . . . "

Ask the third group to read the textbook explanations of evolution and present Darwin's side of the issue. Pretend Darwin is asked to speak to a group of people who have never heard his theory of evolution. He might initiate his speech by explaining how he sees his work in relation to his faith. "I never intended to offend anyone, especially my church, but I needed different answers. The ones I received just didn't fit with what I was learning in my research."

After 30 minutes ask the groups to share their creations. Have the kids point out anything that was especially meaningful to them or facts of which they weren't aware.

Response—Make sure all three groups have Bibles and science textbooks. Distribute copies of Chart 20 and ask your groups to use the Bibles and textbooks to answer the questions. Tell the groups to research their answers rather than depend on their immediate emotional responses.

For answers to *why* we must turn to religious knowledge that is based on the Bible and human experience in relation to God. Religious knowledge provides the meaning and purpose of life. Science can tell us how the world and humanity were created, but our faith tells us why and goes beyond that with concern for where we are headed. What do you think about accepting both types of knowledge? Will this position make a difference in how we interpret the biblical stories of creation? Explain your answer.

Sing a creation song like "I Sing the Mighty Power of

God" from *Songs* (Songs and Creations). Read Psalm 8
responsively. Hold up a Bible and a science book and say,
"No matter how we interpret each of these, we must continue to wrestle with our understandings and our faith to
bring the two together.

"Whether you reject the theory of evolution or integrate
it into your faith, the most important thing is to believe that

---

Chart 20
Discussing Creation

1. Look at the order of the days of creation in Genesis 1.
When was light created? When were the "lights in the firmament" created? What confusion do you see here? How can this
confusion be explained?

2. What is a "firmament"? In Genesis 1:6, what does "let it
separate the waters from the waters" mean? What was the ancient view of the world—the heavens, the waters, the earth and
the underworld?

3. Does either Genesis story allow for a process of creation,
or is the creation of animals and man an instantaneous act? Explain your answer.

4. Many people say Darwin taught that we descended from
apes and monkeys. What does the theory of evolution actually
teach? Why did the churches react so intensely to Darwin's theories? Do you think it's possible to believe in both evolution and
the Bible? Why or why not?

5. Some scientists become overzealous in their support for
the theory of evolution and other claims of science. In some
cases science becomes their religion or faith. Some scientists
seem to need a conflict between science and religion. Can you
name any scientists who have taken that position? Explain.

6. Some theologians teach that we must approach the world
with two basic types of knowledge: scientific and religious. Scientific knowledge looks at the world through the five senses.
The laboratory and the scientific method are key tools. Science
deals with observable "facts"; it describes how things operate,
not why. Religious knowledge, based on the Bible and our experience with God, goes beyond the facts. It provides meaning
and purpose in life. It takes the facts of science and answers
"why?" How can an understanding of these two knowledges
help us interpret Genesis?

God is our creator, regardless of how the world and humanity were made. All of us need to humble ourselves and listen to both sides of this issue."

Close with a prayer like this one:

"Gracious God, Creator of the universe, we come to you with our little minds and our small faith as we confront the big issue of creation. Help us continue to listen to one another and to see your awesome hand at work in the creative forces of nature. Bind us together with our faith in you. Help us continue to try to understand your world. When we cannot understand, remind us to celebrate your goodness and your power in the midst of the mystery and wonder of your creation. In the name of the one who represents the best of your creation, your Word made flesh, Amen."

Options:

1. Arrange for a visit to a science museum. Ask the group to read and listen carefully to the statements in the exhibits. Have your young people look for comments that talk about how certain animals or climates have changed or evolved. Go out for pizza and talk over what you have seen and heard. Help your kids understand that science museums naturally talk about *how* something happens. Help them relate the how to the *why* by using the scripture references and questions in Chart 20.

2. Show *The Creation* (Gateway—New Media Bible Films). What do you think of how the artist "shows" the acts of creation in the film? Does this include all you know or have heard about God creating the world and humanity? Look in your Bibles at Genesis. Where does the film stop? Why?

Were you aware that there are two creation stories in the Bible? Read Genesis 1 and compare it with Genesis 2. Which one seems more like a folk story? Which is more like a drama that would be used in a worship liturgy? Use the Response section from this issue to conclude your session.

3. Check with a high school science teacher for a good film that explains evolution. Then find a quality film that explains the creationist point of view. Order and preview both films. Show and discuss one view one week, and the other the next, or use both films in a retreat setting. Young people from *all* churches, both fundamentalist and liberal, need to be exposed to both sides of this issue.

4. Read and discuss *Inherit the Wind* (Bantam). Compare the kids' opinions with those expressed in the No section of this issue.

ISSUE 25
Are jobs and economic growth more important than a clean environment?

YES, jobs and economic growth are more important than a clean environment.

"My dad says that if the new chemical plant moves in, it will pollute our air and water."

"It doesn't have to be that way, not if the company is careful."

"But they have a record for *not* being careful. The plant in Charleston is one of the worst polluters in West Virginia!"

"That's just talk, Carol. Your dad hasn't been unemployed for almost a year like mine and the others who were laid off when the steel mill closed down. I know our families are more than willing to trade a few chemicals in the air and water for the chance to have an income again. It will be nice to have a chance to provide for ourselves again, plus we won't have to accept others' charity."

When we talk about jobs and economic growth, we must necessarily translate these abstract concepts into human form—the thousands of workers who support their families and operate as a vital part of their communities. There was a time in this country when individuals looked at belching smokestacks and pointed with pride to factories that worked around the clock to produce the goods our nation needed. Other generations looked at those same smoke-stacks and cried "pollution!" More recently, many of the smokestacks have stopped belching smoke—but the unemployed workers stand in welfare lines.

A clean environment is a nice ideal, but we don't live in an ideal world. There can be no such thing as a world without pollution. Even primitive societies create waste that can threaten their environment. To speak of a pollution-free world is unrealistic. Rather, we must talk about acceptable levels of pollution, and this is where the debate begins.

In the last few years the United States has moved from being the world's largest creditor to being the world's largest debtor. We buy more foreign goods than we sell overseas, primarily because foreign nations can now make many things—televisions, VCRs, cameras, cars, steel and clothing—far more cheaply than we can. This foreign competition has put millions of American workers out of work. Some optimists glowingly talk about the changeover to newer high-tech industries, but for most laborers this will be a bitter disappointment. High-tech industries require highly educated workers. Those being laid off from manufacturing industries are mostly blue-collar workers who know little about computers, labs or offices.

If our remaining industries are to compete with foreign markets, we must trim costs and workers must be even more productive. Most foreign manufacturers are not restricted by the elaborate anti-pollution regulations and procedures that add so much expense to American products. We should, therefore, continue to roll back some of the country's pollution regulations and laws.

We cannot have both full employment *and* a clean environment. It's better to have an employed population that is self-supportive than to close factories and shops and dump those workers into the streets. Although we must limit flagrant pollution, the emphasis today should be on production. We need to increase our employment opportunities rather than emphasize our anti-pollution programs.

NO, jobs and economic growth are *not* more important than a clean environment.

"Look, Randy, I might feel the same way you do if my dad had been out of work for so long. But that still shouldn't blind us to what a reckless company could do to our valley."

"You should say *for* our valley. They've promised to put a thousand people back to work. That would make a big difference to the families in our sad-looking town."

"Yes, but at what price? Is a job, or even a thousand jobs, worth it if the company dumps its wastes into our air and rivers and makes our people and wildlife sick, or even kills them?"

We need to keep people employed, but we can't let this financial goal push us backward in controlling pollution and cleaning up our environment. If the important gains we have made over the years are reversed, we might kill ourselves. Then of what value would full employment be?

We live in a world where life processes are interrelated. What happens to one part of our environment eventually affects everything else. It's like one family living together in the same house. If Junior experiments with smelly chemicals in his room, and Sis plays both her stereo and television at full blast, everyone in the house is affected. (Especially if Junior catches his room on fire and Sis opens her door.) With thanks to people like Rachel Carson and Jacques Cousteau we are beginning to realize that our planet is just as interdependent as a household.

We have learned about the food chain, or what happens to the higher forms of life when the lower creatures are destroyed or disappear. In a case like this, everyone suffers. When we throw something into the atmosphere, our actions create a problem for others elsewhere. Our Canadian neighbors continually remind us that they must combat the acid rain our industries create. Even the huge lakes and oceans rebel when they reach their limits and fill with toxic chemicals so that marine life can no longer survive.

We are finally learning how to use our knowledge of ecology. For example, Lake Erie was once so polluted that its fishing industry disappeared and swimming was banned along the shores. Because strict environmental laws were enforced, this great resource has come back. The salvation of this large body of freshwater has cost municipalities and industries a great deal. They had to find alternate ways to handle their wastes that once were merely dumped into Erie's waters, but the result was worth it.

The U.S. auto industry screamed in the '60s when the government ordered it to produce a car that would offer both better mileage and less pollution. Yelling that it couldn't be done, the industry not only met the requirements, but met them well ahead of its "impossible" deadline.

It's wrong to say that we must make a choice. We can, and must, have both full employment and a clean environment. Now is not the time for the people and our government to give up on the campaign to protect our environment. This campaign should have no end, certainly not as long as there are people who try to take shortcuts in making a profit for their companies.

Programming Ideas for Issue 25

Preparation—Gather newsprint, magazines, tape, glue, grocery sacks, paper, pencils, Bibles and concordances.

Chart 21
Is It Possible to Have Both?

**Full
Employment**

**Clean
Environment**

Tape a long strip of newsprint across the front of the room. Write "Is It Possible to Have Both?" across the top. Underneath this question, write the words "Full Employment" on one end and "Clean Environment" on the other end. (See Chart 21.)

Opening—As the kids arrive, ask them to glance through magazines to find pictures and headlines that show the positive aspects of both full employment and a clean environment. Pictures of factories, workers and manufactured goods could represent the advantages of full employment. Pictures of clean rivers and towns plus healthy people and animals could illustrate the positive aspects of a clean environment. Have the young people cut out these pictures and tape them to the newsprint at the front of the room.

If they find examples of how these two ideals clash such as pictures of dead birds and fish coated with oil or lines of asbestos workers picketing the White House for their jobs back, have them cut out the pictures and place them on the floor under the sign.

Program—After the kids have finished taping their pictures to the newsprint, say: "How many of you believe pollution is a major problem today? How many believe unemployment is a big concern? This is a case where two major problems come into conflict. We're going to take a closer look at this conflict and see what some of the issues are." Look at the sign and have everyone choose a position along the wall. If someone favors a clean environment at all costs, have him or her stand at that end of the sign. If an individual feels that the most important thing to consider is full employment, no matter what the consequences, have him or her stand at the employment end of the sign. If some are unsure or have reservations about where to stand, tell them to think of the sign as a continuum and take a place closest to what they think or feel.

After everyone has made a decision about his or her position on this issue, divide the large group into three smaller groups to talk about the position taken. Have the individuals on each end of the continuum form two groups with the undecided people in the third group. Spend about 10 minutes discussing questions such as these: Why did you choose this spot on the continuum? What does this issue mean to our community? our country? our world? What does the Bible say about this issue?

Give a two-minute and then a one-minute warning to wrap up the discussions. Hand each of the three groups a grocery bag and tell them: "Now that you have talked about this issue, go outside and collect as many items as possible that are humanity's mark on the environment. You will have 10 minutes to collect these."

When everyone returns, tell the groups, "With these items, create some junk art called 'Humanity's Mark on Creation.'" Pass out paper and pencils and ask each group to write an explanation of what their junk art is supposed to say to others. Allow about 20 minutes for this process. (If you use this activity at a retreat, extend this section by asking the groups to combine their finished works into one art form and make an explanatory statement at the end of the retreat.)

Response—Call the groups together and have each one present its art form and what it is supposed to say. Encourage the audience to ask questions. After all three groups have presented their creations, discuss the following questions:

1. Did any group involve scripture in its interpretation? Have someone read Genesis 1:24-31.

2. Read Psalm 8. What does it mean for humanity to have dominion over the works of God's hands?

3. Read Genesis 2:8-9; 15-17. What does the concept of man as the gardener add? Whose garden is this? (Another option at this point is to listen to John Denver's song "Whose Garden Was This?" What does this say about our treatment of the earth?)

4. The Bible recognizes the importance of work. Read Ecclesiastes 3:1-13. What is "God's gift to man"? How can we "take pleasure in all (our) toil"?

5. How can overemphasis upon either no pollution or full employment lead to disaster? What are some ways to

progress toward achieving the two goals? (See pictures on the floor under the sign for hints of how these two issues can affect each other.)

Plan your closing for outdoors if possible. Have everyone sit in a circle. Ask the teenagers to turn around to look at the trees, grass, sky and other gifts of nature we have around us. Suggest that everyone say a short, eyes-open sentence prayer, thanking God for some specific natural gifts we have reviewed. When everyone has finished, have everyone turn to the center of the circle and thank God again for some of the special manufactured items we find useful such as a small radio, watch, book, curling iron and so on. Sing, "For the Beauty of the Earth" from *Songs* (Songs and Creations). Close with the following prayer:

"Gracious God, our creator and sustainer of the universe, thank you for all your good gifts. May we never take the earth and its bounty for granted. Keep us thankful for the work you call us to perform. May we strive for a world in which there is beauty and meaningful work for all. We ask this in the name of the master workman, the carpenter, Jesus of Nazareth, Amen."

Option:

1. Divide the group in two sections to work on a slide and tape presentation of this topic. Ask the first group to research scripture passages, poems, hymns and songs for a sound track. (Pete Seegar and John Denver have some great ecology songs that would be appropriate.) While this group is selecting the songs and preparing a sound tape, the other group could equip themselves with cameras. Some could take pictures of factories, streams, hills, animals and people in your community. Others could use cameras with close-up lenses to copy pictures from news magazines and books. After the slides come back from the lab, ask a few of your group members to edit the slides and match them to the words of the songs and scripture passages chosen. Some groups may choose to announce the songs ahead of time so that the photographers can prepare pictures appropriate for

each song. If groups take enough slides, they can use two projectors to create a rich mixture. Preview the show and readjust the slides as needed. Arrange to present this production to various groups in your church and other organizations in your community.

ISSUE 26

Should scientists continue to experiment with genes and other forms of bioengineering?

YES, scientists should continue their experiments with genes and bioengineering.

The researcher shared his dream of the future with his audience. In the year 2000, a young boy named Tom falls on the train tracks near his home and is run over by a fast commuter train whizzing by. Both legs are severed. The emergency squad arrives quickly, administers first aid and delivers the boy to University Hospital, where scientists are experimenting with limb regeneration.

After an analysis and consultation with his parents, the team of doctors begins to subject the boy to an extensive series of treatments designed to stimulate new growth in the tissue and bones in the stumps of the boy's legs. Within a year Tom is walking again on new legs that are his own. The papers call his recovery a "miracle."

Science is a tool for the betterment of humanity. With it we have learned how to control much of our environment, ease pain, travel and communicate with remarkable speed. These accomplishments bring a reasonably good life to most of the people in our country.

Experiments in genetics continue to push back our ignorance and expose our fears as unfounded. Through genetics we have developed superior strains of grain, hardy enough to survive in most of the world. These plants will grow in a wider range of climates and withstand pests that normally destroy valuable food supplies.

We have also probed the secrets of the body's defenses

against disease. Someday genetics may bring us closer to eliminating cancer. Soon we may even learn how to grow individualized replacement organs, using the cells from our own body.

Far from opposing genetic research, Christians should promote it. If we are concerned about its misuse, we should monitor genetic research, how it is used and its progress within the medical community. Many Christian doctors once opposed the use of anesthesia in childbirth because they mistakenly thought women were *supposed* to suffer. The doctors believed the pain was part of the curse put on Eve at the Fall. We should never make that kind of mistake again.

NO, Christians should not be involved in experiments and practices that invade God's domain.

A laboratory worker is transporting a strain of a deadly virus that has been cultivated for study. Suddenly there is an explosion that rocks the lab and tears a huge hole in the wall. The virus container is broken, and the virulent virus escapes the sealed area by riding on the air currents within the blast.

Police and civil defense workers seal off the area. The news media issue warnings for residents to stay indoors, but soon people begin to come down with strange symptoms. A new plague has been created, and there is no known cure. People try to flee the city, but they are stopped at every road by armed soldiers. Despite all these precautions, the plague spreads to nearby towns and cities and gradually begins to march across the country. Millions die in its wake.

It's one thing to use anesthesia or give a person a blood transfusion, but it is something else to begin tinkering with the very structure of life. The genetic engineer is attempting to refashion what God has created. He or she is treading on holy ground, stepping over the appropriate boundaries between God's domain and humanity's.

Who will decide how genetic engineering will be used? Would we want someone to create a series of clones of Adolf Hitler? If we experiment with changing people, will we create a series of monsters or unleash virulent strains of microscopic organisms that will devastate our population? Don't forget the millions of deadly bees that are inundating much of Latin America. These insects are a prime example of humanity's experimentation, bred in a laboratory and released by accident.

Over the years, various prophetic authors have written stories that caution us about going too far with scientific experiments—*Dr. Jekyll and Mr. Hyde, The Golem, Frankenstein* and *The Fly*, to name just a few. Like the story of the ancient Tower of Babel, these experiments remind us that when we try to usurp God's place, disaster results. Listen to these warnings! Just because our knowledge gives us the power to do something is no reason for us to do it. Recent disasters with nuclear power awakened us to the potential of this energy source, but have made us more cautious about using it. We should apply this lesson to genetics as well.

Programming Ideas for Issue 26

Preparation—Ask two of your young people who are interested in science to give a report on current genetic research using introductory material and magazines such as Scientific American or other science journals. Help them research the material available so their findings will be as current and interesting as possible.

Gather newsprint, magazines (preferably scientific ones), newspapers, glue, paper, pencils, markers and scissors. You will also need a Bible for each participant. Cut paper into pieces no smaller than 3×5 cards. Be sure you have a piece for each person in the group.

Make several copies of Chart 22.

Opening—Pass out small pieces of paper and pencils to your group. Ask the teenagers each to draw *one* of these three parts of the body on their paper: a head, an arm or a foot. When they have finished, ask all of the heads to go to one part of the room, all of the arms to go to another part and all of the feet to another. Ask the groups to share their drawings and talk about how many different perspectives there are for one idea. If the groups are not evenly divided, ask some of your kids to move to another group for the discussion session.

Program—Give each small group a copy of Chart 22. Allow 15 minutes for discussion.

Response—Ask the groups to meet together and read Genesis 1:26-30 and Genesis 2:15-17. Distribute newsprint, scissors, glue and magazines. Have the group members

---

Chart 22
Body Parts

● *Arms:* We currently help amputees by making artificial limbs. How far should we go to help the amputee?

by replacing the original limb, if possible?

by learning how to regenerate the cells on the amputee's stump so he or she can "grow" a new arm?

by grafting a limb from another person who has died?

Give reasons for your choice.

● *Heads:* If we could "clone" a person, would it be human in the usual sense? Would it have a soul? Why or why not?

What is a human being? Think of a wide range of famous people such as Hitler and Martin Luther King Jr. Try to think of famous scientists, poets, criminals, statesmen, explorers, writers, Christian leaders, etc. Which of these people could help us today? If we could "clone," or make copies of some of these famous people, who would you choose to clone? Why?

If cloning were a possibility, who would decide who could be cloned? Would this be a wise procedure for our society?

● *Feet:* When the Bible says God has given humanity "dominion" over the earth and the animals, what does this mean in relation to genetic engineering?

Are there boundaries between what is God's and what is ours to deal with?

Give specific examples of things that are in God's realm and things that are in humanity's realm.

make a large mural to interpret these passages in light of their discussions. Their art should express their feelings and beliefs about God's and humanity's involvement in the development of life and the quality of life on this planet. Post the mural on the wall.

Close the evening by asking the group to form a semicircle with the mural at one end. Celebrate God's involvement in life by reading Psalm 8. Celebrate our involvement with God by singing, "I Want to Praise You, Lord" from *Songs* (Songs and Creations).

Option:

1. Invite a Christian scientist and a theologian in to debate this issue. Ask them to debate twice, first using the pure science and pure religion stance presented in the Yes and No sections at the beginning of this issue. Then ask them to change their positions, so that the scientist presents his or her arguments from a religious point of view and the theologian presents his or her arguments from a scientific point of view.

ISSUE 27

Would the discovery of life on other planets affect humanity's view of the Bible, Christ and faith?

YES, if we discovered life on other planets, it would definitely affect our view of the Bible, Christ and our faith.

"Don't call in the press. That's the worst thing we could do at this time!" General Bedell slammed his fist on the table.

"But General, this is one of the greatest moments in human history—the first contact with someone from another planet!"

"Dr. Jameson, you're a scientist. You're used to sharing your discoveries, but you haven't thought about the consequences of such an announcement to the public. It could create panic both in the streets and on the stock market. Remember Orson Wells' broadcast in 1939!"

"But that was a fictional invasion. These people, or beings, are real and have come to us in peace. We can't keep this kind of thing from the public."

"But we have to. Most people couldn't handle this kind of information; it would be much too stressful for them. We'd have every religious kook and doomsday prophet in the world stirring up fear and irrational behavior."

The discovery of life, especially intelligent life, on other planets would profoundly impact our faith. Those who accept a literal interpretation of scripture will be affected most. They would probably respond in fearful disbelief much like people did when Copernicus and Galileo announced their theory that the sun, not the earth, was the center of the solar system, or when Darwin presented his theory that human beings were not the unique result of creation's sixth day, but part of a continuous evolutionary process.

When science first discovered data that seemed to oppose the teachings of the Bible, the church authorities fought back. They often excommunicated and even imprisoned those whom they thought were guilty of "heresy." If the church had possessed the same power during the 19th century, Darwin, Aldous Huxley and other scientists who questioned humanity's place in the scheme of things would most likely have met the same fate. This same fearful reaction may arise from Christian leaders today when, and if, we discover intelligent life in other parts of the universe.

Disturbing questions could arise about where human beings fit into the pattern of creation. Long ago, astronomy removed the earth from its central place in the universe by disclosing that this small planet actually encircles a small star near the edge of one of a million galaxies. That piece of information was difficult for theologians to accept at first, but they reasoned that at least human beings were unique; they were created by God to be special. Then Darwin and Huxley attacked that sense of uniqueness with their theory that human beings are related to the animals as part of a long evolutionary process. Millions of Christians do not accept this teaching; they believe it goes directly against the teachings of God's Word.

Discovering other life in our universe also raises the question of how Jesus Christ fits in. In several of Paul's letters, he portrays Christ as a cosmic figure, not bound to earth alone. "He is the image of the invisible God, the first-born over all creation. For by him all things were created: things in heaven and on earth, visible and invisible, whether thrones or powers or rulers or authorities; all things were created by him and for him. He is before all things, and in him all things hold together" (Colossians 1:15-17).

Is Christ the Savior for human beings only, or was his sacrifice for other life forms too? Does the Fall, described in Genesis 3, apply only to humanity, or does it involve other beings? What kinds of religion will other life forms have? Will there be points of mutual understanding and communication? Will they understand the concept of sin, of Adam's Fall? Or could there be a race that did not fall into Adam and Eve's trap like the race in C.S. Lewis' Space Trilogy? If so, where would such a race fit into the scheme of things? Would they be like the angels or other heavenly creatures we find mentioned in the Bible?

What should the relationship of our churches be to other races? Would we send missionaries to convert them? Or would we need to? Or would *we* be the targets of missionaries from another planet? What if their spirituality was more developed than ours?

To discover other intelligent life forms today would challenge the Christian faith much more than the discoveries of Copernicus 450 years ago. Millions of Christians would raise questions that their leaders would have great trouble answering, especially if their beliefs supported the inerrancy of scripture and the literal interpretation of the Bible.

NO, if we discovered life on other planets, it wouldn't necessarily affect our view of the Bible, Christ or our faith.

"I think we should study the Corillians more before any of us send missionaries to their planet."

"We already know plenty about them from our contacts. It's plain they are a heathen race. Our duty is to proclaim the Gospel to them as soon as possible."

"I'm not so sure about their being heathen. They speak of a Grand Life Force. Their concept of 'mohktu-la,' their concern for the preciousness of life, sounds a lot like Albert Schweitzer's 'reverence for life.' I think we're . . . "

"Are you suggesting these beings are operating on the same level we are?"

"I'm just saying that we don't really know. Until we know more than we do now, we should proceed with caution. These beings may have a great deal to teach *us* about God and faith."

The discovery of life on other planets may be a problem for some Christians, but most will simply take the event in stride as one more example of how science and experience increase our faith. Each new discovery is simply another opportunity to enlarge our concepts of God and the universe.

When the Bible was written, humanity's view of the world was small because experiences were limited. Most regarded the earth as a flat disc floating on the waters. A hard shell called the firmament lay over the earth and protected it from the waters above. The heavenly lights—the stars, planets, moon and sun—shone through the firmament, and above these was heaven. Beneath all of this lay the realm of the dead, or Sheol. Presiding over this world was the God of Abraham, Isaac and Jacob, perceived at first as a tribal deity interested in Israel alone. As centuries passed, the prophets revealed that God was the Lord of *all* nations and concerned with the welfare of *all* people. Jesus Christ further expanded humanity's understanding of God when he illustrated the power of God's love by the cross. As the Apostle Paul says, "For in him the whole fulness of deity dwells bodily" (Colossians 2:9).

Since the time of Christ, human beings have fluctuated

back and forth in trying to make society's laws conform more closely to Jesus' teachings.

Just as customs and laws that deal with the less fortunate have matured through the centuries, so has our knowledge of the physical universe expanded. Since the advent of science, human beings have realized the world is a huge expanse of stars and galaxies, not the closed, comfortable system envisioned by the biblical writers. The stars, instead of being just a few thousand miles away as theologians once thought, have proved to be hundreds of millions of miles instead. During King David's reign, there wasn't even a number in the Hebrew language that could cover this concept. (The highest number in Hebrew was 10,000; the Hebrews merely started over again when they reached 10,000 and counted another 10,000, keeping track of the number of 10,000s they had counted.) Today our mathematical concepts testify to God's power and make us realize even more how great God is.

Human beings have struggled with the ego-deflating assessment of our special place in creation through studying the geological and biological sciences. Once thought to be special creations of God, human beings now understand that we actually evolved from the animal world, different from them in that we developed our brains and our spiritual awareness. We are made in the image of God, but Genesis teaches us that we were formed from the clay of the earth, like all of the other creatures. This new self-understanding does not come easily or without opposition. Many Christians still refuse to accept these findings of modern science.

Those who have integrated the understandings of science with their faith can cope with the discovery of intelligent life in other parts of the universe. They know that God is concerned with all of life. Like the older child who listens with excitement about the birth of a new brother or sister, human beings will merely have to make room for and learn to accept the "new" arrival as part of the family. We will expand our own understanding of God's vast and complex universe when we realize that God keeps track of each of the many worlds and children he has created.

If Christ is, as we firmly believe, the revelation of God, then we must look for some evidence of his presence within the alien culture. This evidence need not repeat the story of Jesus as we know it, but it must contain some form of self-giving, some life-transforming act of self-sacrifice to be authentic.

All of these ideas assume we can establish communication and friendly relations with the aliens. If these beings turn out to be hostile like those in some of the current science fiction films, our need for self-preservation will probably take over and we will fight for our lives. As we come face to face with entities that look upon others only as slaves and a source of food, our perceptions of evil in the universe would deepen.

It is also possible that these beings may not have fallen into sin, which would *really* stretch our theological imagination and understanding. Such a case, we would have to accept gracefully. Christians would have to be especially careful that they guarded the alien beings from the exploitation, greed and callousness of other destructive human beings. Ray Bradbury expresses this concern in *The Martian Chronicles*, a wonderful collection that reverses the old science fiction theme of evil aliens trying to take over or destroy the earth.

Our religion is one of faith, conceived as a relationship with the God of our Lord Jesus Christ, not just an assent to a list of beliefs. The propositions of faith may change; some may be dropped or modified when experience and new knowledge indicate they are childish or have been outmoded. Our relationship to God is not destroyed by these changes, but enhanced, for change is the process of growing up in the Lord. The discovery of intelligent life on other planets will not threaten our faith; it can only add depth and challenge to it.

Programming Ideas for Issue 27

Preparation—Decorate the meeting room with aluminum foil stars and silver tinsel. Dim the lights or use candles. Have the kids come dressed as aliens. Buy fruit or Mars candy bars to award kids' costume creativity.

Locate a picture or a slide of a galaxy or a star cluster. Use an opaque projector or a slide projector to show this on a screen.

Gather paper, pencils and Bibles.

If you decide to close with a movie (see Option 1), reserve the video and VCR. Set up and preview the film to be sure everything is operating properly. With either movie, this program would be longer than normal and would lend itself to a retreat setting or an overnighter.

Opening—Begin the session with an "out-of-this-world" fashion show. Let kids model their alien costumes. Award prizes for costumes such as "Out of This World," "Scary" or "I'd Like to Meet You."

Show the picture or slide while one of your young people reads Psalm 19:1-4. Tell the group, "You are about to face some important questions about your faith and the rest of the universe."

Program—Divide into two groups and role play the first encounter between humans and aliens. One group will play the aliens. The people in this group will decide what kind of civilization they have including their religion, government, art, the position and relationship of the sexes, if there are any, and so on. They will decide ahead of time whether they will seek a friendly relationship or a hostile contact, but of course, they won't tell the other group what they have decided. The humans will talk about how their culture has developed and discuss how they will try to communicate with the aliens. At least one person in each group should represent the opinion that the other party should be attacked and exterminated.

The setting for the first meeting will occur on another planet far from both groups' home planets. Both groups will be a part of exploratory expeditions that stumble across each other as they investigate this neutral planet.

Response—After the role play, have the groups talk

about the beliefs and values that determined how each group reacted and related to the other. Ask questions like the following:

1. What do you think about the concept of life in the rest of the universe? Is it fiction or fact? (If anyone is into astronomy, ask him or her to share what the current thinking is among astronomers.)

2. What would the discovery of other intelligent life do to our concept of God? How would Jesus Christ fit in? Read Colossians 1:15-20. Would this scripture passage still apply to our faith? Would it apply to the aliens as well? Why or why not?

3. Describe historical events and discoveries that have radically challenged old ways and views.

Some events you may wish to discuss include:

● The Gentiles' large-scale acceptance of Christianity, transforming this religious experience from a purely Jewish movement.

● The fall of the Roman Empire.

● The Crusades and travel to the Orient.

● Copernicus' theory that the sun, and not the earth, is the center of the solar system.

● The discovery of the New World and the realization that people were already living there.

● The Protestant reformation influenced by Martin Luther.

● The publication of Darwin's *Origin of Species* and his theory of evolution.

● The acceptance of the U.S. Constitution which legally separated church and state.

● The rise of the Industrial Revolution.

● The dropping of the atom bombs at the end of World War II.

4. Read Genesis 3. What if the aliens had never experienced a fall or separation from their creator? What if they had continued to live in perfect harmony with each other and their environment? What kind of reaction would you expect from humans? Why?

5. React to the following statement: "As part of our contact with an alien race, we would need to study their culture and religion. We might discover points of contact with our own faith—the concept of a deity of grace, plus stories of a figure who teaches love, respect and giving oneself sacrificially. The terms and names may be different, but the basic concepts might be the same if we have 'eyes that see and ears that hear.' " What does this mean? How can this statement relate to our faith?

Close this session by asking the group to form a circle. Remind everyone of the advertising slogan for the movie, *Close Encounters of the Third Kind*. It was, "Search the skies, we are not alone." Tell the group: "For Christians, this slogan can have two meanings—One, the Creator of the heavens is always with us, and two, there may be other races reaching out to us. There is no way we can know what new things will come in the future, but we can face all our tomorrows without fear because we know we are not alone."

Ask someone to read Psalm 139:1-12. Sing, "In Christ There Is No East or West" from *Songs* (Songs and Creations). Close with the following prayer:

"Gracious God, we realize that the vast reaches of space with its countless galaxies are but a speck of dust to you. Yet you have assured us through your Son that you are aware of each sparrow that falls and the number of hairs on each of our heads. You are indeed a wonderful God. Thank you for your watchful care. We pray that our faith and understanding will continue to grow throughout all our days. May our relationship with you continue to mature and develop steadfastly. This we ask in the name of Jesus Christ our Savior, Amen."

Options:

1. A good follow-up to this session would be to view the film *Close Encounters of the Third Kind* or *Enemy Mine*. Reactions will be mixed to both presentations, so plan some time for questions and discussions.

2. If anyone has read Ray Bradbury's *The Martian Chronicles* (Bantam), ask the person to tell about the priest who tries to communicate with the Martians and discovers that they have not fallen from grace. Others may share insights from C.S. Lewis' Space Trilogy (MacMillan) in which the reader finds a similar concept.

3. If there is a planetarium or science museum nearby, arrange for a group visit. Ask if any staff member is prepared to lecture on the possibility of extraterrestrial life. Invite your pastor to accompany your group and guide a theological discussion through what you have just experienced.

CHURCH AND STATE ISSUES

C hristians must operate as citizens of their nation. But they must also function as citizens of yet another "kingdom"—the kingdom of God. Jesus taught this when he proclaimed that " . . . the kingdom of God is near" (Luke 21:31). He told both his enemies and his disciples, "Give to Caesar what is Caesar's, and to God what is God's" (Matthew 22:21).

Most of us have little difficulty giving to God or Caesar (our country); tithing and taxes are clear-cut. But we occasionally struggle with the uncertainty of exactly what belongs to Caesar and what belongs to God. We watch our nation's leaders debate whether to approve or disallow school prayer while they attempt to keep the government neutral in religion. Christians disagree on how involved they can be in the political process without identifying their political programs with the kingdom of God. Jesus instructed us to welcome and feed the stranger, but our government says we shouldn't help certain strangers. Our civil law threatens to punish us with fines or imprisonment if we protect people who enter our country illegally. How do we know what to do?

Newspapers and television bombard all of us with stories of the struggles between the church and state. As our government's activities grow larger and more complex, the world seems smaller. Conflicts between church and state occur more often. The early church debated many similar issues, and so must each succeeding generation, including our own. Christians will continue to question their allegiances as long as they operate as citizens of more than one kingdom.

ISSUE 28

Should prayer be allowed in public schools?

YES, prayer should be allowed in public schools.

"How do you like your new school, Bart?"

"It's different. More strict, and every class or activity starts with prayer."

"You pray before phys-ed and class meetings? That's a lot of praying."

"Yeah, but it gets you on the right track. There's certainly a lot less griping and fighting than there was at Jefferson High."

"So you don't miss being in public school?"

"I miss my friends—and the sports. I just wish the government had left us alone so we could've continued to pray in school. Then my church wouldn't have had to set up a separate Christian school."

Deeply religious people founded this nation. Many came to this country so they could worship in freedom and hope. Generations of Americans grew up in schools where they recited the Lord's Prayer or the 23rd Psalm at the beginning of each day. To ban prayer from the classroom is to turn our back on our precious religious heritage.

We continue to print "In God We Trust" on our money. Congress begins each session with a prayer from one of its chaplains. Our country continues to celebrate Thanksgiving, the holiday proposed by Washington and instituted by Lincoln, to give God thanks for the blessings we have received. We provide chaplains in our armed forces to look after the moral and spiritual needs of military personnel and their families. There is a wall that separates church and the state, but not religion and the state. Belief in a Supreme Being is too intertwined in our history and culture to abolish it. The Declaration of Independence, the very document that established our country as a nation, acknowledged the fact that we are "endowed by (our) Creator with certain unalienable Rights."

In most communities the majority of the people would support beginning each day with a class prayer. It isn't fair that a minority should thwart the will of the majority. If parents or a child object to this practice, teachers could excuse the child from the activity. Schools have handled the objections of the Jehovah's Witnesses to the Pledge of Allegiance this way for years.

Many children come from homes where religious training does not exist. Their parents do not take or send them to church or Sunday school. These children lose the most when prayer is removed from the schools. The practice of classroom prayer would teach them that there is a Supreme Being who cares about them, and it would provide at least a sample prayer for them to use.

Banning prayers from our schools goes along with the moral decline of our nation. The increased use of drugs, teenagers' lack of respect for their elders, disrespect for the flag and the national anthem, the rising tide of violence in our schools and on our streets, the laxness in sexual mores, and the tremendous problems of teenage pregnancy, venereal diseases and abortions—all are symptoms of a nation that has turned its back on God. Allowing the schools to use prayer again would be one small step toward cleaning up the moral climate of our nation and setting us again on the path of greatness. Therefore we should not only allow prayer in our public schools, but we should encourage it.

NO, we should not allow prayer in the public schools, if we mean using a prayer sanctioned by the school board or a teacher.

"Esther, you'd like our Christian school much better. It has smaller classes and we all feel we belong to something really special."

"I'm not so sure, Sally. I really like Madison High. Except for you, all my best friends go there. We also have some excellent teachers that I'd miss . . . "

"But ours are even better; they're Christian. They start every day and each class period with prayer."

"My classes start that way, too."

"What do you mean? The Supreme Court outlawed prayer in the public schools."

"No, it didn't. It merely forbade schools to demand that students repeat the canned prayers written by school boards or officials. There's no law against offering my own prayer. I just close my eyes for a few seconds, thank God for what I am about to receive and ask for guidance in what I'm about to experience."

Asking children to recite an official or printed prayer is a definite violation of separation between church and state. Schools are designed to educate, not teach or enforce religious practices. Teaching children how to pray and read scripture is a responsibility that belongs to the church and parents.

Actually, the Supreme Court did not ban prayer in our schools. And even if it did, no authority on earth could keep a student from saying a personal prayer at the beginning of the day, before a test or at some other moment during the day. What the Supreme Court banned was the official prayer sanctioned by New York's state Board of Regents. In this famous decision, the Court said there could be no official prayer that all students must recite in school. When some schools tried to get around the Court's decision by having a devotional moment at the beginning of the day, the Court ruled that school officials could not do this either.

The prayer suggested by the New York regents said very little about the deity to whom it was directed. Christians weren't satisfied because we pray in the name of Jesus. Jews, who pray to "the God of Abraham, Isaac and Moses," didn't recognize the deity in this prayer either. The prayer had been watered down to the point it wouldn't offend or exclude anyone. But in doing so, the regents actually included no one. The concept of God in this prayer was a cosmic blur. But even this much reference to a higher power was too much for the citizens who didn't believe in any form of a Supreme Being. They resented any form of prayer being forced on their children.

Non-denominational prayers, and especially the Lord's Prayer, repulse a large number of Jewish children who attend our public schools. With the rising number of Muslim and Buddhist families who have entered our urban areas, any attempts to force the use of Christian prayer in our school system would be resisted even more in the future.

This is why a number of Christian denominations such as the Methodists and the Presbyterians have gone on record as supporting the Supreme Court's decision. It's not that they agree with Madalyn Murray O'Hare's atheistic philosophy; these denominations just believe in fairness to all. They regard any form of coercive prayer as wrong. They realize it is not only impossible to write a prayer that would satisfy all the different religious groups, but even if it could be done, it's not right to force students whose families are opposed to prayer to either join in the exercise or be singled out by non-participation.

Making a class recite a standard prayer cheapens the act; it deprives prayer of any real significance. Prayer becomes simply one more exercise that everyone goes through with little thought or meaning, much like singing the national anthem or reciting the Pledge of Allegiance. Prayer is meant to be a form of communication for those who want to talk with God in a personal way, whether it is during congregational worship or personal devotions at school.

Again, there is no law, nor any possibility of one, that actually prevents genuine prayer at school. Parents and church leaders are the ones who should teach children how and when to pray. Students are free to offer their own prayers at the beginning of the day or at other moments when they need or want to celebrate God's presence. This kind of personal communication with God is far more effective than having students repeat a prayer written by others. Churches need to teach students how to offer their own prayers, rather than depend on someone else's words. We will not become a praying people by forcing children to mumble empty words handed to them by some authority. We must encourage our young people to pray from their own hearts and minds, both in and out of school.

Programming Ideas for Issue 28

Preparation—Prepare a copy of Chart 23 for each member of the group. On separate 3×5 cards tape a situation from Chart 24. Place all cards in a box.

Gather at least 25 boxes for the wall of separation in the Response section. Ask some of your young people to wrap the boxes with newsprint ahead of time. Gather newsprint, tape, scissors, pencils, magic markers and Bibles. In the meeting room, stack the wrapped boxes like a wall. Label one box with "In God We Trust" and another with "Military Chaplains."

Make a sign stating each of the following positions and place the signs on opposite walls.

Position One: The job of the school is to educate and the job of the church is to pray and worship. The two shouldn't be mixed.

Position Two: Schools need to pay more attention to the moral and spiritual aspects of their students' lives by bringing God back into the school day.

Opening—Ask the group, "When do you talk with God?" Pause for a response or two. Continue with: "Where do you talk to God? at church? at home? at school?" If no one responds to the phrase about school, ask the group: "Is it okay to talk to God at school? What does the law say about this?"

Tell the group: "During this session we're going to take a look at both prayer and school. Can the two go together? Some say no; others say yes. For many Christians this issue has become a very emotional issue, at least when prayer and school are mentioned together."

Program—Pass out the Personal Prayer Lists (Chart. 23). Explain: "Each one of us has ways he or she communicates with God. This list will help us discuss what we think and how we talk with God. Take a few minutes to complete this form and be prepared to share it with one other person in the room." Allow five to 10 minutes for this activity.

When everyone has finished, ask your young people to find prayer partners and share their lists. Explain that one person will share his or her prayer list for about three minutes and then the other person will share for the next three minutes.

Talk with the group members about prayer at their school. Ask the kids if their school encourages them to pause for a moment of silence, or if their school continues to use public prayer, as some do, in defiance of the Su-

Chart 23
Personal Prayer List

I need to talk with God about:

I usually talk with God when:

From my prayers I expect:

Permission to photocopy this chart granted for local church use only. Copyright © 1987 by Edward N. McNulty. Published by Group Books, Inc., Box 481, Loveland, CO 80539.

preme Court's decision. Ask if their school simply ignores prayer. Talk about what the students think about each position.

After discussing personal attitudes and the school's position toward prayer, pass the box of Situation Cards and ask each pair of prayer partners to draw one of the cards and discuss it in light of their prayer lists. Ask everyone to read the situation and talk about his or her personal position, the school's position and the position of the church in each of these situations.

After five minutes of discussion, have the prayer partners share their situations and ideas with the total group. Ask others to respond to each situation if they have any further insights or ideas. After all the prayer partners have shared their situations and the group members have responded, ask the kids to look at the signs on both walls and stand under the sign that most closely represents their point of view.

After everyone has taken a position on either side, give the two groups the following assignment: "You are the school board for your community. Work together to write a prayer that will not offend or exclude any person of any faith." Remind the group members to question each other's words and ideas to be sure this prayer could be accepted by people of all faiths.

After about five minutes, have the groups share their prayers. Ask the groups to describe any difficulties they experienced. Ask them to describe the god of their prayers. Was the god well defined or fuzzy in concept?

Talk about how we pray as Christians. To whom do we speak? How do we close our prayers? In whose name do we pray? Can a general prayer really satisfy Christians? Why or why not?

Response—Point to the wall of boxes you set up earlier. Remind students: "Thomas Jefferson talked about the wall of separation between church and state. What are some of the gaps in this wall? What are some of the evidences of a breach between church and state?"

Ask each young person to take a box and a marker and

label the box with some practice that breaches this wall of separation between church and state. Show the kids your sample boxes with "In God We Trust" (on U.S. coins) and "Military Chaplains" (in the armed forces). Tell them they can work as teams of two or three if they wish.

Chart 24
Situations

1. You have just seated yourself in the classroom where you are to take a big test. You studied hard the night before but you feel frightened about how well you will do.

2. You sit down to take an important final. Last night you chose to watch television instead of studying because you always get uptight when you study hard.

3. Today is your first day of chemistry. You know science is not your easiest subject.

4. Your team is about to play in the final game of the state volleyball tournament. The other team meets in the center of the court and bows for prayer.

5. The principal has just canceled the trip to the amusement park because three class members were smoking in the bathroom. You and your friends don't think this is fair but you've never confronted the authorities at school.

6. You and your friends have just seated yourselves for lunch time in the school cafeteria. Everyone knows you are a Christian and active in your church youth group.

7. You've wanted to attend the homecoming party all week, but now that you're here you're nervous about meeting all these new people.

8. Your best friend is going into surgery at 10 a.m., right in the middle of your third hour English class. Your teacher claims to be an agnostic and has little patience with anything religious.

9. Your school's custom is to begin classes each day by reciting together the Lord's Prayer. Your new classmate is a member of the Jewish synagogue. You notice that she is nervous and visibly upset after the prayer is over.

10. You and your Christian family have moved to another country where classes begin each day with readings from the Koran. Everyone knows you are a Christian.

Here are some other suggestions of practices that breach the wall of separation between church and state. Your young people may find even more.

1. Chaplains in Congress offering prayers.

2. Annual issuance of Christmas stamps by the post office.

3. Baccalaureate services during high school graduations.

4. The addition of "under God" to the Pledge of Allegiance.

5. Thanksgiving Day proclamations by the presidents.

6. Singing Christmas carols and having Christmas concerts at school.

7. Memorial Day practices that combine religious services to commemorate military sacrifices.

8. Words of the Declaration of Independence.

9. State and federal aid to parochial schools.

10. Tax-exempt status for churches.

11. References to God made by the president and other politicians in their speeches and public comments.

12. Historic traditions that have grown up around our country's Founding Fathers, like Washington kneeling in prayer.

After everyone has written his or her idea on one of the boxes for the wall, have individuals bring their boxes forward to rebuild the wall, leaving space between the boxes. As each one presents his or her idea, ask the group: "What do you think of this practice? Is it harmful to any minority? Does the good outweigh the harm?" After everyone has helped to rebuild the wall, ask, "Is it really possible to have total separation of church and state? Why or why not?"

Say that there are ways to pray at school without breaking the law. Talk about those moments in the school day when prayer would help. Discuss the concept of sentence prayers—those simple prayers of thanks for special moments of relief and victory during the day, or those quick cries for help at stressful moments.

For those who want more than private or individual

prayer, suggest they choose prayer partners for school. Have the partners agree to meet daily a few minutes before classes begin, to share any needs or concerns they have for that day. Suggest they work out a code or hand signal to indicate, "Hey, I need your prayers!" A partner could use this signal when passing in the halls or across a classroom to let another partner know that he or she needs support during that moment of stress or need.

Close by reminding the group that our nation consists of many individuals who must work together to make our country function properly. Baptists, Pentecostals, Catholics, Greek Orthodox, Lutherans, Methodists, Presbyterians, Jews, Buddhists, Muslims, Jehovah's Witnesses, Hare Krishnas and atheists—all have their place in our country, each contributing to the whole. All of us have the right to pray, or not to pray, as we wish. As individual Christians there can be no barrier to prayer at any time. Our God invites us to speak with him at any time, in any place.

Ask someone to read Ephesians 6:18-19. Close by inviting group members to offer sentence prayers of thanksgiving or requests. After a suitable time, which might include more silence than words if the group isn't used to this form of prayer, conclude with everyone praying together: "May the Lord watch between you and me, while we are absent, one from another. Amen." (Try this sentence prayer several more times at other meetings if there isn't much response at first.)

Option:

1. Use this Bible study as a follow-up session for this issue. Explore what the scripture says about prayer. To determine why, when and for what we should pray, survey the Psalms, the prayer book of Israel. Divide group members into four smaller groups and assign a portion of the Psalms to each group: Psalms 1—36; Psalms 37—75; Psalms 76—115; and Psalms 116—150. Ask the groups to scan the Psalms in their section and complete the following activities:

● Make a list of the types of prayers or moods you find.

● Determine whether the individual Psalms are personal or group prayers.

● Find out how the various Psalms were being used.

Allow about 30 minutes for this research. Then call the groups back together to share their findings.

Jesus offers several examples of when to pray and gives his followers specific examples of how to pray and what to expect. Read Mark 1:35 and Matthew 14:23. What was the writer trying to illustrate by including these experiences from Jesus' life? (Does this mean we should not pray with others? If anyone should say "Yes" to this, then read Acts 4:23-31.)

Read Matthew 6:9-13 and Luke 11:1-4. Compare both versions and point out the basic elements of this model prayer.

Ask individuals to read the following scripture passages: Matthew 7:7-8; Matthew 21:22; Mark 11:20-24; John 14:13; and John 16:24. Will God answer all of our prayers? Does Jesus really mean "anything," or is there some qualification? How does praying in Jesus' name affect our prayers? For example, is it possible to pray for harm to come to an enemy and conclude the prayer in Jesus' name? Or if we pray in Jesus' name, does this transform our desires so that we want only those things that would please Jesus? Read Matthew 26:36-44 to see this concept at work in Jesus' personal prayer life. What was Jesus' desire at this moment? How was Jesus able to put aside his human desire when he prayed? Read Genesis 28:16-22 and compare Jesus' prayer with that of Jacob's. Who seeks to strike a deal with God? How is this kind of prayer an attempt to use God? Do you find yourself praying more like Jacob or Jesus? Do you see examples of bargaining prayers around you?

Paul sees all of life as a prayer. Read Ephesians 6:18 and 1 Thessalonians 5:17. How can we make these scripture passages real in our own lives? Talk about the concept of sentence prayers—the short, one-line prayers we can use when we're on the way to school, in the halls or in the classrooms.

ISSUE 29

Should the church involve itself in meeting people's spiritual needs rather than promote peace and justice issues?

YES, the church should stick to meeting the spiritual needs of people.

"Look, I know there are hungry and homeless people. I just don't think it's the church's job to get involved in social, economic or political solutions to complex problems. Our job is to preach the gospel, to save people's souls."

"But helping solve problems that hurt people is preaching the gospel in a very practical way."

"No, not when it gets into social issues that divide people and get them angry and worked up. When people begin to concentrate on social issues, they soon forget about the gospel. They dilute the efforts of the church to minister to people's souls, and the church becomes just another social service agency. Look what's happened to the 'Y'!"

"The Y? What do you mean?"

"The YMCA was once a strong Christian movement concerned with helping young men understand and use their faith. Then it began to stress individuals' recreation and physical needs to the exclusion of their spiritual concerns. Now the Y has become just another health and social club for the middle class. That kind of change could happen to the church if it gets too wrapped up in changing society rather than meeting people's spiritual needs. The church could forget that its basic mission is to spread the gospel and witness to Jesus Christ."

Jesus said, "Go into all the world and preach the good news to all creation" (Mark 16:15). The church's job is evangelism; it has no business getting involved in social or economic affairs. Jesus told Pilate, "My kingdom is not of this world . . . " (John 18:36). Those who promote a social gospel disregard Jesus' words when they call upon the church to take a stand on every issue that comes along.

The church should channel all of its time, money and energy into seeing that everyone on earth hears and understands the gospel. Peter, Paul and other apostles concentrated their efforts on spreading Jesus' message after he returned to his Father. The book of Acts and the letters of the New Testament testify to their ability to successfully delegate social concerns and concentrate on fulfilling their spiritual mission. They didn't lobby with the emperor to abolish slavery, establish equal rights for women or debate the necessity of armaments. They preached the gospel; that was their job, just as it's ours today.

The church will create controversy and conflict within the congregation when it meddles in social issues. Sincere Christians may take either side of an issue. When their church takes a stand on one side of an issue, congregation members who disagree with the church's position may feel betrayed. Members who give to their church for spiritual purposes may be angered when their funds are used to advance the social causes they oppose. Division may occur.

The church too often takes a stand in economic issues and international affairs where it doesn't have all the facts or any significant expertise. What do ministers know about economics, the intricacies of foreign affairs, nuclear armaments or military tactics? Church leaders should stick to what they are trained for—studying and preaching the Bible.

NO, the church must reach beyond meeting people's spiritual needs and involve itself in serving peace and justice needs, too.

"But don't you see? It's specifically because we are Christians that I want our youth group to join the demonstration tomorrow!"

"No, Alex. All I can see is that you're going to join that mob of radicals who picket all the missile sites. That installation is here to defend our nation."

"That missile site houses weapons that could destroy millions of lives. As church members we cannot support any possibility for such total destruction of life."

"That still doesn't make it right for Christians to picket such a site. This kind of social protest could lead to violence, and I can't imagine Christ approving such action!"

"Oh, really? What about the time he got angry in the temple? Remember when the priests and merchants set up tables to sell religious paraphernalia and animals for sacrifices? Jesus didn't just scold these people and preach to them about their actions. He staged a forceful and violent demonstration, all on his own. He even destroyed other people's property! But he got his message across and people listened. Sometimes it's necessary to do something unusual to get people's attention."

Jesus talked about the importance of feeding the hungry, clothing the naked and visiting those in need. He promised that individuals who concerned themselves with these issues would be welcomed into his kingdom, whereas those who ignored such needs would not be admitted (Matthew 25:34-46). His story about the Samaritan who helped the robbery victim and proved himself the true neighbor condemned the lack of action by the priest and Levite who passed by (Luke 10:29-37). He recognized the efforts of those who worked for peace by calling them sons of God (Matthew 5:9).

The apostles did not lobby for social causes early in their ministry because they were desperately concerned with the survival of the gospel. The early church was still just a tiny minority of the population. Yet even then many implications of the gospel led some Christians to take a stand on certain issues such as refusing to serve in the army or in the court system. Christians felt this kind of involvement could lead them to kill another human being in war or condone killing criminals or political opponents. Later, when Christians became more numerous, many chose to protest social policy. In A.D. 404, the monk Telemachus protested against the gladiatorial games. He lost his life in the Colosseum when he tried to part the gladiators. Prudentius had also appealed to the emperor to ban the games.

This Roman official, who wrote the words to the hymn "Of the Father's Love Begotten," joined other Christian senators to ban the altar and statue of the Roman goddess Victory from the Senate chamber.

We are part of a society where individual citizens have the right to speak out and promote the issues in which they believe. Unlike Paul and members of the early church, today's Christians can actually help to formulate laws. We the people are Caesar. Christians can unite their efforts to work through the electoral and lobbying processes of our government.

Many Christians come to the church with expertise in a multitude of fields. When churches become concerned about an important issue, they can continue to examine their concerns in the wisdom of scripture, but they can also utilize the knowledge and experience of their members. Today Christians serve in the military and attain upper-level positions in the government. Some work as college professors, while others are college students. Many operate large and small corporations, while some work with the labor unions. Many struggle with the law on a professional basis, and others wrestle with international affairs. When church boards and committees study an issue today, they can draw upon a broad range of expertise within the church itself. No longer is the final decision of a church board or assembly based solely on what the pastors believe. Intelligent decisions rely on the collective wisdom of God's people, under the guidance of the Holy Spirit.

Some issues are so important and have so many moral and ethical implications that for the church to remain silent or refuse to offer any guidance is to ignore an important part of the gospel. In Germany only a handful of Christians spoke against the evil teachings and practices of the Nazis. Most German Christians believed they should simply obey whatever the government said and never question its dictates. They forgot Edmund Burke's dictum that all it takes for evil to win is for good people to stand by and do nothing. They preferred to look the other way and denied that

Chart 25
Spiritual Vs. Peace and Justice Issues

Abortion	Capital punishment
Anti-Semitism	Prison reform
Birth control	Ecology and pollution
Civil rights and racism	Nuclear power
Economic policy	Nuclear warfare
Gambling	War and peace issues
Gay rights	Multinational corporations
Feminist concerns	Farm policies
Poverty	Children's needs
Hunger	Government family policies
Welfare reform	Tobacco use
Alcohol and drug abuse	Sexuality
Censorship	Pornography
Education reform	

Permission to photocopy this chart granted for local church use only. Copyright © 1987 by Edward N. McNulty. Published by Group Books, Inc., Box 481, Loveland, CO 80539.

Chart 26
The Church: Spiritual or Social?

Yes	Yes/No	No
(The church should be involved in important social issues.)	(Not sure.)	(The church should speak and act only on spiritual concerns.)

anything was wrong. They chose safety while their Jewish friends were beaten in the streets and their shops smashed. Even later, when they smelled the stench from the concentration camps' ovens, they refused to get involved.

Christians too often use evangelism as an excuse to look the other way and avoid controversial topics in the church. Evangelism will take care of itself if Christians work to meet the needs of the poor and the oppressed. Our best witness is made with deeds, not words. As people witness Christians feeding and clothing the hungry and fighting for the rights of the oppressed, they will recognize the influence of Jesus Christ as the inspiration of the church. Our deeds, not our words, will win others to Christ.

Programming Ideas for Issue 29

Preparation—Gather newsprint, markers, tape, paper, pencils, scissors and Bibles. For each participant, make copies of Charts 25 and 27.

Tape a large panel of newsprint across the front of the room and prepare it as a decision board. See Chart 26 as an example.

Write the following scripture references on a small sheet of newsprint: 1 Peter 2:9-10 and James 2:14-17.

Select about 15 minutes of prerecorded hymns that include a mixture of praise, piety and social concerns. Set up a record player or tape player and have these playing during the Opening part of your program.

Opening—Give each young person a copy of Chart 25. Ask each person to label each box on the chart with his or her initials. Tell the kids to cut the issues apart and tape the cards on the decision board where they think the issue belongs. Tell them to choose Yes if they think the church should speak out on or become involved in the issue; Yes/No if they're not sure; and No if they think the church has no business dealing with the issue.

Start the music after you have completed your explanation of this activity, and wander about the room to answer any questions kids might have. Be careful not to influence them as to where to place the issues on the decision board.

After everyone has put his or her cards on the decision board, ask each person to go to the board and count the number of cards he or she placed in each category. Announce that those who put more than half of their cards on the Yes section should gather on the left side of the room, and those who had more cards on the No section should gather on the right side. Those who have over half of their cards in the Yes/No section must choose the group they will join.

Program—Have the young people each find a partner on their side of the room. If there is an extra person, ask him or her to join with one of the pairs. Partners should tell each other why they are in the Yes or No group. They can do this by selecting one or two of the issues and giving their reasons for placing the issue cards where they did. Allow 10 minutes for this sharing.

Now have pairs from one side of the room join pairs from the other side of the room. If there is a triad on both sides, these groups should join so the No's and Yes's in each new group are equal. Ask each person to tell again why he or she wound up on the Yes or No side. Instruct individuals to use one or more specific issues but try not to use the issues they talked about before. Allow 20 minutes for this activity. Pass out Bibles to each small group. Ask them to look up the two scripture references you have posted on the wall. Tell the small groups to discuss these passages and select the one they think best describes the purpose or work of the church.

After 10 minutes ask the small groups to share their thoughts about this experience. Was it hard to choose a scripture? Did everyone agree? Did the group choose both scripture passages? What were some of the highlights or most important parts of the discussion?

Response—Pass out copies of Chart 27. Give each group a Bible plus copies of your current hymnal and some older ones you may have. Allow 20 minutes for discussion.

Gather the small groups and read Matthew 28:18-20. Tell the group: "The church has been sent on a divine mission: This mission includes proclaiming the name of our Saviour, but it also includes speaking out whenever injustice threatens people. We must respond to the prophets in Isaiah's time and learn to do good and to seek justice." Have someone read Isaiah 1:10-17.

Sing, "Servant of All" from *Songs* (Songs and Creations). Invite the group members to bow their heads and offer sentence prayers for the church and its mission. Close with the Lord's Prayer.

Options:

1. Poll your congregation on this subject. Secure the cooperation of the pastor and other staff. Make sure you have permission from the official church board. Distribute Chart 28 before or after a service or during the coffee hour. If preferred, young people could use the same form to conduct personal interviews with church members and youth group members.

Chart 27
Mission Discussion

1. Compare the church's purpose to the purpose for a newspaper or an ad agency. List and discuss their similarities. List and discuss their differences.

2. List and discuss how the church is similar to a social welfare agency. How is it different?

3. Scan Matthew 5, 6 and 7. Is this just a collection of laws or ethical principles? Read Matthew 7:21-27. What does this scripture passage say about what you just scanned?

4. Scan through copies of our church hymnal. Hymns typically reflect our views of the church and its mission. How many hymns deal with praise? adoration? repentance? salvation? Are there hymns that deal with social justice? peace? other social issues? Check the subject index of the hymnal. Turn to some hymns in each category and examine the lyrics. Discuss their messages.

Compare your current hymnal with one of the older ones. Examine the subject index in both hymnals. What kinds of hymns have increased in the modern hymnals? What kinds of hymns have decreased? What do these changes reflect about the church's view of its mission?

Ask some of your young people to tabulate the answers. From these results determine whether your church is conservative, liberal or middle of the road when it comes to social concerns. Share the results with your pastor and congregation through your church newsletter.

2. Find where your denomination stands on the church's

Chart 28
The Mission of the Church

1. Which of the following statements best describes your view of the church's mission?

 a. The church should stick to preaching the gospel and not get involved in social issues.

 b. The church should place more emphasis on helping people who are hurting and suffering injustices in our world.

 c. The church should be concerned about both spiritual matters and social issues. It must preach about Jesus and call people to believe in him, but it must also help hurting people by speaking out against anything that oppresses them, even if this means stirring up controversy and personal persecution.

2. On the following issues the church should:

 a. Take no stand.

 b. Speak out or act upon it.

 c. I don't know.

Abortion	Capital punishment
Anti-Semitism	Prison reform
Birth control	Ecology and pollution
Civil rights and racism	Nuclear power
Economic policy	Nuclear warfare
Gambling	War and peace issues
Gay rights	Multinational corporations
Feminist concerns	Farm policies
Poverty	Children's needs
Hunger	Government family policies
Welfare reform	Tobacco use
Alcohol and drug abuse	Sexuality
Censorship	Pornography
Education reform	

involvement in social issues. Your pastor can help you by showing catalogs and publications from your church's national office. Check to see which of the 27 issues your denomination has dealt with.

What about the other churches in your community? Are there issues they stress and others they ignore? Why? Find a list of social pronouncements from these denominations. Many churches provide lists of printed materials for their members so they can make up their own minds on the issues. List the churches represented in your community and assign different young people to check with the other pastors before your next meeting.

ISSUE 30
Should Christians, especially pastors, become involved in political causes as leaders or candidates?

YES, Christians and their pastors should involve themselves in politics as much as they desire, just like all other citizens.

"Did you see the Senate corruption hearings on the news last night?"

"Yes, I'm afraid so. What's this country coming to? It seems there aren't any honest politicians anymore."

"That's why I'm supporting the Rev. Jim Starr for the presidency."

"But he's a TV evangelist. What does he know about running a national government?"

"He's done pretty well building up his TV ministry. It's now a $200 million a year business. He's also met and talked with many of the world's political leaders during his travels. Most of all, he can bring a sense of morality and decency to public affairs."

"That would be a welcome change!"

"You bet! Maybe we could at last get someone in the White House who would do something about abortion and prayer in the schools, not just talk about it!"

In a democracy like the United States, it is a Christian's duty to participate in the political process. When public morality seems to be at a low ebb, it's important for Christians to bring their ethical and moral concerns to the political system.

Christians are concerned about many causes: abortion, gambling, war, nuclear energy, education, prayer in schools, textbooks, the rights of women and minorities and so on. Christians who feel deeply about these issues and how they are resolved have every right to voice their support or opposition to these concerns. After all, if women, blacks, homosexuals, teachers, labor unions and business groups have the right to stand up for their causes, so should Christians.

This kind of concern may even prompt a pastor or church leader to voice support for particular candidates. During the elections of 1980 and 1984, many pastors and some TV evangelists openly supported President Reagan. They agreed with his positions to prohibit abortion, oppose the Equal Rights Amendment, revive school prayer, reinstate the death penalty and build up the military to establish "peace through strength." His public profession of his faith also appealed to individuals who felt our nation needed a strong Christian influence who would lead us back to our roots of faith and morality.

Large groups of evangelical Christians examined not only President Reagan, but many candidates for other governmental offices. These concerned Christians supported some candidates and openly opposed others. When the elections were over, several evangelical leaders expressed pride in the apparent success of their efforts to defeat candidates who opposed the fundamentalist social agenda.

Liberal critics expressed concern about the political activities of these evangelicals. Some liberals even announced that Christians had no right to get involved. These individuals obviously forgot that numerous liberal Christians marched for civil rights and demonstrated against the Vietnam War during the '60s. What is fair for one group of Christians ought to be fair for others, regardless of where they stand on the issues.

Some Christian pastors and leaders not only express support for specific candidates for political office, but have run as candidates themselves. The Rev. Pat Robertson, the TV evangelist and talk show host, and the Rev. Jesse Jackson, the black minister who has fought for civil rights, both considered the presidency. Many believe William H. Hudnut III, Presbyterian minister, has served as one of the most successful mayors in the history of Indianapolis.

Christians should involve themselves in politics as much as their convictions and desires dictate. Their religious beliefs often give them a perspective and sensitivity about issues that others might not have. Our country can only be richer for the participation of Christians in the political process.

NO, Christians and their leaders shouldn't become personally involved in politics.

"Did you hear that Reverend Gables is running for mayor?"

"How can he do that and still be our pastor? Doesn't he have enough to do here at the church?"

"My mom says she's worked with him on the service committee for the last few years, and she's impressed with how well he can organize people and activities to help others."

"I knew he was good at helping others. He's always at the school to work with students who need help or emotional support. Wouldn't he serve best by using his time to educate church members and be an example of how they can serve?"

"But he's such a neat person. We need people like him in politics."

"Yes, we do, but Reverend Gables' first priority has to be the church. He chose the ministry. He can serve best by helping others understand and support the Christian point of view. Think about how many people he can influence to serve him in public roles like mayor, councilman or even senator. Reverend Gable could actually influence more people as a pastor than he could as mayor."

Christian leaders and pastors have no business getting involved in politics as candidates for office or supporters for political issues. There isn't enough time for these people to serve both positions. Christian pastors have already chosen their place of service. They have committed themselves to the church. If pastors serve their congregations effectively, they have plenty to do where they are. The church operates like a large family, God's family. When pastors and church leaders become overly concerned with activities outside the church, they fail to serve the needs of the congregation.

Jesus recognized a need to remain totally involved in his mission. After he fed the 5,000, the people were overwhelmed and decided to make him king (John 6:15). They recognized his greatness, but they were confused about his purpose. Later on, Jesus explained to Pilate, "My kingdom is not of this world . . . " (John 18:36). Jesus had no desire to be king. He acknowledged others' reactions to his leadership, but he added that those who understood his real mission would not demand this kind of leadership position from him.

Strength and power can be outstanding qualities, but they must be used correctly. Jesus knew who he was and why he was here. Leaders in the church must maintain that same sense of direction. Even when their abilities and interests indicate that they could serve others in some powerful political office, they must stay alert to their purpose. Christian pastors who have developed their thinking and organizational skills must use their God-given talents to serve God's purposes.

If Christian pastors do decide to run for office, they should definitely resign their church position. They should never involve their churches since some members may oppose their party or their candidacy. Pastors should never claim that God is only on their side. At the height of the Civil War, Abraham Lincoln had to remind a delegation of pastors that God was on neither the North's nor the South's side. With courage and theological insight, Lincoln prayed to a God whom he saw as above both parties in the war. This kind of humility saved him from fanaticism and self-righteousness.

Self-esteem and personal value feel good to those in leadership positions. Few people can resist the tug of glory or praise from others, but Jesus realized these feelings are temporary. He could see that people's attempts to recognize leadership don't last. Jesus could reject these temporary ego trips because he knew that these experiences with power and the human need for acceptance and adoration would mean nothing later. When the disciples struggled with an issue, they asked Jesus who was greatest among them. He surprised them by saying, "If anyone wants to be first, he must be the very last, and the servant of all" (Mark 9:35). This was hardly what these loyal followers expected as a response to their question, but from this answer they gained new insight into the role of leadership, especially Christian leadership.

Programming Ideas for Issue 30

Preparation—Select a committee to decorate the room with red, white and blue streamers and balloons. Add some political posters for president. Include some real ones and make some of your own. Include leaders from the past like Abraham Lincoln, John F. Kennedy, Martin Luther, Peter the disciple, Paul the apostle and other positive examples you may think of.

Gather paper, pencils, newsprint, posterboard, art supplies (markers, poster paints, brushes, crayons), masking tape, an offering basket, a tape recorder or a video camera and blank tapes, 3×5 cards and Bibles. Prepare copies of Chart 29.

This session will require at least two hours. Plan ahead for extra meeting time, or arrange to stop at the end of the Program section and continue the following week. This session could also be used at a weekend retreat.

Opening—Have the kids look around the room at the posters on the wall. Ask each person to choose the individual he or she would like to see serving as president today. After each person has decided, have individuals share their choices and explain why they chose that person. List the reasons for their choice on a sheet of newsprint at the front of the room. Tell the group: "In this session each of you will enter the political process in a deeper way than ever before. We will explore how Christians can influence politics no matter how they choose to be involved. Remember the qualities you just listed as you work with the next part of this program."

Program—Ask the kids to count off by twos. All the ones will be in Group One to set up a campaign for a Christian candidate. All the twos will be Group Two to work out ways for Christians and their leaders to influence the government to make positive choices and decisions.

Group One will go into a separate room to work on a campaign for a Christian candidate. This candidate can be real or fictitious. Ask the group to do the following:

1. Select a party chairman to coordinate everyone's work and ideas.

2. Talk over the basic content of your Christian candidate's party platform. What issues will he or she address in this particular election—capital punishment, abortion, women's rights, etc.?

3. Divide into three task force groups after you have agreed on the basic issues of your party platform:

a. The Issues task force will work on brief statements to the public that will explain your candidate's position on these issues.

b. The Media task force will create slogans and campaign posters. Some may use a tape recorder or video camera to design advertising spots for radio and television.

c. The Strategy task force will work on an overall campaign strategy—how your candidate will appeal to the public, the place of the churches and the media in the campaign, the tone of the campaign and so on.

Select one individual from each task force to encourage an exchange of ideas and coordinate each groups' efforts.

Group Two will discuss how Christians and their leaders can influence the current political process without being totally involved. Ask the group to do the following:

1. List the issues about which Christians should be concerned (abortion, gambling, sanctuary for aliens, poverty, world hunger, prison reform, drug enforcement, nuclear power, nuclear warfare, racism, apartheid and so on).

2. Put a checkmark by those issues you believe are nationally important today. Circle the issues that are strictly concerns of the church. Place a star by those issues that involve both the church and federal or state governments in some way.

3. List methods such as writing letters, sending telegrams to government officials and voting at election time that Christians and their leaders can use to influence the government about their concerns. (The following list of suggestions may help the group, but don't share it right away since it may short-circuit the group's brainstorming. Use it only to supplement what group members come up with, or to stimulate their thinking if they can't get started or get bogged down.)

Join a political party and work within the system to make your viewpoint known.

Write letters to newspapers and magazines.

Call radio talk shows and raise the issues that concern you. Alert your church members to this opportunity to share and discuss.

Bring the issue to the attention of your school through articles in the school newspaper or during panel presentations at a school assembly.

Write a short play or vignette dramatizing the issue and present it to church groups, school classes and community service clubs.

Create a slide and tape show or a videotape of the issue and show it at church, school or in community groups.

Talk over the issue with your pastor and elicit his or

her help if possible.

Organize study groups at church to explore the issues through films and speakers. Encourage people to attend by having a family supper or an ice cream social.

Write pamphlets and magazine articles to explain your position and distribute them to the public.

Talk with friends and acquaintances to make them more aware of the issues.

Work on church and denominational committees that are concerned with the issue.

Organize and participate in public meetings on the issue. Use speakers, debates, films and any other media that explain your position.

See that the issue is dealt with on TV talk shows. Appear as a guest or get other knowledgeable people to do so.

Go to Washington to meet with the government officials concerned.

Join organizations concerned with doing something about the issue. (If there isn't such a group, organize your own.)

Organize and join in demonstrations that call attention to the issue.

4. Look at the issues you starred earlier. Ask two or three individuals to choose an issue and design a campaign to convince government officials that they should adopt a Christian position. Use any or all of the methods on your list.

Allow one hour for Groups One and Two to work on their plans and projects. Ask each group to decide how they will present the result of their planning to the other large group. Allow 15 minutes for this planning, then call both groups together again.

(If time is limited, have the groups make their presentations at the next meeting. Close this meeting with prayer.)

Response—Since each group invested a large amount of time and energy in their presentations, it will be difficult for the group members to listen to each other with complete objectivity. Pass out Bibles, pencils and the evaluation

form (Chart 29) to help individuals analyze and react to
what they hear. Read through the form and tell the groups
to make notes as they listen to the other group's presentation.

After both sides have offered their presentations, ask
the young people to examine the notes they have made. After about five minutes go through each item on the form
and invite everyone to share his or her thoughts and reactions. Talk about what they have learned from this exercise.
Ask if they see any parallels in current or recent campaigns.

Have everyone sing the first verse of "America the
Beautiful" from *Songs* (Songs and Creations).

Remind the groups: "Even though our nation is far
from perfect, we do have a system that allows us to live
and work together despite our religious differences. In
countries like Lebanon, Ireland and India, political differences often lead to violent conflict and death. Let's pray
that no matter what stance we take in regard to Christian
leadership, each of us will work to strengthen our ability to

---

Chart 29
Evaluation of Involvement Vs. Influence

1. What problem(s) did this group raise?

2. What solution(s) did they offer?

3. How realistic are their ideas? (Is the problem or the solution presented in a simplistic way?)

4. Would their solutions create even more problems? Explain your answer.

5. Read Micah 6:8 and Matthew 22:34-40. Does the presentation reflect the ideas presented in these scripture passages?
Explain your answer.

accept others as they are." Pass out 3×5 cards and have individuals write one thing they can do to influence Christian decisions in our government. Then pass an offering basket.

Invite the group members to offer sentence prayers for our country, its leaders and its citizens as they deposit their ideas in the basket. Close the meeting by having three young people alternately reading the ideas offered by the group. Ask them to read the cards as "I" statements. For example, "I will pray each day for our president and his Cabinet," or "I will spend one hour each weekend working for the Rev. Starr's campaign."

Options:

1. If there's an election in progress, have the group study the candidates and their tactics. Check to see if Christian leaders or groups support any candidate. Check speeches and publicity materials to see if candidates have solicited support from Christian groups by the way they address the issues or by the issues they emphasize. Investigate whether the candidates' current campaign claims agree with actual records. For incumbent candidates, check with the League of Women Voters about their voting records. Look closely at the problems and solutions suggested by the candidates. Are the issues stated in overly simplistic terms, or are their statements and claims realistic?

2. Have volunteers look up information about the political situations in Northern Ireland, Iran, Lebanon, Italy and France. What role have churches and religious leaders taken in these countries? Has religious involvement helped or hindered the resolution of problems in these countries? Has the mixture of religion and politics led to peaceful and just ways of working out differences? Give examples to support your answers to these questions.

ISSUE 31

Should churches provide sanctuary for illegal aliens?

YES, churches should provide sanctuary for illegal aliens.

264 ► Controversial Topics for Youth Groups

"But providing sanctuary is against the law! I think those ministers and their church members ought to be caught and punished."

"Maybe it is against the law to help illegal aliens, but it's a lousy law if it keeps us from helping people who come to us in trouble. I think those sanctuary workers are really brave."

"But they've still broken the law. Our government has told us that we can't help refugees from Central American countries. We have to obey that law and turn these people over to the immigration authorities. Even the Apostle Paul says we must obey our governing authorities."

"But Jesus says to feed the hungry and welcome the homeless, and that's enough for me. If some ragged individual who spoke English with a Spanish accent knocked at your door some night to ask for food and shelter for his family, would you turn him away? And if you did, could you still look at yourself in the mirror and call yourself a Christian?"

Participation in the sanctuary movement continues Christ's ministry of welcoming the stranger, a practice that dates back to the times of Abraham and Moses. In the Old Testament the Israelites were commanded to establish sanctuary cities for fugitives from justice. Families of victims were not allowed to pursue and punish criminals when they fled to a sanctuary. The church carried this concept into the Middle Ages when it offered its buildings as sanctuaries to those accused of political and other crimes.

The sanctuary movement began in this country when Christians in the Southwest helped Central Americans who were fleeing from their countries. At first, church pastors and other leaders tried to work with immigration authorities to receive political refugee status for the aliens. This status was almost always denied since authorities claimed the refugees were here to seek better jobs, not freedom from oppression. According to our State Department, countries like El Salvador and Guatemala had almost abolished their human rights violations of the past, and these refugees were ordered back to their countries.

Despite the claims of the State Department, too much evidence backed the refugees' stories of persecution and torture in their homelands by their own governments. New refugees reported that many who had been forcibly returned to their countries had been threatened, arrested, beaten and sometimes killed. Thus, the Christians in this country felt they had no choice but to oppose our government and help these people. They were prodded by the inspirational stories of the underground railroad of pre-Civil War days when thousands of Christians helped runaway slaves escape to Canada. Helping escaped slaves was against federal law, but the people believed helping their fellow human beings followed a much higher law. They wouldn't think of returning an escaped slave to the brutal punishment and hopeless bondage that awaited all who were caught and dragged back to the South.

Members of today's sanctuary movement believe they too must obey that higher law. The teacher who said, "I was a stranger and you welcomed me" set the example for today's sanctuary workers. Most U.S. citizens realize that they jeopardize their own freedom when they attempt to help these refugees; several have even been convicted in federal courts. But these individuals believe the U.S. government has refused to grant Central Americans political refugee status because the government would have to admit to the state-sponsored terrorism that exists in these countries. The testimony of people who live in Central America and the reports of Amnesty International prove that thousands of people are being tortured or have been killed while in detention with our allies in countries like El Salvador and Guatemala.

Despite convictions of sanctuary workers in Texas and Arizona, the movement continues to grow. Churches all over the country have declared themselves as sanctuaries. They have agreed to assume responsibility for finding food, shelter, clothing and transportation for these illegal refugees, passing them on to the next church or group on the long road to Canada. Several city and state governments have also declared themselves as sanctuaries. The officials, who are moved more by compassion than political arguments, have joined church leaders and refused to cooperate with federal immigration officials.

NO, churches shouldn't provide sanctuary for illegal aliens.

"Maybe their country is poor and run by tough leaders, but that doesn't mean our church should get involved in hiding refugees from there, not when it's against the law."

"But isn't there a higher law than the Immigration and Naturalization Service? What about God's law that tells us to help our neighbors when they come to us in distress?"

"I understand God's law, but sanctuary isn't that simple. Encouraging refugees to come to our country could lead to a lot more problems. This flood of people could bring an increase in disease and crime and could cause overcrowding and unemployment for our own poor. We would be modeling disrespect for the law and those who try to enforce it. Aliens could assume that since it's okay to break one law, it's probably okay to break others. I hope our church thinks twice before it gets involved in this popular social movement."

Christians should welcome and try to help refugees when they come for aid. Providing food, shelter and counseling are appropriate actions for the church, but illegally hiding individuals from our government violates the law. The church must obey the law. It must report illegal aliens and hand them over to authorities.

Individuals in our society openly flout the law every day. Disrespect for the law is already rampant among our citizens. For example, how many drivers on the highways obey the speed limit laws? If the church goes against the laws of our government for any reason, it would lower respect for the law among both church members and the rest of the public. If church members won't follow the law, who will?

We cannot select laws we like or with which we agree and obey only these. We must respect and obey the law in its entirety. Otherwise, chaos would exist in our country as everyone makes up and follows his or her own regulations. Our State Department and immigration officials have more facts about Latin America than the average citizen. It is not up to us to disregard government policies, but to accept them. If government officials say that those who come from a certain region need not fear violence or intimidation back in their own countries, who are we to disagree? The refugees could be making up stories about their plight to win the sympathy and support of softhearted church people.

The sanctuary movement is just one more example of how the church sticks its nose into areas in which it doesn't belong. The church should attend to the needs it has already identified—sending missionaries overseas, fighting against abortion and pornography and reviving the faith of our people and our nation. Christian churches should have nothing to do with this illegal movement of do-gooders.

Programming Ideas for Issue 31

Preparation—Select 10 to 15 people to present the following role play: Juan, his wife, and their three teenage children knock at First Church's door. They are from Central America and claim that they need help. They had paid a man to smuggle them into the United States and find them a job, but he had dumped them at the side of the road once they were into the country. Their oldest son had been a university student who participated in a student demonstration. He was arrested and tortured and his body was left outside the family's home as a warning about any form of disobedience.

A few days later the minister and two of his church officers meet to decide what to do. While they are meeting, federal officials come to the church to ask about a Central

American family reported in the area.

Gather newsprint, posterboard, markers, pencils and Bibles. Prepare three signs labeled "Aliens," "Sanctuary Workers" and "Government," and tape them on the wall in three different locations in the room. Prepare copies of Charts 30 and 31. Locate a copy of Emma Lazarus' poem *The New Colossus*, which is inscribed at the base of the Statue of Liberty. Ask a group member to prepare to read this aloud for the closing.

Opening—Set the stage for the role play with the following explanation: "A flood of people pouring across the southern borders of the United States has become a great problem and is raising the question, 'Are these people coming just to escape the great poverty of their native lands, or

---

Chart 30
Role Play Discussion Questions

Aliens. Discuss why aliens would leave their country and try to stay in this country, even though it's illegal. What would cause thousands of people to leave their homeland and flee with only a few belongings? What are some of the problems or obstacles they must face?

Sanctuary Workers. Why would these individuals break the law and risk prosecution and punishment? Should we always obey our government's laws, or is there a higher law that sometimes demands we confront our society or our government? Could this kind of decision lead to a breakdown of law and order? Make a list of arguments for and against the actions of the sanctuary movement.

Government (the U.S. Border Patrol and officials of the Immigration and Naturalization Service). What is your viewpoint of the aliens? What do you think of those who give them sanctuary? What is your view of the law? How would you feel about arresting church leaders?

are some of them political refugees whose lives are actually in peril?' International law states clearly that political refugees must be granted asylum in the country to which they flee; our own law agrees. According to our State Department, those leaving El Salvador and Guatemala are not in danger. Those democratic nations are allied with the United States against the threat of communism in Nicaragua and have committed few human rights violations. Despite the stories of political killings, arrests and tortures reported by refugees and agencies like Amnesty International, our government has maintained its position of granting few individuals refugee status when they come from these Central American countries. When these refugees have appealed for help from some of the Christian churches, church leaders and members have decided to help the illegal aliens even though this action opposes the policy of our government. This movement is known as the sanctuary movement and has produced much controversy, especially since government officials have arrested several church leaders and convicted them of violating the immigration laws. This situation gives rise to the question, 'Should Christians break the law in order to help someone?' To dramatize this issue, a group of your friends have agreed to present the following role play."

Program—After the role play divide the kids into three groups. Have each group meet by one of the signs. Ask the kids to pretend they are members of this group of people. Ask them to think about the role play, read the discussion questions (Chart 30) and respond to how this particular group in the role play would think and feel.

After about 10 minutes, ask the groups to rotate clockwise around the room to the next sign. Have the kids pretend they are members of this group of people and discuss the questions.

Change groups a third time and repeat the same procedure.

Response—Pass out the questionnaire (Chart 31) to each small group. Ask kids to assign the scripture passages at the top of the page to individuals within the group and take turns reading them aloud. Ask everyone to decide which group the scripture passages support. Allow about 20 minutes for this activity.

Read Emma Lazarus' poem *The New Colossus* written in honor of the French people's gift to the United States—the Statue of Liberty. Explain that today it is not always easy to follow the ideals of this poem. Good people disagree about this important issue. Our government is sincerely concerned about its current citizens and the flood of refugees pouring into our land. Others have been called to pay a high price for helping those whom they believe are being oppressed. As Christians we must concern ourselves with all individuals who need our help and realize we are called to serve everyone in the name of Christ. Both groups need our prayers.

Close this session with the following prayer:

"O God, our creator and sustainer, we know you understand when we pray for those who have fled their homelands. For you ordained that our governments should rule over us to provide order and promote justice. Hear our prayers as we offer concern for all our brothers and sisters—

for those who struggle to escape their homelands, no matter what their motives are,

for those who seek to minister to these aliens' desperate needs,

and for those who are called to enforce the laws of our land, even when the result is painful for all concerned.

May the comfort and guidance of your Spirit be with all those caught in this great dilemma of our age. We ask these things in the name of Christ, who is the Lord of all, Amen."

Options:

1. If you live in or near a large city or close to a university, people who know about, or are involved in, the sanctuary movement would probably be available to come and speak to your group. Follow this presentation with someone from the Immigration and Naturalization Service or U.S. Border Patrol who can present the other side of the issue.

2. This issue of whether to follow God and our Chris-

Chart 31
The Bible Supports . . .

Which of the three groups do the following scripture passages support? (Write "A" for aliens, "G" for government agencies and "S" for sanctuary workers in the blank to the left of the scripture passage.)

____Exodus 3:7-9   ____Mark 12:17

____Numbers 35:9-15   ____Acts 5:27-32

____Deuteronomy 10:12-19   ____Romans 13:1-2

____Psalm 146   ____Hebrews 13:1-2

____Matthew 5:3-12   ____James 2:14-17

____Matthew 25:35   ____1 Peter 2:13-17

1. Several of these scripture passages seem to conflict at first, so examine them closely. For example, reread the passages in Romans 13 and 1 Peter 2. Do you think the authors meant to always obey the government no matter what its orders are? Lutherans and Catholic Germans accepted this interpretation during World War II when they followed Hitler's orders and betrayed their Jewish friends and neighbors.

"For rulers hold no terror for those who do right, but for those who do wrong. Do you want to be free from fear of the one in authority? Then do what is right and he will commend you" (Romans 13:3). Is helping a scared, penniless refugee family the right thing to do? Does this act follow Jesus' teachings in Matthew 25:35? People have been arrested and prosecuted for feeding, clothing and caring for the sick when the recipients of their aid entered the country illegally. When individuals and church groups have turned illegal aliens over to government authorities, these aliens normally have been returned to their native country. What should a Christian do when each decision he or she might make will violate a cherished belief?

2. Jesus taught us, "Give to Caesar what is Caesar's and to God what is God's" (Mark 12:17). But what if Caesar or our government authorities demand what is God's? Whom do we obey? Reread Acts 5:29. Why did the apostles refuse to obey their rulers' commands not to preach the gospel?

tian conscience or the laws and customs of our country is an old one in America. Ask individuals to locate information about the following and bring it to your next meeting:

● Henry David Thoreau's "Essay on Civil Disobedience." Ask someone to read the essay and describe it to the group.

● James Russell Lowell's hymn "Once to Every Man and Nation." This hymn was written to protest the Mexican War. Lowell believed this conflict was being fought to extend the territory of slavery. For more information on this hymn, refer to Albert E. Bailey's book *Gospel in Hymns* (Scribner).

● The abolitionists and the underground railroad. What Supreme Court decision did these people, most of whom were church members, violate? What did the law say they were supposed to do if a runaway slave came to their door?

● The suffragette movement. Describe some of the tactics used to secure passage of the constitutional amendment that granted women the right to vote.

● Martin Luther King Jr.'s "Letter From a Birmingham Jail." What Southern laws were broken to secure equal rights for blacks? What were some of the charges made against King and the civil rights movement?

● The Founding Fathers of our nation. Were the first patriots law-abiding citizens, or radicals who believed that citizens had a right to rebel against the laws and government they deemed oppressive and unjust? For example, did those who took part in the Boston Tea Party respect the property of their opponents? What laws of the time did they violate?

● Sanctuary movement. Ask a young person to do some research on this topic and report his or her findings. Magazines such as Sojourners, The Other Side and Christianity Today have run articles on the sanctuary movement.

ISSUE 32
Should Christians ship food to countries that don't practice birth control?

YES, Christians should ship food and aid to any country that needs it, regardless if it practices birth control.

"Did your youth group participate in the UNICEF trick or treat campaign?"

"Sure. We gathered the children at Sunday school, helped pass out the boxes and brochures, transported and escorted them to their areas and prepared a party for when the kids returned with their money boxes."

"Our church doesn't believe in working with UNICEF. This organization gives some of the money to communist countries and others that don't deserve it."

"What do you mean by countries that don't deserve aid?"

"Like those countries where people refuse to practice birth control. If they won't even try a simple means to help themselves, then they don't deserve our help either. The children we help in these countries will only grow up to starve later because of overpopulation."

"Sounds like you've got it all figured out, haven't you? I wonder what Jesus would say to that. I thought the Bible said something about feeding our enemies. I don't remember Jesus putting any conditions on our help."

Experience indicates that poor people become more interested in helping themselves if they can help plan and participate in the aid itself. Poorer countries should promote some kind of birth control, without including abortion. This kind of responsibility would prevent the runaway population growth that gobbles up any increase in food production that aid programs create. Implementing birth control programs isn't always possible. There may be religious or cultural reasons why families hesitate to adopt birth control. In many societies where children are regarded as precious assets, the more children the higher the status of the parents or family. Some birth control methods are so complicated that poor, illiterate families have difficulty understanding how to use them. Our insistence on birth control is often regarded as an attempt to interfere with or even run their country.

Most Westerners fail to understand that large families are the social security of the poor in Third World countries. With no government programs to care for the elderly, parents have large numbers of children to ensure that at least a few of them will survive infancy and childhood and can care for their parents in their old age. Experience in several countries indicates that when health care improves, more babies survive the first few years, and when the food supplies are more stable and assured for families, the birthrate drops dramatically.

Churches and governments should continue to aid a needy country, even if its population doesn't promote birth control. Such programs can be suggested, but they shouldn't be forced on people along with a threat to withdraw food. Jesus teaches us to feed the hungry. He never said anything about adding conditions for offering that food. Jesus simply instructed us to feed the hungry and that is exactly what we should continue to do.

NO, Christians shouldn't ship food to countries that don't practice birth control.

"No, I'm sorry, Clark, but I can't sponsor you on the CROP walk for world hunger."

"But the money isn't for me, it's for the hungry people of the world."

"I know you believe that. I'm sure you honestly believe you're helping people, but I've read a lot lately—about the different groups that have jumped on the hunger bandwagon, even the rock music groups."

"Yeah, isn't it great that so many people are getting involved?"

"To be honest, Clark, no, it isn't. Even if all that money got through to all of the starving countries, it would still be a waste. We may save a few babies now, but their parents would continue to have more and more children— more mouths to feed, more mouths to starve. I think we should stop helping those countries who show little concern for any population control and give aid only to those nations where our help can do some lasting good."

"That sounds pretty callous!"

"Actually, I think it's even more cruel, as well as useless, to aid some country that refuses to promote birth control or encourage other self-help projects. With our limited resources, the church must look carefully at the countries that want our aid and give only to those who continually strive to get out of their mess. Some have worked hard to develop better economic and trade policies that encourage Western business. Others have instituted self-help programs and encourage special programs for birth control."

Christians ship millions of dollars worth of food, tools, medicine and clothing to foreign lands each year. Church World Service and CROP (Church Relief Overseas Project), World Vision, CARE, Lutheran World Service, Bishops' Overseas Relief Fund and a host of denominational and private agencies are channels for the generous aid of millions of Christians who follow their Lord's command to feed and clothe "the least of these brothers of mine."

Such aid is good, and it's desperately needed. In fact, when all the aid from Christian and private agencies is added together, it barely affects the huge mountain of poverty and hunger in the world. Thus, Christians need to be careful that their limited funds make as big an impact on the problem as possible.

It does little good in the long run to feed people who will reproduce even more babies than their nation's gains in food production can accommodate. These needy governments and their people must do something about overpopulation, their source of misery, in the future. In many Third World nations, the birthrate is so high that no matter what emergency measures are taken, like feeding the people or improving their health, an even greater disaster awaits. When more babies arrive and old people live longer, the population increases to the point it surpasses the nation's food production. And that nation is confronted again with terrible famine and hunger.

Some nations have introduced birth control into their culture to try to stem the birthrate. We should direct our aid to these nations where it will do the most good. Other nations will see that our country is willing to help those nations who try to help themselves. When these people face less and less scarcity as the years go by, the program will take effect and other nations will follow this example.

Christians will want to have some input about the methods of birth control nations might choose, especially since China and Japan have chosen abortion as a way to curb population growth. Abortion can be effective like it is in Japan, but Christians cannot condone this act as a method for birth control.

Christians should carefully select those countries who are willing to help themselves and offer their aid. An effective plan for population control should be a basic requirement for any aid given.

Programming Ideas for Issue 32

Preparation—Ask the parents of your group members to help plan and prepare a meal for hunger. Tell them you will want to serve food that can be provided in large, family-style containers like bowls and casserole dishes. Prepare a separate dessert table.

Ask your young people to plan ahead and decorate for the hunger banquet. They might want to order special place mats from CROP that have hunger statistics printed on them. They could also use pictures and maps of Third World countries to decorate the walls. Agencies like UNICEF also have catalogs which may help you find appropriate items to decorate the tables.

Prepare meal tickets with the same number at both ends of the ticket. Set up only enough tables and chairs to accommodate one-fourth of the group you expect to attend. Place extra bowls and spoons at each table.

On separate 3×5 cards, tape the activities listed in Chart 32. Add other ideas that would work well for your group. Prepare a set of cards for each table. Gather bibs, peanuts, silly hats and other items you will need for these activities.

Preview several hunger films and select the one you want to use for your event.

Opening—Welcome the group and make sure each person has his or her meal ticket. Ask the kids to tear their tickets in half; put half in the basket that is being passed and hold on to the other half. Explain that tonight's meal will be part of an experience to explore the issue of merely feeding the hungry or establishing conditions for our aid, especially birth control. Select a number of tickets that represent one-fourth of those present. Explain that this lucky minority represents North America, Europe, Japan, Australia and the affluent world. Ask them to seat themselves at the tables. Those who were not selected will stand around the tables. These people will represent the Third World countries who must wait for the affluent to determine whether or not they will eat.

Chart 32
Suggestions for Activity Cards

- Sing two stanzas of a hymn.
- Tell the person who offers you the card what a great person he or she is.
- Hum "The Star-Spangled Banner" while standing on one foot.
- Roll a peanut (or small ball) around the room with your nose.
- Promise to wash dishes after the meal.
- Read a special love poem to the group. (Bring a mushy one along!)
- Hop on one foot to the dessert table to get something for the person who gave you the card.
- Walk around the room with a book or other object balanced on your head.
- Wear a bib and a silly hat for the rest of the meal.
- Recite the 8s and 9s of the multiplication table.

Offer a prayer for the food and ask those who are serving to bring in the food.

Program—While the lucky ones pass the food and begin to eat, the others will stand around and watch until they are invited to come to one of the tables. Do not set up extra tables and chairs, only enough for those who represent the affluent nations.

Each table should have a stack of activity cards for the affluent to offer the Third World representatives. These cards will tell people what they must do to obtain their food. Shortly after the meal begins, tell those who are seated at the tables to call one or more of the Third World people to the table and give them a card. The recipients of the cards must do whatever is on the card in order to receive any food.

Give out small portions of food and serve in bowls with spoons. Tell the Third World people if they are hungry, they must continue to ask for more and must perform another task each time they ask for food. Third World representatives must sit on the floor to eat and they cannot ask for more until their bowl is empty.

Serve dessert only to those individuals seated at the tables. Regardless of pleas or enticements, allow no Third World members to eat the sweets. (Well, maybe a bite to someone who offers an exceptionally ingenious plea.)

After dessert, show a short film on world hunger such as *The Hungry People* from World Vision (write: 919 W. Huntington, Monrovia, CA 91016).

Response—After the film divide into four small groups for discussion. Be sure to include some of the affluent in each group. If there is a film guide, incorporate some of its questions with the following:

1. How did you feel during the supper?

Ask the affluent: "Did you feel strange or guilty? Did anyone do anything to make you feel even more awkward? Did you feel superior? How did you feel about the ability to command someone to do something?"

Ask the Third World representatives: "Did you feel upset or cheated? Did you express your feelings, even though this was a game? How did you like having to do something in order to get fed while the others just sat and ate? Was this experience humiliating? Did those in power try to rub this in? If yes, what did they do? Did anyone offer to slip you some food against the rules? Were you tempted to take it? How did you feel about not getting dessert?"

2. After listening to one another's feelings, have you learned anything in particular about how others feel in each situation? Give an example of what you have learned and explain what you mean.

3. List some of the ways you know that affluent countries try to help those in Third World countries. How many of these efforts are controlled by the government? private organizations? church agencies?

4. Some individuals have suggested there are so many hungry people we cannot help them all. They have proposed that we limit our aid to countries and people where we can make the most difference. These same individuals suggest that we abandon countries that aren't willing to adopt self-help measures like birth control. What do you think about this kind of limited aid?

5. Did Jesus attach any conditions to his commandments to feed and care for the needy? Ask individuals to read aloud Matthew 25:31-46; Mark 6:30-44; Romans 12:20-21; and James 2:14-17. Did Jesus or his followers ever encounter the magnitude of such situations as mass starvation and overpopulation? Support your answer with specific examples.

6. What are the motives for the different forms of aid from governments? private businesses? churches? How might Third World people react to the aid they receive from these different sources? How might these people react to the condition that they adopt a stringent program of birth control? (Recall comments that the Third World representatives made about how they felt when they had to do something for their meal while the smaller group just sat and ate.)

7. Talk about how certain conditions like birth control might, or might not, fit into a nation's culture or religion. For instance, could all Christians in our own country accept the condition of birth control? In Third World countries like India, Bangladesh or Ethiopia, would having just one or two children be practical or make sense? How would this condition affect these countries' concept of manhood? Would this condition actually help? Can we impose such a condition on a culture or group, or must they come to this conclusion on their own?

Remind the group that hunger in the Third World countries is not an abstract problem but one that involves human beings. Ask someone to read Romans 12:20a. Offer a prayer like the following:

"God, you have created this beautiful world and filled it full of good things to delight our senses—the ear, eye and palate. Through no effort of our own we have been born in a land overflowing with food, while many of your children lack even the basic necessities of life. We realize our greed and lack of compassion have created this disparity. Through your Son we also realize that when we have been given a great deal, much is also expected. Help us be nurtured by your Spirit to become more compassionate and willing to share what we have with others. Inspire us to increase our awareness and our sharing. We ask that we may never rest as long as one child remains hungry. Help us serve each person's need for bread—of the earth and of life. We ask this in the name of the one who broke and shared his loaves with the multitude, Jesus Christ our Lord, Amen."

Options:

1. Invite a CROP worker, a missionary, a Peace Corps volunteer or some other knowledgeable person to speak on world hunger. If you can't secure a speaker, rent or borrow a film from the local library, the school, the denominational office or a local peace and justice center.

2. Involve your group in a hunger action program. Some possibilities you may want to consider are these:

● A CROP walk. Sponsors pay participants so much for each mile they walk for the cause.

● UNICEF drive. Your group could help younger children trick or treat for UNICEF on Halloween.

● Hunger fast or a hunger meal. Collect a typical amount for a meal at church and serve only crackers and water. Watch a film on hunger. Give the proceeds to a hunger fund.

● Food collection. Collect food for a local food closet or soup kitchen. Ask one of the staff members to talk about hunger in your immediate area.

3. Create your own media presentation for this issue. Divide the group in two and work on multimedia presentations for each side. Incorporate hymns and hunger songs, scripture passages and narrative into the sound track. Secure low-cost slide sets from the UNICEF catalog or equip your 35mm cameras with close-up lenses and go through back issues of Time and Newsweek for lots of photos to copy. Look for local scenes to photograph—your community food closet or kitchen, a CROP walk or other hunger fund-raising activities. Put the sound and slides together and present the program to your group, congregation, schools, community clubs and organizations.

RIGHTS ISSUES

R ights groups have multiplied within recent years: civil rights, women's rights, Native American rights, welfare rights, gay rights, prisoners' rights, victims' rights, employers' and workers' rights—even children's, animals', students' and non-smokers' rights. With so many rights groups, it's hard to know who's right and who's wrong.

In the past, many of our ancestors put up with discrimination and other injustices—only occasionally bursting forth resentfully in open rebellion. During these times a new awareness emerges among the downtrodden—they do not have to tolerate oppression. They can work for and win their rights. For many of the oppressed, Exodus is the scriptural focal point and the chief inspiration of their hope.

Most of us agree that all people are entitled to their rights. Uncertainty arises when considering where the rights of one group end and those of another begin. Often the rights of two groups conflict. For example, society's right to protect itself from addictive drugs conflicts with an individual's right to privacy. The right of a child afflicted with AIDS conflicts with the right of fearful parents to protect their own children from AIDS. An employer's right to set employees' wages conflicts with workers' rights for protection against exploitation by business leaders. The freedom of the smoker to do as he or she pleases conflicts with the right of a neighbor to breathe clean air.

Such conflicts of rights are not easily resolved, even by good will or good wishes. Some conflicts may not be resolvable at all, but youth group members must deal with them sooner or later. The sessions in this chapter can help prepare kids to deal with conflicting rights issues in a sane, rational and considerate way.

ISSUE 33
Should employers have the right to pay minors less than the minimum wage?

YES, employers should have the right to pay minors less than the minimum wage.

"Sorry, Billy, I can't hire you again this summer."

"Oh, no! I was counting on the job, Mr. Mahler."

"Well, I'd like to hire you; you're a good worker. But all the regulations the state requires employers to follow— especially the higher minimum wage we're supposed to pay—make it tough. It's just getting too expensive to hire summer workers. So my wife has been pitching in when I need extra help here at the store."

Abolishing the minimum wage requirement for teenagers would be more practical for employers as well as more beneficial for teenagers. The minimum wage might have been useful several generations ago when wages in general were so low, but today minimum wage is more of a problem than a help. The minimum wage law hinders a lot of teenagers from working and makes it difficult for many employers to find affordable help. Grocery stores and fast-food restaurants are especially affected by the minimum wage law. These service industries provide low-level, first-entry jobs into the market. They call for unskilled people who can be trained to perform simple duties. These industries also often need people to work various shifts or during peak business hours.

The minimum wage is now so high that employers have a difficult time affording help. Service industries operate on a low profit margin; they depend on high-volume business to make a profit. Hiring employees at the minimum wage level or higher prevents these companies from making much of a profit—especially when hiring teenagers at minimum wage. These industries must devote far more time to training young people, most of whom won't stay with the store for very long, so the industries may hire adults instead.

Adults give these companies a more seasoned and dependable work force. However, to avoid paying even higher wages and to get around some of the regulations, employers often schedule their employees to work under 40 hours per week. This isn't good for adults who need a full-time job; and it shuts out most teenagers from what could be valuable work experience.

Teenagers are among the largest unemployed age group. This is especially devastating in the cities, where idle teenagers get into so much trouble. If employers could be exempted from the minimum wage requirement, they would hire more teenagers. Smaller businesses would be able to take on another employee. These small owner-operated businesses often need more part-time workers, but can't afford to hire them under the present laws. So the owner works more hours. If owners could hire someone at the actual wages they could afford, many would do so.

Over the last 50 years, our country has become terribly entangled in rules and regulations and bureaucratic delays. At one time, an employee and employer simply made their own agreement without anyone else interfering. "This is what the job pays. If you want it, fine. If not, I'll look for someone else." And the job seeker could try to bargain with the employer, or he or she could look elsewhere.

Today there is such a layer of rules and regulations that even experts have trouble figuring them all out. These rules and regulations have made the small business employer all the more reluctant to take on extra help, especially teenagers, who are known for their high rate of turnover.

It would be better for both teenagers and employers if the minimum wage law did not apply to them.

NO, employers should not have the right to pay minors less than the minimum wage.

"Hi, Mom. You're home early today. I got some good news to tell you—and you sure look like you could use some!"

"Yeah, I sure could! I was laid off."

"You're kidding!"

"I wish I was. Most all of us working the counter were let go. The store changed its policy since the minimum wage law was lifted. The company has hired a bunch of kids who can work part time at lower wages than they're paying us."

"Oh, no! That's terrible! What a dirty thing for them to do."

"Yeah. But you said you have some good news. Tell me. I can sure stand some."

"Oh boy, I guess it isn't so good after all!"

"What do you mean?"

"On the way home from school I saw the 'part-time help wanted' sign in the store window where you work. So I went in, and the manager hired me!"

Abolishing the minimum wage law would be taking a step backward. It would undo much of the good that has been accomplished over the past 50 years in the area of labor relations. And it could mean the creation of new problems.

The myth of the equal bargaining position that once existed between the employer and the employee is false. There was never any equality in this relationship. Employers were always in the superior position. They had the economic power of their business. Large companies could always use this power and offer extremely low wages. Workers could do nothing, until they began to organize into unions. And this was a long, bloody process, since employers fiercely resisted. The government stepped in and made the rules and regulations to keep greedy employers from exploiting their help. Nothing has happened to human nature in the past 50 years that indicates improvement. Rules and regulations are still needed.

If employers could hire minors at below minimum wage, then employers would fire the more costly adult workers and hire the cheaper teenagers. Teenagers could be hired to work shorter shifts, and the employer could pocket quite a substantial savings. In the meantime, adults would be out of work and on unemployment benefits or welfare, since many of these people do not have the skills for higher paying jobs. In the long run, society would have to pay for employers' increased profits.

A better course of action to deal with the very real problem of teenagers and unskilled adults in the work force is for the government to subsidize employers who are willing to hire minors. The subsidy could make up the difference between what the employer could afford and the current minimum wage. Safeguards from abuse and other details would have to be worked out, but such a program could lead to the hiring of more teenagers without risk to adults in the low-paying job sector. But until there is such a program, employers should not have the right to pay minors less than minimum wage.

Programming Ideas for Issue 33

Preparation—Prior to this session, ask several young volunteers to survey community employers on the status of their teenage employees. They can use a survey similar to Chart 33.

Invite several area employers (a supermarket manager, community recreation director, fast-food manager, etc.) to be part of "Ask an Expert" and a "Job Fair." Explain to the employers that you want to provide a time and place for youth to ask questions and discuss job opportunities and requirements. Ask them to come to the session 30 minutes after it begins. This will allow time for the young people to prepare questions to ask the employers.

At various locations in a large room, set up one table for each employer. Use posterboard and markers to make large, attractive signs identifying each place of work.

Promote the Job Fair at school and among other church

groups. Advertise in local newspapers and on radio stations the young people listen to.

One week prior to the session, prepare the young people by telling them the session will be divided into two parts: Ask an Expert and Job Fair. Give young people copies of the Yes and No positions on minimum wage. Have kids write any questions they have about minimum wage and rules and regulations employers are required to follow. Ask them to bring these questions for the first part, Ask an Expert.

Ask young people to search the want ads for employment opportunities. Encourage them to write any questions they might have about employment (qualities employers look for in employees, interview tips, specifics about differ-

---

Chart 33
Job Survey

Employer	Number of teenagers employed	Average hours per week	Minimum wage?
1.			
2.			
3.			
4.			
5.			
6.			
7.			
8.			
9.			
10.			

ent businesses). They can ask these questions at the second part, the Job Fair.

Allow at least two hours for this session.

Opening—Try a little impromptu acting to get the kids thinking about job issues. Ask a volunteer to read the parable of the workers in the vineyard (Matthew 20:1-15). Ask the others to act it out during the reading. One person could be the landowner, another could be the foreman and the rest could be divided into the three groups of workers who were hired at various times of the day—for the same wage. A fun, modern-day adaptation to this exercise is called "Workin' at the Carwash Blues" from *The Giving Book*, by Joani Schultz and Paul M. Thompson (John Knox Press).

Ask the landowner to describe difficult aspects of being a boss. How did he or she feel when the workers grumbled? Ask the workers how they felt when they were first hired. How did they feel when they discovered all workers were being paid equally for varying hours of labor? How could negative feelings affect a work relationship? Does an employer have the right to set wages for his or her employees? Why or why not?

Say that relationships between employers and employees have not changed much over the years. This session will give the young people an opportunity to find out what is happening in the job market in their own city.

Ask the volunteers who surveyed local businesses to present their findings. How many businesses employ teenagers? How many teenagers? How many hours do they work per week? Are they paid minimum wage?

Describe the two parts of the session: Ask an Expert, which is a time to ask area employers questions about minimum wage; and Job Fair, which is a time to find out more about each business, qualities employers look for in employees, interview techniques and suggestions, and any other questions kids have.

Program—Introduce each employer like this: "And now, ladies and gentlemen, I'd like to introduce to you expert No. 1—Joe Summers from Super Grocery on Fifth Street. Welcome him, please . . . Expert No. 2 is . . . " and so on until all employers are introduced.

Allow 20 to 30 minutes for kids to ask questions on minimum wage and other rules and regulations employers must follow. Questions can include:

1. Do you think minimum wage is fair for the employer? Why or why not?

2. Do you think minimum wage is fair for the employee? Why or why not?

3. How much control should the government have on an employer and his or her business?

After Ask an Expert, tell the young people that now they will look beyond the issue of wages to the work itself. Ask the employers to move to their assigned tables.

Divide kids into groups (one group for each employer). Give them 10 minutes to ask questions and talk with the employer. If kids are interested, encourage them to set up interview times with the businesses that interest them. After 10 minutes, signal participants to rotate to the next station. Continue this format until all kids have visited all employers.

Response—Gather as a large group to discuss any further questions. Form a circle alternating young person and employer. Ask them to cross their arms, right over left, and join hands. Close with this prayer:

"God, you created the world with your hands and gave each of us work to do. We thank you for this and for your many blessings that make life so rich and rewarding. Be with us as we go out in the world and spread your love to all people we meet. Amen."

On "Amen," have all participants (still holding hands) turn clockwise (under their right arm) to the outside of the circle. Arms are "miraculously" uncrossed as members face outward to the world and their new challenges.

Options:

1. Plan a follow-up Bible study for the next session. Encourage kids to discuss questions such as: What seems to be

the attitude of a great many people toward their work? What are different ways people describe or refer to their jobs? (The grind, the rat race, the salt mines, the pits, etc.) Say: "The term TGIF (Thank God It's Friday) also reveals much about people's attitude toward their work. This negative attitude is old. The ancient Greeks disdained manual work, thought to be fit only for slaves. In the Middle Ages a gentleman was one who never soiled his hands. However, the reformers Martin Luther and John Calvin discovered in the Bible a dignity of labor."

For this biblical view of work divide the group into teams of three or four and assign them the following passages:

● God as worker: Genesis 1:31-2:3; Psalm 19:1; Proverbs 8:22-31; Isaiah 40:21-31; 45:9-13; 64:8.

● People as workers: Genesis 1:27-28; 2:15; Exodus 20:9; Psalm 104:19-24, 31; Proverbs 6:6-11; Ecclesiastes 3:1-13; 1 Thessalonians 4:11; 2 Thessalonians 3:10.

● The curse that work has fallen under: Genesis 3:16-19; Ecclesiastes 2:1-11; 18-23; Luke 12:15-22.

● Christ the transformer of work (and worker): Matthew 9:35-38; John 4:31-38; 1 Corinthians 3:5-9.

2. Do other countries issue rules and regulations governing minimum wage? Research countries such as Japan, England, Sweden, Germany and so on.

3. Delve into the issue of job hunting by setting up mock interviews. Divide kids into pairs. One person is the interviewer, the other is the interviewee. Take turns interviewing each other. Then discuss questions such as: Why are interviews difficult to go through? How did the interview go? What questions were surprises? Was it difficult to confidently answer the questions? Explain. Is interviewing a person difficult? Why or why not? How can you apply this interview to your job-seeking skills?

ISSUE 34
Should school authorities have the right to search students' lockers?

YES, school authorities should have the right to search

students' lockers.

"Well, Glen, what do you think? That's the third student in a week who's been caught with drugs. Think it's time for more drastic action?"

"I wish I knew, Carter. I'm glad at times like this that you're the principal and I'm the assistant. I don't think that the student council officers will be of much help."

"I know. They were awfully quiet when I made my appeal to help us uncover the drug pushers here. The old code of 'us versus them,' of not telling on a fellow student, is too strong."

"I'm afraid it is. And yet I don't like the idea of surprise locker searches. That somehow smacks of police state tactics. The kids are going to feel that way, too—and resent it."

"(Sigh.) Yes, I'm sure they will. No one hates playing 'Narc' more than I do. And yet we've got to try to find the source of the problem before drugs really get out of hand. Even if we don't catch them right away, we can throw the guilty students off balance by several searches so that it will be more difficult for them to hide the drugs on school property. What else can I do?"

Locker searches are necessary at a time when many drugs are circulating around the school. Locker searches are also necessary when authorities need to find a stolen object. In some urban cities, searches are necessary to find knives, handguns or other weapons.

The right to search should not be used often, but this right should be used when necessary. During school hours, authorities are in charge of the students' welfare. If school authorities are to look after the students, they must have the same rights as the parents do at home. Students do not own their lockers, they merely use them during the school year. The public actually owns school property, since their taxes pay for it. Authorities act on behalf of the public when they watch over school property and the students.

Students' right to privacy is an important right, but it

must take second place when the entire student body's welfare is at stake—as in the case of drug abuse or storing weapons in a locker. Oftentimes the only way drug pushers can be identified is by an unexpected locker search.

Students who have nothing to hide should not mind such searches, and they should be willing to cooperate with the authorities, since the searches are for their own welfare. Locker searches cause inconvenience, but it is similar to the inconvenience endured by airline travelers who are subject to screening before they board a plane. No one likes this, but all put up with it because they realize the necessity of preventing someone from sneaking a gun or bomb into the plane.

It's too bad that we live in the kind of world in which lockers must be searched, but many times, the safety of the entire student body makes locker searches a necessity.

NO, school authorities should not have the right to search student lockers.

"Boy, did this morning's locker search catch me unprepared! I'd been meaning to clean my locker for a month."

"Yeah, me too. And Ol' Lady Sweeney blew her top when she saw my rock poster taped inside my locker door. You'd have thought I had a Playboy centerfold taped there!"

"And did you hear how embarrassed Marty was when they found that package of condoms tucked into his biology text?"

"I would love to have seen that. Though what happened to Jane wasn't so funny."

"Oh? What happened?"

"They found the can of baby talc that she uses after her gym shower. It's the non-scented kind, so they thought it might be coke or something. They called her into the principal's office while the police checked it out."

"It doesn't seem fair. We're pushed and pulled, told what to do and what not to do. Not even the bathrooms or our own lockers are private!"

"There ought to be some place that we can call our own. It's a creepy feeling to have someone searching your personal stuff."

"And all because of a few jerks who sneak in drugs. It isn't right. It really makes me mad!"

Our nation prizes privacy, yet denies this right to students. This is not a good way to teach democracy and fair play.

The risk of drugs at school is great, but not great enough to violate the basic rules of a democracy. Such a practice fits in better with a police state like the Soviet Union.

If the school authorities are really serious about combating drugs on campus, they should try to enlist the students themselves in the fight. They should bring their concern to the student government and the student body and see what ideas they have. Although students do not want to become informers, they might be able to think of some creative ideas. If given an opportunity to deal with the problem, students are harder on each other than adults are.

If school authorities want the students to respect them, then the school authorities should respect the students. Surprise locker searches are demeaning to all concerned and do more harm than good—even if the guilty are caught. There must be a better way to deal with this problem than to search lockers and intrude into all students' privacy.

Programming Ideas for Issue 34

Preparation—Gather newsprint, markers and Bibles.

Opening—Read the following two statements. If students agree with the statement, have them stand; if they disagree, have them sit down and cross their arms in front of them.

● Society must protect itself from the danger of drugs, even if we must give up a little of our personal right to privacy.

● No one has the authority to invade another's privacy, even for a good cause.

Say that during this session, the students will discuss these issues, learning more about their opinions and why they feel as they do.

Program—Ask the kids to turn in their wallets and purses. Watch their reactions. Tell them it's very important that they do so—a police officer is coming and wants to inspect them.

After a moment or two of mass confusion, tell the kids to keep their wallets and purses, and that you wanted to see their reaction. How did they feel about the request? uneasy? upset? scared? Do their parents search their bedrooms without their permission? If so, how do the kids feel about it? How many keep a diary or journal? How would they feel if someone were to read it without their permission? Do school authorities ever search students' lockers? If so, how do they feel about this practice? What is the school's official policy on this issue? How about other schools in the area?

Compare the previous four practices: searching wallets or purses, searching bedrooms, reading diaries without permission and searching lockers. How are they similar? different? What is the one "right" they all violate? (The right to privacy.)

Make two columns on newsprint: pros and cons. Ask group members to list reasons under each column why each practice should or should not be allowed. Discuss these reasons. The old conflict between private and public rights will probably emerge (the individual's right to privacy versus the group's right to protect itself). Can this conflict ever be completely resolved? Why or why not?

Read Romans 13:1-5. How do these verses apply to locker searches? Should anything be done about these searches? Explain.

Read Ephesians 6:1-4. On campus, school authorities are regarded as exercising authority in place of parents, so what does this passage say about the situation? Should students just accept what is said and done without question?

Why or why not? Are there qualifications placed on the authority in either of these passages? In other words, should authorities recognize certain limitations? If so, explain. Does our government apply any limitations to the misuse of authority and abuse of privacy? What are they, or what are they called? (The Bill of Rights, the first 10 amendments to the U.S. Constitution.)

Response—Some kids may totally agree that locker searches are justifiable for the school's protection; others may totally disagree and think locker searches violate students' privacy; still others may think locker searches are okay in some instances. Whatever the students' opinions, discuss the idea that someday on some issue, kids may need to try and influence or change school policy.

Make another list on newsprint of ways students could change school policy. For example:

1. Write editorials and letters to the editor of school and community newspapers.

2. Write and circulate a petition to the principal, school board and the student council.

3. Discuss the issue at a parents meeting.

4. Discuss the issue at a student council meeting.

5. Organize students to prepare and distribute leaflets advocating a change.

Close with a prayer such as the following:

"God, we thank you that we live in a democratic society in which the young and the old have a voice. Help us to be aware of any wrongs. Give us the wisdom to see what we can do to correct these wrongs, and the courage to act accordingly. But above all, give us love that we might see the humanity in those who disagree with us. Help us to listen so that we might learn from them and never allow our passions to blind us to the good in them. Be with us now as we go forth from here, and bless our plans that are in accordance with your will. Amen."

Options:

1. Invite a school official to speak to the group. Ask

questions concerning the school's policy on locker searches and other means of maintaining a safe environment in the school.

2. Distribute copies of the U.S. Constitution. Read the Bill of Rights and discuss whether or not sections apply to the kids and their situations at home or school.

ISSUE 35

Should minorities be given preference in college scholarships, jobs, housing and other areas?

YES, minorities should be given preference in college scholarships, jobs, housing and other areas.

"It doesn't seem right, Mom. We were slaves for over 300 years. And then when we got our freedom the whites started to take it away with Jim Crow laws. Whites kept us down on the poorest land and gave us schools that weren't fit to store cotton in. And we're expected to compete with the sons and daughters of doctors and lawyers who've gone to the best of private schools."

"Now listen, Son. You can drop out and become bitter, or you can work hard in high school and get a scholarship to a good college—something none of us ever had a chance at."

"But how could I ever get into a really good school like Harvard or Yale?"

"Just as I said. By trying your best while you're here in school and by taking part in plenty of school and church activities. When school authorities see that you're black, they'll look at your record far more favorably than that of a white person with the same grades. And you'll find that's true when you're looking for work later on—at least with a lot of companies and government jobs."

"How come? Is this another handout?"

"No, it's a hand up, if you'll take it. Your daddy and I may not be very educated, but we know about affirmative action. It's a way of making up for all the years that we've been kicked and kept down. It doesn't guarantee that you'll be a success, but it does give us a chance to get our foot in the door and succeed or fail. Before the government started affirmative action we couldn't even get in the door."

Affirmative action is the practice of giving preference to members of minorities in hiring and giving out scholarships. The program includes blacks as well as other minorities. When it began, affirmative action was justified on the basis of the three-century-long maltreatment of blacks. Throughout their history in America blacks have been held down—uprooted from their native lands, sold and bred like cattle. Families separated at the whim of their masters. Even when blacks were finally freed after the Civil War, they were the victims of Jim Crow laws in the South and more subtle prejudice in the North. They went to inferior schools. Very few of them graduated; many dropped out for economic reasons.

Many blacks have been the last to be hired and the first to be fired. Even today some craft guilds and unions fail to recognize blacks. Thus it's right that our society should attempt to make up for the centuries of wrong inflicted upon our black neighbors. Affirmative action with a measurable quota system is one way to give blacks a chance at the scholarships, jobs and public housing from which they have been excluded for so long. A similar case could be made for other minorities as well.

Many people say that affirmative action is wrong. When testing for certain jobs, whites may be better qualified than blacks, yet blacks are hired first to satisfy a quota. Some of these tests are unfair. They don't show the true qualifications of the applicants. Many of the tests are slanted toward the white culture. Affirmative action guards against this bias.

Martin Luther King Jr., who fought and died for equal rights for all, frequently quoted Amos 5:24: "But let justice roll on like a river, righteousness like a never-failing stream!" By giving minorities preference, we will help the waters of justice flow through and heal our land.

NO, minorities should not be given preference in college scholarships, jobs, housing and other areas.

"What do you mean you didn't get accepted at Harvard?"

"That's what the letter says, Mom."

"But you were in the top 5 percent of your class!"

"I know. And even more strange, Randy was accepted!"

"What? Why, he wasn't anywhere near you in class standing."

"I know, he just barely made it into the upper third of the class. But he's got something I don't."

"You mean his black skin?"

"Yeah. How can you beat that? It just doesn't seem right, Mom. Blacks are moving into more of our neighborhoods; they're getting special treatment at schools; and the government is making companies hire them before more qualified whites. What's a white person to do?"

Blacks and other minority members should have to compete for scholarships and job openings like everyone else and win them on merit, not the color of their skin. Affirmative action has rightly been called by some "reverse discrimination." And it's just as wrong as any other form of racial discrimination.

Blacks and other minorities have suffered greatly from discrimination over the centuries, but so have many other groups such as the Irish, Jews, Italians and Eastern Europeans. Each group was ridiculed and excluded because they were different. This is a part of the darker side of our history. But each group, through hard work and tremendous sacrifice and courage, has found acceptance in our society.

Although the skin color of blacks singles them out and makes their acceptance more difficult, in time acceptance will come. Many have achieved greatness in every field of endeavor and have become accepted.

Quotas and affirmative action programs demean blacks and create smoldering resentment from rejected whites. These programs say that now a person will be hired not because he or she is competent, but simply because he or she is a member of a minority. This is especially galling when two people are interviewed and the white has far more experience and training. The employer has to say to the white, "Sorry, we have to hire this other person, even though you scored higher on the tests." No wonder a number of whites have filed suits to overturn such a practice.

Many police departments, fire departments and other government agencies have had a difficult time finding minority members whose scores are high enough to be hired. In some instances the quality of recruits has declined because such a large number of people, who once would have been unacceptable, were hired. A large number of white applicants with excellent credentials were turned down and may never become a policeman or fireman.

Discrimination of any kind is wrong, even when it is done to correct a centuries-old wrong. There must be other ways to redress the mistakes of the past. Preferential treatment of minorities is not one of them.

Programming Ideas for Issue 35

Preparation—Go to your local library or school resource center and secure a recording of Martin Luther King Jr.'s *I Have a Dream* speech. Also check out picture histories of the civil rights movement or of Martin Luther King Jr.'s life. Lay the picture histories around the meeting room so that early arrivers can leaf through them.

Type the following scripture references on separate 3×5 cards: Luke 10:25-37; Acts 10:34; 1 Corinthians 13; Galatians 3:27-28; Ephesians 2:14-18; 1 John 4:7-21. Make three to five copies of each scripture—enough so each participant has one card. Gather several Bibles.

Set up a table for poster making. Supply poster paints, brushes, pencils and white sheets of posterboard.

Prepare copies of Chart 34.

Opening—Play a portion of Martin Luther King Jr.'s *I Have a Dream* speech and talk about the picture histories. Say: "Everyone needs a dream, especially those who are oppressed. But one person's dream can become another person's nightmare. At least that's what some whites feel about affirmative action programs. Who knows what affirmative action is?''

If nobody knows, explain that affirmative action programs try to redress or "make up for" years of racial biases.

Program—Divide into groups by counting off in twos. One group represents blacks and other minorities; the other group represents whites. The groups are to meet separately for about 15 minutes and think of reasons for supporting or opposing affirmative action. Distribute copies of Chart 34. Encourage the kids to discuss these questions from their group's perspective.

Ask the groups to go to the table with the poster-making materials. Have the young people make posters to express their position. For example, a student could paint a poster showing two different-colored hands reaching toward each

---

Chart 34
Affirmative Action

1. Does the long history of blacks in America handicap them in our competitive society? Explain.

2. Does a white society owe blacks and other minorities a big debt? Why or why not?

3. Is affirmative action a good way to pay such a debt? Explain.

4. What can be said about the past wrongs committed by society against blacks and other minorities?

5. Do these wrongs justify denying whites their rights (as some people say affirmative action programs do)? Why or why not?

6. Can you fight discrimination by discriminating against those who are supposedly better off? Explain.

other. At the top of the poster is a heart with a cross on it, and the words "Love one another."

After 15 minutes, call the two groups together and have them share their arguments, statements and posters. Display the posters in the meeting room.

Say, "Scriptures don't deal with such a modern issue as affirmative action, but they do deal with the basics of our relationships with others." Randomly distribute the scripture cards. Ask the young people to call out their passage and find those who have the same card. Once kids find their partners, distribute Bibles. Ask them to read the scripture and discuss how it applies to our relationship with people of all races.

Call the groups together and have them share their scriptures. Say: "These passages may not settle for us the issue of affirmative action, but what do they tell us about racial prejudice? How should we treat people—no matter what color their skin?"

Response—Suggest that Christians must be sensitive to all individuals' concerns and viewpoints—even if we differ strongly. We can do this because of Christ's reconciling work. And we must especially work for the establishment of justice through Christ's love.

Gather students in a circle. Have them place their arms on one another's shoulders. Close with a prayer such as the following:

"Dear God, you have given all peoples and nations one beautiful planet on which to dwell. Yet we have not treated it or each other well. Forgive us for accepting old prejudices and stereotypes of other peoples. By your Spirit, help us to walk a mile in the shoes of a brother or sister of another race, that we might gain a better understanding of another's experience. This we ask in Jesus' name. Amen."

Options:

1. Complete a community survey. Obtain census figures or demographic facts from local organizations such as the chamber of commerce, a social welfare agency or church

denominational office. What are the percentages of minorities in your community? Where do they live? work? go to school? How would you describe their status or acceptance in your community? Are minorities confined to certain areas (often called "ghettos" in large cities)? Do you find many of them in the professions and service industries of your community? Are any of them your friends? Explain. In what areas is there still need for progress?

2. If there is an NAACP chapter or other such group in your area, check with them to see if a member could speak to your church on this topic. If your youth group is predominantly white, plan a joint meeting with a black youth group. If your youth group is predominantly black or other minority, plan a joint meeting with a white youth group.

3. Martin Luther King Jr.'s Birthday, observed on the third Monday in January, is a national holiday, the first to so honor a black. Celebrate this holiday by organizing an event titled "Is the Dream Still Alive?" or "What Does His Dream Mean Today?"

ISSUE 36
Do smokers have the right to smoke wherever they please?

YES, smokers have the right to smoke wherever they please.

"Hi, Conrad, welcome to the Black Hole of Calcutta."

"Hello, Sybil. Whew! They've certainly put us in a dingy place for smoke breaks!"

"I'll say. I sure miss the days when I could light up at my desk. It just doesn't seem fair. Just because a few people don't like our smoking!"

"No, it isn't fair. Why, the other day in a restaurant I took out a cigarette to light up, and several people gave me the dirtiest look. One even asked me to put the cigarettes away, claiming that it was a non-smoking section."

"Something like that happened to me coming up in the elevator yesterday. I tell you, these non-smokers are becoming real tyrants. I wish they'd just leave me alone. I don't try to get them to smoke. They should learn to live and let live!"

"Maybe we should start our own organization, something like 'Citizens for the Preservation of the Freedom to Smoke.' We could head up petitions and print bumper stickers and buttons and all."

"Not a bad idea. Somebody needs to stand up for our freedom. Count me in if you go ahead."

An American's right to smoke should be protected. Some concessions must be made for safety's sake—for example, no smoking in auditoriums, around gasoline pumps and while an airplane is taking off and landing. But restrictions should be as few as possible to avoid interfering with individuals' rights.

Our country is supposed to be the "land of the free, the home of the brave," and yet everywhere we look we see examples of our rights eroding. There are so many restrictions on property and houses that owners have to get a permit for almost anything they wish to do—remodel, build, rewire the house, etc. Homeowners can't even rent or refuse to rent to just anyone. And gun owners must fight against those who want to take away their right to own and carry guns. In every area of life government intrudes with its restrictions and rules.

The attempt to limit or ban smoking is one more example, perhaps all the more galling since smoking is a personal choice. People who smoke find great pleasure and relief by lighting up during a break or during a stressful work period. Part of the fun of dining out is being able to enjoy a cigarette right after a good meal. It isn't right to deny this pleasure because a few people don't like cigarette smoke.

It might be true that tobacco is harmful to health, but so are a lot of other things—like overeating and excessive drinking. "To smoke or not to smoke" is a choice each person should have. People should not be forced into a decision against smoking. If a person wants to smoke, it's his or her life, not someone else's that's at stake.

If people want to take a chance on the questionable odds of contracting cancer because they enjoy smoking so much, they should be able to do so. It's still a free country. Let's keep it that way!

NO, smokers do not have the right to smoke wherever they please.

"I saw you leave the meeting early last night, Roger."

"Yeah, I got to feeling a bit sick from the cigarette smoke. I moved twice, but both times someone around me lit up a cigarette, and the smoke drifted my way."

"Why is it that the smokers' pollution almost always drifts away from them and into the non-smoking area?"

"I don't know, but it seems to work that way. Anyway, I couldn't take it any more, so I left."

"I almost did, but I managed to stay. I'm not allergic to smoke as you are, but it still bothers me a lot. I'm so tired of having to put up with the smoke at meetings or in restaurants."

"Yeah, me too. That's why my wife didn't come last night, even though she wanted to. She knew the smokers would be too much for her."

"Well, maybe someday our turn will come. It just doesn't seem fair that a few inconsiderate people should be able to stink up the air for the rest of us! I don't throw my garbage onto their lawn; they shouldn't mess up my air!"

If people want to indulge in this offensive and un-healthy vice, they should do it at home, in their cars or outdoors. Smoking should be banned in most every other place.

Smokers seldom realize how offensive the clouds of smoke are to the non-smoker. Millions of people suffer through meetings because clouds of smoke invade the non-smokers' space. Fine meals have been ruined at restaurants because non-smoking diners had to breathe tobacco smoke. Non-smokers endured such indignities for years in silence, but they are no longer willing to do so.

This issue is far more than one of courtesy and comfort, it is also one of health. The old argument that "it's *my* body" is no longer true. Growing scientific evidence points to the fact that residual smoke, the smoke that others breathe in from a smoker, is as dangerous, and maybe even more so, than the smoke which the smoker inhales from his or her cigarette. Thus the health of family members at home, fellow workers at the office, and strangers in a restaurant or other public place is also at stake whenever smokers light up. Smoking is not just a private affair.

The public has a right to protect itself. A ban on smoking—this should include a ban on all forms of cigarette advertising and giveaway programs also—is a good step in the right direction. Educational campaigns are useful for protecting the young from those who would trade on their health for profit, but they convince very few smokers to give up. Indeed, some smokers have grown hostile to any attempt to suggest that their vice is harmful and thus should be curbed. Therefore, it's necessary to add the force of law to that of peer pressure and educational campaigns to curb the harmful effects of smoking—upon the innocent as well as the guilty.

In 1 Corinthians 6:9-20, Paul says that our bodies are meant for the Lord, that the body "is a temple of the Holy Spirit who is in you . . . " He warns, " . . . You are not your own; you were bought at a price. Therefore honor God with your body."

It's impossible to argue that a practice which threatens the health of both smokers and those around them can be a way of "honoring God with your body."

Programming Ideas for Issue 36

Preparation—Contact your local county health office, the American Cancer Society or other health agency and ask for posters or display items on smoking. Pick up the material and display it in your meeting room.

Have a student check with the pastor to find out your denomination's stance on tobacco and smoking.

Gather several Bibles, pencils and copies of Chart 35. You'll also need one chair for each person.

Opening—Welcome the kids, then have them sit on a chair in a circle. Instruct them in the following Pile-Up-On-People's-Lap game. Say that when you make a statement, they will either move to the right or to the left according to their answer. They must sit on the chair no matter how many others are sitting there. Here are some statements:

1. If you have a close friend who smokes, move three chairs to the right.

2. If your mom or dad smokes, move two chairs to the left.

3. If you think people have a right to smoke wherever they please, move five chairs to the left.

4. If you think all public smoking should be banned, move one chair to the right.

5. "It's my body and my life, and I'll do as I please with it. No one can tell me what to do." If you agree with this statement, move four chairs to the right.

6. If you disagree with the statement in No. 5, move three chairs to the left.

Program—Unscramble yourselves from the game, then say, "This session's topic will explore the relation between smoking, our health and our faith."

Take a poll of how many kids think smokers should be able to smoke wherever they wish. Those who agree give a thumbs-up sign; those who disagree give a thumbs-down sign. Divide into two groups according to their viewpoints. Have the groups think of reasons to support their stance. (If almost all your kids oppose smoking, stay as one group. Try to get them to think of some reasons smokers would list.)

After five minutes, gather as a large group. Distribute pencils and copies of Chart 35. Have kids from both sides of the issue share their reasons. Encourage students to write the ideas in the appropriate space on the handout. Which reasons are self-centered or self-indulgent? Mark an "O" by these. Which seem based on a concern for other people?

Mark an "X" by these.

Pass out Bibles and have the young people reflect upon the following passages: 1 Corinthians 3:16-18; 6:9-20. What does Paul mean when he says that he would not be enslaved by anything? What does he mean when he says that we are not our own; we are bought with a price?

Give kids five minutes to look at the health display in the room. Then ask: "Is it only the smoker's own lungs that cigarette smoking harms? What evidence do you see in the display (or have heard about) that tobacco smoke is harmful to those around the smoker as well? Are smokers responsible for others' health and comfort? Why or why not?"

Ask the young person to report on your denomination's stand on this issue. (Some churches react against dancing, card playing and movie attendance, as well as smoking. Some clergy themselves smoke. Discuss this.)

Response—Say: "Whether or not you smoke, the issue confronts you, and will for a long time. May your response to it be based on a Christ-centered concern for the welfare of others. Remember not to be judgmental to those who smoke or to those who don't smoke. Our God is a forgiving God. We should be the same."

Offer a prayer:

"Lord, you made all things, but we know that not everything is good for us or for our neighbor. Help us to be considerate of each other. Increase our knowledge and understanding of what it means for our bodies to be temples of your Holy Spirit. Give us an increased sense of responsibility toward our bodies, and those of our neighbor. We ask this in Jesus' name. Amen."

Options:

1. Invite a medical expert, perhaps someone from the local cancer or lung society, to come and speak on the topic.

2. Invite a person who smokes to come and talk to the group. How did he or she start smoking? Does he or she

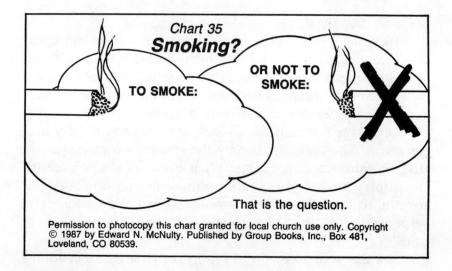

Chart 35
Smoking?

TO SMOKE:

OR NOT TO SMOKE:

That is the question.

want to quit? Why or why not? How does the person feel about the anti-smoking feelings of so many people? Has the person experienced rude non-smokers in restaurants and other public places? If so, how do they handle these situations?

3. Contact a local health office or cancer society and obtain a film on smoking and health. Show it to your group and discuss its message.

4. Send group members to the library to find more articles on this timely topic. Have them share their findings. How widespread is smoking at your school? Why do many of your peers take up smoking? Are the educational efforts on television and at school very effective? Why or why not? Do efforts to prohibit smoking work very well? Explain. Should efforts be made to create a "smokeless" society? Where do members in your own church smoke? Should areas in your church be designated "non-smoking"?

LEISURE ISSUES

C hristians of the so-called First, or developed, World are among the most privileged human beings to have lived, for we have the gift of leisure. In the past, only a few people in each society were free from endless drudgery. This is still true for the majority of the world's population. To achieve even meager earnings, most of the world's people must toil long hours. For some, their very survival demands that they constantly sift through the refuse dumps of the affluent.

In each civilization that came before ours, the rich and powerful were the people who enjoyed leisure time. This luxury was usually attained strictly through heredity, so masses of people were bound to the soil or the desires of their masters. No wonder festivals were so popular. The Hebrews were among the first people to establish a break in the work routine with the Sabbath. The Fourth Commandment was literally a God-sent break, not only for human beings, but for the beasts of burden as well. Society hasn't always honored this commandment. Some businesses often forced men, women and children of the lower classes to work in wretched factories and mines as late as the early 1900s.

Only after food production became somewhat stable did leisure arise for even a few. With this free time, people began to study the world, accumulate knowledge and develop the arts. In fact, the word scholar comes from the Latin word meaning leisure. Today Americans are blessed with an abundance of leisure, and leisure industries continue to develop. Besides the entertainment industries of film, radio, television, music, amusement parks and game manufacturers, the sports industries have expanded and even lobbied for more leisure time.

Like all our endeavors, leisure presents its own problems. How much leisure should Christians enjoy? Do we abuse our leisure? How can we balance our leisure concerns with our service to God? Are some forms of leisure so corrupting that Christian young people should not indulge in them? Such issues become increasingly important, especially since kids have more money, leisure time and freedom than ever before.

ISSUE 37
Should Christians view R-rated films?

YES, Christians should view R-rated films.

"Hi, Cindy. Can you come to my house tonight? A bunch of us are getting together to watch a movie on our VCR."

"Sounds great, Gloria, but what movie is it?"

"*Ordinary People*. This movie came out a few years ago, but only a few of us got to see it. Those who did, want to see it again."

"Oh, I remember when it came out. I also remember why a lot of us didn't get to see it. It's an R-rated film. I'm sorry, but I won't be able to come."

"But it's not a dirty movie or anything like that, Cindy. It deals with a family who has trouble relating to one another. It's also a sensitive portrayal of how a family deals with death and suicide. There are some swearwords, but you hardly notice them."

"I would. In the first place, my church believes it's wrong to attend such movies. My parents don't approve either. I guess I won't be there. Actually, Gloria, I don't think we should support movies that play up sex and swearing and violence."

"I agree, Cindy, we shouldn't support those kinds of movies. I don't go see the *Rambo* movies or the blood-and-gore horror shows or most of the garbage that Hollywood

aims at us during the summertime. But there are some excellent films like *Ordinary People* that show life as it is.
The sex or swearing in these films isn't put there to tease
us, it's part of the reality of the situation. I'm sorry that
you're missing a chance to see this with those of us who
are concerned about the issue of suicide. Our school counselor recommended it because all of us are still confused
about Jamie's suicide. Think about it, and if you change
your mind, come over about 7 o'clock."

Even though Christians may not appreciate some of the
content, they should see good films, even if they are R-rated.
We live and seek to serve our Lord in an X- and R-rated
world from which we cannot retreat or hide. Although a
large percentage of R-rated films are worthless trash that no
Christian should waste his or her time viewing, some R-rated
films are worth viewing and discussing. Christians should
view such films for the following reasons:
- To keep in touch with what the rest of the country,
especially young people, are viewing and valuing.
- To observe many areas of life we normally know little about.
- To make connections between the world of the
scripture and theology with our modern culture.
- To gain a better understanding of the gospel from
the insights of modern storytellers. (Sensitive film makers
actually create many of today's parables.)
    Like it or not, most young people and adults in or out
of our churches go to the movies. Films like *Rambo* or *Star
Wars* affect a lot of people. Christians ought to know something about these films. Although one *Rambo* film may be
more than many of us want to sit through, we should see it
so we can discuss it with others and point out how the
values of this kind of film conflict with those of our faith.
Christian leaders should also see at least one horror show a
year to better understand what many of their junior high
kids are watching. (Rent a film in videocassette form so as
not to waste too much money!)

On a more positive note, R-rated films take us into places we don't ordinarily go and introduce us to people we would not otherwise meet. We are introduced to the dark, violent world of crime and law enforcement in films such as *The Godfather, Prince of the City, Manhunter, Tightrope, To Live and Die in L.A.* or *Fort Apache: The Bronx.* The costly horror of war is presented in *The Deer Hunter, Apocalypse Now, Platoon* or *Full Metal Jacket. Sophie's Choice* and *Plenty* illustrate the bleakness of life without hope or faith. *Raging Bull, Purple Rain, All That Jazz* and *Soldier's Story* demonstrate the terrible price that various forms of sin exact. These films do not include detestable language, sex scenes and violence to exploit these negative aspects of our society. They include these scenes because they depict the world as it really is, not as we Christians wish it were. Their characters talk and act like real criminals, street people or police, at least as much as is possible in a film made for mass consumption. Of course, not all R-rated films reflect this kind of responsibility to authenticity. Most, like the *Porky's* or *Halloween* series, seek to exploit a sensational theme in order to draw a large audience. But Christians should learn how to tell the difference; they should observe carefully how the film maker treats his or her characters and decide whether the film maker honestly portrays the result of self-centered, manipulative behavior or uses sex, swearing and violence as a technique to enhance sales.

Christian leaders need to help their people make connections between the Bible and modern culture. Some call this process a "dialogue with the world." For example, when we talk in the church about the sin of Adam and Eve, we can gain understanding about that story by watching the film *North Dallas Forty.* Two older football players are being tempted to sell their integrity as a way to stay on the team. One does, amply illustrating Jesus' warning about "gaining the world" but losing our souls. The other athlete holds out; when his buddy tosses him the football, he lets it fall to the ground without attempting to even touch it, a beautiful symbolic moment that concludes the film.

We gain insight about the concept of grace when we see *Out of Africa*. When Karen loses her farm in Kenya, she comes to the reception for the new governor and drops to her knees to beg for protection for the tribespeople who live on her land. She shocks the dignified guests. Karen is not a Christian, but in this moment she illustrates what Christians mean when they talk about grace.

Just as Jesus illustrated his great teachings by telling stories, the modern film maker spins stories that embody important insights into human nature, ethics and relationships, both between people and between individuals and God. In *Saturday Night Fever* Tony realizes that his world, the disco dance hall, is actually a world of illusion. When the crowd and the owner of the club choose Tony and his partner as winners of the big dance contest, he is awakened to the unreal quality of his world. He has just watched his main competition, a Puerto Rican couple, perform, and he knows they are better. He realizes the couple were passed over because of prejudice. Too honest to live with a lie, Tony accepts the trophy, walks over to the couple, gives it to them and walks out of the disco for the last time. This act begins a new chapter in his life. This interesting variation of the prodigal son story is especially poignant in the disco scene when Tony "comes to himself." But in this version there is no loving father; in fact, Tony's parents are part of his problem.

Films can illuminate the great doctrines of the Bible and the church. "The wages of sin is death . . . " (Romans 6:23) takes on new meaning after we see the main character in *All That Jazz* try to use everyone around him, burn the candle at both ends and struggle with a heart attack and death.

The meaning of the cross, or risking your reputation and life for something bigger than yourself, is powerfully displayed in *Silkwood*. This true story of Karen Silkwood, an uninvolved woman of loose morals, finds her taking up the cause of industrial safety when one of her friends, and then herself, become tainted with radioactivity in the nuclear plant where they work. Although this film is not overtly religious it nonetheless opens and closes with the hymn "Amazing Grace." The film maker is obviously suggesting that the relatively short life of this feisty woman was divinely touched.

Films help us understand our faith and the world in which we live as they force us to wrestle with the ambiguities, failings and triumphs of life. For example, Christians always discuss the communion of saints, but Robert Benton actually illustrates the meaning of this celebration in the last scene of his film *Places in the Heart*. As the trays of bread and juice are passed through the small congregation, the viewer is astonished to see several characters who, earlier in the film, have been killed or left town. A lot of people are puzzled by this scene, but Christians who celebrate the communion of saints understand the film maker's point—there are places in the heart, symbolized by the communion service, where we are bound together with all those who have gone before us, as well as with those present or those who will come after us.

Christians should examine a film beneath its surface before judging whether it is good or bad. Many PG-rated films are far more dangerous than R-rated films if they teach that sex is a cheap thrill and violence is the best way to settle disputes or deal with our enemies. As long as film makers do not use sex, violence or profanity just to titillate the audience, Christians should keep an open mind about the value of films.

NO, Christians should not view R-rated films.

"George, I'm not sure I ever want to go back to that theater again."

"I understand, dear."

"Hi, Mom, Dad. You're back early. Didn't you stay for the whole movie?"

"Certainly not, Judy! I haven't heard that much dirty language since I left my job at the plant. Even your father was upset."

"I sure was. I had enough of that kind of talk when I was in the Navy, and there was no way to get away from it there. But I don't have to put up with it now, even though we did pay $4 apiece!"

"Judy, I thought you said this movie was a comedy."

"It is, Mom. It's supposed to be one of the best of the season. The critics love it."

"Well *we* didn't. You know, your dad and I aren't prudes, Judy, but I felt like we were being rubbed in the dirt, and the longer we sat there, the dirtier I felt. I can put up with a 'hell' or 'damn' occasionally, but listening to people constantly taking the Lord's name in vain really bothers me. I couldn't believe that every other word was another form of profanity. I didn't realize people actually used all those words, especially on the screen."

"I was more concerned about the casual view of sex this movie portrayed. It seemed as though sex was just like an itch that you scratched whenever you wanted to relieve it. A few weeks ago I argued with our pastor when he said we shouldn't attend films anymore, but now I can understand his concern."

Living a Christian life in today's world is difficult enough without subjecting ourselves or our children to the garbage that comes out of Hollywood under the guise of entertainment. Christians shouldn't expose themselves to films that contain so much foul language, cheap sex and gruesome violence.

Hollywood has long been known for the disgusting lifestyles of many who work in the motion picture industry. Some stars go through husbands or wives one right after the other. Parties become wild with liquor and drugs. Women trade their bodies to their producers or directors as payment for a part in a picture. People live rich, pretentious lives, totally absorbed in the deal for their next picture. It is difficult to find anything good that comes out of this corrupt and hedonistic environment. For example, *Fort*

Apache: The Bronx is supposedly a good show, but when the hero goes to bed with the girl he's attracted to as if this behavior were perfectly acceptable, Christians have to be concerned. The characters' language is even more unaccept- able. Some films seem to go out of their way to profane the Lord's name. The crude Anglo-Saxon terms for sexual inter- course and excrement are bad enough, but taking the Lord's name in vain so many times is especially upsetting to Christians. It's time Hollywood writers and producers began to realize how offensive their products have become. Two good ways Christians can protest these products include staying away from the theaters and writing to the Holly- wood studios to let them know how offended we are.

The world of Hollywood films is totally secular. God is mentioned only in curses, and his presence is rarely recog- nized except when characters are in trouble and need help. People live, eat, make love and work as if God didn't exist. Rarely does a film portray a family saying grace before a meal or going to church on Sunday even though millions of American families do so regularly. When the characters face difficult moral choices, they rarely pray for guidance or mention their faith or Christian values as motivating factors. In short, the examples our young people see in today's movies are primarily godless individuals.

Hollywood films portray sex as simply an appetite you appease, much like taking a drink of water when you are thirsty. In the popular film *Saturday Night Fever*, Tony's friends climb into the back seat of a car and couple with girls like animals. When the guys are through using them, they push the girls aside until they want them again.

In film after film the hero and the heroine go to bed together with seemingly no question about whether the act is right or not. Love is equated with lust, sometimes justi- fied by an "I love you" from one of the parties involved. Boys meet girls and almost immediately climb into bed. Modern films and novels make virginity look like a ridicu- lous state a person has to apologize for.

It's little wonder so many teenagers get into trouble.

The irresponsible behavior portrayed by their favorite Hollywood stars makes kids believe love justifies anything they want to do with their bodies. These young and immature people enter into marriage relationships built solely on feelings and wonder why their feelings don't remain intense like they do in the movies. When disputes occur, which is inevitable when two people live together, the couple begin to think they are "falling out of love." Rather than work at their relationship to arrive at a more mature understanding of themselves, they head for an affair or the divorce courts. Hollywood has sold these young people a big lie about love relationships and has produced a large number of twisted and hurt young lives.

Hollywood films also glorify violence. The Sylvester Stallone series of *Rocky* and *Rambo* depict in full color and slow motion muscular men pummeling, slashing, stabbing, shooting and burning each other in scene after scene. Even the critically praised film *My Bodyguard* seemed at first to suggest there are better ways to stand up to bullies than beating them up, but in the end our two young "heroes" seem to enjoy smashing the bad kids' noses. In the first *Dirty Harry* film, the film maker manipulates the feelings of the audience. He makes the villain so slimy that everyone actually cheers when Clint Eastwood stomps him to death. Our young people need not be exposed to such anti-Christian trash.

Even worse are the horror films many kids love to watch. Many theaters now have "fright nights" or "midnight madness" on weekends, where they feature some of the worst pictures of the past few years. In these productions monsters or sick human beings slash and gash their victims. Evil vampires suck people's blood. Witches cast their spells over their helpless targets so that no mere mortal can stand against them. These irresponsible works glorify the powers of darkness and portray them as victorious in their struggles for people and their souls. Such movies stimulate fear and superstition in young minds. As a society we need to heed James' words, " . . . Resist the devil, and he will flee from you" (James 4:7).

In view of all the filth and immorality presented in R-rated movies, Christians should boycott these films. When a large segment of the public refuses to buy tickets or rent these movies, Hollywood's corrupt industry may realize it has gone too far. Besides attending only G- or PG-rated films, Christians have the alternative to rent one of the Christian films that are available. Many churches provide this alternative for their membership because these films are not only clean, but they deal specifically with Christian concerns like witnessing, missions and family relationships. They portray families who actually pray at mealtime and sincere individuals who witness to their friends about God's saving love in Christ. These films offer exciting stories and adventures and support the Christian film makers.

Programming Ideas for Issue 37

Preparation—Cut out the movie sections from several different newspapers. Gather newsprint, tape and three different-colored markers. Tape two or three sheets of newsprint to the wall at the front of the room. Decorate the room with movie posters. Ask to borrow some from your young people or talk with your local theaters.

Rent the videocassettes of *Ferris Bueller's Day Off* and *All That Jazz*. If you don't want to use *Ferris Bueller's Day Off*, substitute *The In-Laws*, a popular film that values deceit and self-centeredness. Contrast with *All That Jazz*, or use *Salvador* or *Silkwood* instead. Preview the films ahead of time and select the scenes you wish to use. Set up your VCR and monitors before your meeting and have your videos ready to use.

Bring your back issues of GROUP Magazine to the meeting.

Prepare a media display. Include a video camera, a reel, a copy of a play or skit, a VCR cartridge and a Bible.

Opening—Ask for a show of hands of who has gone to the movies recently. Ask: "How many go more than once a week? weekly? twice a month? never? How many watch movies on television or cable? How many have a VCR for watching films?" Spend 10 or 15 minutes having the group list all the films they have seen, while a volunteer writes them on a sheet of newsprint. Ask the group these questions:

● "Which movies had a lot of bad language?" Put a red "L" next to each film mentioned.

● "Which movies contained excessive violence?" Put a green "V" next to the titles.

● "Which films presented lots of nudity or sex scenes?" Use a blue "N" to indicate nudity and a purple "S" for sex scenes.

Now ask the kids to look over the film list again. Ask them:

● "Which films promote unchristian values or false relationships and are obviously trash?" Think about those that portray people using each other or engaging in promiscuous sex with no consequences from their sin. Many movies glorify violence or picture deceit as cute. In some productions, the humor and language deal mainly with sex or body wastes. Draw a line through these movies on that list.

● "Which films say something important about life or relationships and seem worthwhile?" These films may show that violence affects the perpetrator as well as the victim, like in *Full Metal Jacket*. Others indicate that "free sex" has a high price tag in damaged lives or that there is hope in this dark and dangerous world when people respond to each other in loving ways rather than in manipulative ones. Circle these films on the newsprint.

Transfer the circled titles to another sheet of newsprint along with the markings with each title. Ask the group to examine this reduced list. Ask: "How many titles have one or more letters beside them? What does this mean?" Give the group time to think. If there is no response after three minutes, ask: "Does this suggest you can't always tell a good movie from a bad one by the language or the amount of skin exposed? Which is important—the attitudes and beliefs of the film maker or the amount of bad language and

sex used in the film?" Ask the kids to support their answers
with reasons.

Program—Gather the kids around the TV monitor(s).
Tell them: "We are going to watch scenes from two movies, *Ferris Bueller's Day Off* and *All That Jazz*. One film is
R-rated and the other is PG-rated. See if you can determine
why these movies are rated this way."

Show one of the scenes in which Ferris lies to his parents or to school authorities. Then show a scene from *All
That Jazz*. Ask group members: "Can you determine which
film is R-rated and which PG-rated? Which film seems less
moral? Why?"

Tell the kids: "Critics praised the Ferris Bueller film because the hero was cute and fun-loving. A closer examination
of this film, however, reveals its primary message—deceit
and lying are okay; in fact, they're cute if you get away
with this kind of behavior." Ask the group: "Is this true in
real life? What if Ferris were one of your friends? How
would your group react to his constant lying and manipulation of people?

"Many viewers are shocked and disgusted by many of
the scenes in *All That Jazz*. In this movie the main character tries to indulge in a life of booze and free sex, but he
eventually has to pay the consequences. The strange, erotic
dance scene that shocks so many viewers is actually a warning. When the dancers finish their performance, the film
maker uses an eerie light to make their faces resemble death
masks and symbolize his message that the wages of sin is
death.

"Contrast the difference in these two messages. Do the
ratings make sense? Why or why not?"

Response—Pass out back issues of GROUP Magazine
to each person in the group. Ask individuals to look for
"MediaWatch" in the contents. Have a group member list
the movies suggested in different issues. Come to a consen-
sus on a film your group would like to watch and discuss in
its entirety. Set a date and time different from your regular
meeting time. (If everyone has seen the suggested movies,

decide on a more recent film and use the Generic Film Discussion Guide found in the Options section.) *Always* preview a film before showing it to any group. You don't want to be surprised with any content.

Be sensitive to the fact that younger teenagers probably are not ready for a film like *All That Jazz*, but the more mature kids in your group can handle a challenging discussion. Mixed groups can explore the other, less explosive subjects like integrity in *North Dallas Forty* or standing up against evil in *On the Waterfront*.

Inform parents and other church staff about the plans for your group. Some parents won't care what you show their sons and daughters. Some will allow their children to see strong material if you explain what you will be doing. Others won't want their children to see a controversial film no matter how carefully you explain the program. As youth leader, respect each parent's decision. If a young person skips a controversial meeting, affirm the maturity of those who came and educate them about positively accepting others' decisions. Never allow derogatory remarks about absent members. Affirm kids' right to make their own decisions.

Acknowledge the video display you set up ahead of time. Say: "Through the magic of photography and intricate machinery, we can capture the motion, color and drama of the world around us. But the human mind and soul have a choice—they can combine these developments into a work of art that helps us understand our world a little better, or they can produce just another piece of junk. As viewers, we can influence this decision by our critical responses to the films produced in our culture."

Close with the following prayer:

"God, Creator of this beautiful and exciting world, thank you for the many opportunities we have to experience life through film. We appreciate the opportunities we have to laugh and cry, become angry or feel good about life and all its challenges. Thank you for the film makers and actors who care deeply about their professions and who work so hard to bring us the best possible form of their art.

Give us eyes that see, ears that hear and minds that are open to your truth. Help us become discerning Christians who can effectively evaluate what we should and should not see and support. Hear our prayers as we present them in the name of the great storyteller, Jesus Christ, our Lord. Amen.''

Options:

1. Do your young people agree that a particular film contains too much offensive language, sex or violence? Plan a letter-writing session. Divide members into teams of two or three people. Tell them to talk about what bothered

---

Chart 36

Generic Film Discussion Guide

1. Describe your favorite scene or one that is especially significant for you. (Go around the circle so everyone has an opportunity to join in this discussion. Remember there are no "right" answers for this question.)

2. What contributed to the effectiveness of the scene you selected—the acting, music, camera or lighting techniques, special effects, sound, dialogue (or lack of it), setting or scenery?

3. Name the main characters. What are they like? How do they view life? How do they relate to other characters? Are they manipulative or competitive, or do they support others in loving ways?

4. Are the characters pictured in a favorable or unfavorable light? What are the results of their mistakes or unethical ways? Where in the film do you see sin and its consequences?

5. Do any of the characters seem to exhibit any form of faith? If so, how is religion portrayed—phony or authentic? hypocritical or helpful? Do the characters regard God as supportive or as a distant, uncaring being?

them in the film, decide on what to include, and compose the letter. After 30 minutes, ask each team to share its thoughts. Criticisms should be specific. Tell the groups to talk about what specifically upsets them and have them word their concerns in a reasonable manner. Send the best letters to the film company. (Theater managers can provide addresses.) Encourage other youth groups to do the same thing. Be sure to write about good films too.

2. One good source for film discussion and study guides is Culture Information Service (write: Box 786, Madison Square Station, New York, NY 10159). Frederic Brussat provides short reviews of almost every film and in-depth

---

6. Are there any "crucifixions," places where characters assume another person's burden or the consequences of another's act in a redeeming or helpful way? Are there moments when good confronts evil and sacrifices itself in order to help other characters?

7. Are there "moments of grace" in the film, incidents when one character gives or receives help in an unexpected way? Are there times when a ray of hope bursts forth in an unexpected, but dramatically logical way, like Han Solo's last-minute rescue of Luke Skywalker at the conclusion of *Star Wars*?

8. What is this film about? Is it just light entertainment or does it offer important insights into the human condition? If it is more than an escape, what insights are offered? How close are they to the teachings of the gospel? Are the situations in the film realistic? If the film deals with the darker side of life (as in *Full Metal Jacket, Prince of the City* and *Blue Velvet*), does it glorify or exploit the theme? Does the film maker show the destructive consequences of a lifestyle or set of values and allow the viewers to draw their own conclusions? Give examples to support your answers.

9. How did you feel at the end of the film? Did you gain any new insights or ideas? Was the film maker warning you about the destructive consequences of a character's values and lifestyle? If the film was a comedy, does its humor build people up or tear them down? Support your answers with examples.

discussion guides for major releases. This Lutheran clergy-man's insights are far more helpful than the reviews in secular magazines like Time and Newsweek.

3. If you can't locate a quality discussion guide for the film your group has chosen, copy Chart 36. With this tool the leader isn't expected to be an expert who dispenses information and theological wisdom, but a facilitator for the group. This guide will help your young people share and discover their own insights.

4. If your youth group would like to watch and discuss some films, suggest they come an hour earlier than usual on the first Sunday evening of each month. Introduce some of the great films of the past like *On the Waterfront, Cool Hand Luke, Citizen Kane, Zorba the Greek* and so on.

5. Films could be divided into four categories. Write Popcorn Features, Poison, Slice of Life and Visual Parables on a sheet of newsprint and tape it up in the front of the room. On another sheet of newsprint, ask the kids to list the films they have seen. Explain the four categories and then have the kids place each film in the proper category.

a. Popcorn Features—Relatively harmless trash you see and soon forget. If you go out for popcorn during the show, you haven't missed much.

Example:

● The summer teenage comedies.

b. Poison—Dangerous trash that peddles sex, sadism, unethical or manipulative lifestyles and foul language.

Examples:

● *Ferris Bueller's Day Off*—lying and using people are okay if you're cute and entertaining.

● *Rambo* series, Clint Eastwood, Chuck Norris and Arnold Schwarzenegger films—violence is not just the best way to deal with enemies, it's the *only* way.

● Teenage summer releases like *Animal House*, or *Porky's*—sex and dirty language indicate someone has grown up.

● Horror and "slash'm and dice'm" features—

sadism from the safety of your theater seat.

c. Slice of Life—The film maker takes you into areas most of us would never experience. Life is often pictured in the raw with the audience expected to draw its own conclusions.

Examples:

- *Platoon*—the horror of what can happen to the "good guys" in the midst of the passions and pressures of war.
- *Prince of the City*—sin as a web of entanglement that destroys both the guilty and the innocent.

d. Visual Parables—films with meaning and a message. Some of the better Christian films (that don't hit the audience with the message, but allow them to struggle to find the answer) would be included in this category.

Examples:

- *The Mission*
- *Salvador*
- *Cool Hand Luke*
- *Zorba the Greek*

ISSUE 38

Can Christians do anything they wish in private?

YES, Christians can do anything they wish in private, as long as it doesn't hurt someone else.

"That was some sermon, wasn't it?"

"Well, the pastor certainly laid into us, if that's what you mean. I think he went a little overboard."

"Overboard? You mean when he denounced so many of today's immoralities?"

"Yeah. There are plenty of negative influences on our lives such as lying, cheating and killing, but he included card playing and viewing movies in the privacy of our own homes."

"Well, the church has to take a stand somewhere. Some of those movies are pretty bad, almost as bad as the dirty magazines."

"I'm not so sure about some of the films he men-

tioned. Some of those are classics. And even if they are
dirty movies, when a person views them in the privacy of
his own home, what's the harm?"

"Plenty, I would think."

"Why? Didn't Jesus say that it's not what goes *into* a
person that makes him evil but what comes out of him? I'd
just hate to see our church turn the gospel into a negative
set of rules with everyone afraid to do something because
it's wicked."

We have just come from an era when churches tried to
control the thoughts and actions of their people. Today we
see people seeking new freedom from the outmoded restraints. Christians are no longer willing to accept the
church's dictates about what they should think or do in the
privacy of their homes. For example, pastors once preached
about the evils of playing cards. While there is still debate
about whether Christians should play for money since it is a
form of gambling, claiming that a friendly game of cards
with one's friends at home is a great sin hardly seems
reasonable. Yet preachers once bellowed from their pulpits
against all forms of card playing. These sermons rarely dis-
couraged card playing; church members merely drew the
blinds as they brought out the cards. If the pastor or a strict
church member came to the door; they hurriedly hid the
cards.

Today such hypocrisy is unnecessary. Many churches
have realized that card playing can be a fun activity for families and friends. Many churches have also relaxed their
stand on drinking and dancing. More and more churches
have recognized the privacy of the home and allowed their
members to make their own decisions about what they do
at home or in other private places like their businesses.

In his letter to the Galatians, Paul writes: "It is for freedom that Christ has set us free. Stand firm, then, and do
not let yourselves be burdened again by a yoke of slavery"
(Galatians 5:1). This passage clearly supports the idea that
individual Christians, as long as they do not harm anyone

else, should be free to do as they please, especially in the privacy of their homes.

NO, Christians are not free to do anything they wish in private.

"Gary, what in the world are you doing with a copy of Hustler magazine?"

"I'm taking it home to read. Look, I'm old enough to vote and I don't have any kids at home, so what difference does it make?"

"I just don't think Christians should be reading that kind of thing."

"Well, I figure I need to release some of my sexual tension somehow, and reading is far better than making out with a prostitute. Besides, as long as I do this in the privacy of my own apartment, who's to know?"

"Well, God for one. Need I take it any further than that?"

What we do in the privacy of our homes does make a difference. Even if no one else should find out, God would know. Reading pornographic magazines, engaging in deviant sex practices, drinking oneself into a stupor or taking drugs can affect an individual and his or her interactions with others even if no one is aware of what that person is doing. Christians should be as responsible in their private lives as they are in their public conduct, for the two can't really be separated.

Paul explains this personal freedom when he says: "You, my brothers, were called to be free. But do not use your freedom to indulge the sinful nature; rather, serve one another in love" (Galatians 5:13). He goes on to say that we should live by the Spirit and not give in to the desires of the sinful nature, since the two are in conflict with each other. He lists the acts of the sinful nature as immorality, hatred, jealousy, drunkenness, selfish ambition and the like while the fruit of the Spirit include love, joy, peace, patience and so on (see Galatians 5:16-25).

From Paul's argument we understand that the conduct of a Christian is like a seamless robe; there can be no division between one's private and public life. If a person turns to self-centered vices in private, these experiences will affect his or her whole person, including his or her public life. John understood this when he quoted Jesus' words: "This is the verdict: Light has come into the world, but men loved darkness instead of light because their deeds were evil. Everyone who does evil hates the light, and will not come into the light for fear that his deeds will be exposed" (John 3:19-20).

Christians should live by the principle that they will do nothing in private that they would be ashamed to admit before their fellow Christians. Long ago the psalmist answered the question of who will ascend to the Lord and stand in his holy temple: "He who has clean hands and a pure heart . . . " (Psalm 24:4).

Programming Ideas for Issue 38

Preparation—Gather newsprint, markers, 3×5 cards, pencils, a basket and Bibles. Tape two sheets of newsprint to the wall at the front of the meeting room. Title one sheet "Appropriate/Inappropriate—Why?" Title the second sheet "Activities Justified by Privacy." On another sheet of newsprint, write the Bible verses and discussion questions found in the Program section. Post this sheet at the front of the room.

Opening—Ask everyone to sit in a circle on the floor. Dim the lights and ask the group members to think about things they like to do when they are alone such as reading a book, taking a walk or fantasizing about what it would be like to walk in space. After a minute ask them to narrow their thoughts to the things they like to do alone but don't tell anyone about (for example, dancing to their favorite music, making silly faces in the mirror, or practicing their acceptance speech as the new president of the United States). Tell the group: "All of us do and think things in our private moments that we don't want to share with others.

Sometimes it's because we're too shy to share a talent or a dream, sometimes we're afraid others will think we're silly or stupid and sometimes we're embarrassed to let anyone know what we're doing or thinking."

Pass a 3×5 card and a pencil to each person in the group and ask him or her to write a statement or draw a picture of something he or she likes to do when alone. Tell the group members not to identify themselves on the cards because you will share the cards with everyone. After five minutes collect the cards in a basket. Share the cards with the total group.

Program—Using the first sheet of newsprint you have posted in the front of the room, tell the group: "List the activities you do that could be classified as appropriate or inappropriate to do alone like getting dressed and undressed, brushing your teeth, talking loudly or playing your stereo. These activities are neither moral nor immoral. Whether or not we indulge in them depends upon our circumstances. List other activities and suggest when these are appropriate and when they aren't." Suggest that some activities touch more on morality. Tell the group: "Some people say it is all right to do certain things alone in the privacy of one's home such as reading pornographic magazines, getting drunk to 'drown one's sorrows' or using drugs to forget everything for a while. List activities that could fit this category. What kinds of things do people justify by saying, 'It's no one's business if I do this alone,' or, 'I'm not bothering anyone else'?" Write these activities on the second sheet of newsprint you have prepared at the front of the room.

Divide into groups of four or five and have each group select one activity from the second sheet of newsprint. Tell each group to talk about this activity—how it might affect the individual, how it might affect his or her relationships with others, or how it might create a bad habit that would affect others.

Assign the following scripture passages and questions to the different groups:

● 1 Samuel 16:7: " . . . The Lord does not look at the things man looks at. Man looks at the outward appearance, but the Lord looks at the heart." How does this scripture apply to doing things in private?

● Matthew 6:4, " . . . Your Father, who sees what is done in secret, will reward you." Do you want to hide certain activities from your earthly father? your Heavenly Father? Explain.

● Matthew 18:20, "For where two or three come together in my name, there am I with them." Is God present only when we are with other people? Is God present only when we are alone? Explain.

● John 3:19-21: "Light has come into the world, but men loved darkness instead of light because their deeds were evil. Everyone who does evil hates the light, and will not come into the light for fear that his deeds will be exposed. But whoever lives by the truth comes into the light, so that it may be seen plainly that what he has done has been done through God." What do these verses tell us about secrecy? How do these verses apply to other areas of our life?

After the small groups read the verses and discuss the questions, share responses with the total group.

Response—Form a circle and ask the group to read Psalm 138:1-8 responsively. Those on one side of the circle would read even-numbered verses, and the other side would read the odd-numbered ones. Encourage the group to think in silence about the psalmist's intimate view of God and whether anything we have talked about or anything we might do in private would threaten that close relationship with him.

After a few moments suggest that everyone pray silently that God will help each person with his or her personal struggles and temptations. Ask everyone to sing the Lord's Prayer together, and close by praying the following prayer:

"Lord, our God, from whom no secrets are hid, we thank you that you are merciful and loving. As our Creator, you know us as we really are—no smiles or sweet words can mask our true selves from you. Yet within the Bible, you declare a love for us that never ends, never gives up, and accepts us even though we disappoint you over and over again. May the healing power of Jesus' cross continue to work within our lives, reaching into those secret places to transform each of us into the image of your Son. We pray this in his holy name, Amen."

Option:

1. Offer your young people a chance to see how their private lives can affect their public lives. Suggest that each individual give a part of his or her private life as a gift to God. Ask each person to think about a private act he or she might want to change, a personal goal he or she might want to accomplish or a thought he or she might want to develop. For example, a shy person may want to become more outgoing, or a teenager may want to schedule a daily devotion time.

Pass out paper and pencils to individuals and have them write letters to God about what they would like to do. After individuals have finished their letters, hand out a long envelope to each person. Ask individuals to insert their letters in the envelopes and write their names and addresses on the front of the envelopes.

Encourage your young people to work on their gifts to God during the next month. Ask the young people to keep track of their daily growth, the steps ahead and the steps backward. At the end of the month, send the envelopes to the kids as a reminder of their gifts to God. When they receive their envelopes have them evaluate their progress. Have they accomplished their goals?

ISSUE 39

Should Christians place a high priority on their health and physical appearance?

YES, Christians should place a high priority on their health and physical appearance.

"Hey Trev, why don't you join us tomorrow afternoon

after school for some jogging. We're meeting at the church.''

"You can't get me to your worship service, so now you're going to try jogging. You're certainly persistent, Jack. I have to hand it to you.''

"Trev, this isn't a plot to get you in the church. We really do have a jogging group that uses the church grounds and the parking lot. It's safer and more pleasant than running along the roads. You've been complaining about being short-winded; it won't take long before you feel better and look better, too.''

"Maybe you're right, Jack. I have let myself go lately. I've been so busy at school and my job, I haven't exercised much.''

"Okay, meet us in the church parking lot at 4 tomorrow afternoon. After our run we'll work out on some of the equipment in the church gym.''

"Your church has a gym and exercise equipment?''

"Sure, why not? We believe God created our bodies and wants us to take good care of them. At our church we have a sanctuary and chapel for the soul, a library and classrooms for the mind, and a gym and equipment for the body.''

Christians should be concerned about their health. Strength and energy are necessary to do God's work. Without healthy bodies, Christians would have difficulty fulfilling their calling and might become a burden to others as well.

Although some people overdo it, the current emphasis on physical fitness can be beneficial. People are improving their health through jogging, aerobics and weight-loss programs. They are educating themselves about nutrition, eliminating fatty foods that produce a high cholesterol level and refusing foods with chemical additives. They are learning how to reduce stress. As individuals develop trim, firm bodies, they feel better about themselves, their work and their families.

More facts have surfaced to concern the public about smoking and its health risks. Although the tobacco industry has seduced many of our young people into smoking, more and more adults are eliminating their habit. Today there are far more non-smokers than smokers, and many vocalize their concerns about the harmful effects of secondary smoke. Some encourage more stringent laws aimed at those who continue to pollute the air in public places or their work space.

Those who drink are becoming concerned about the effects of alcohol. Beer companies have responded to this concern by promoting "light beers" with fewer calories and less alcohol. It's possible that one day the "beer belly" may be a thing of the past.

Virtually every town offers fitness classes in health clubs, YMCAs or YWCAs. Many churches offer aerobic classes. Recognizing this trend, record companies have responded by releasing aerobic albums featuring contemporary Christian music.

All this concern about physical fitness is leading to a healthier, happier population. Christians who believe the body is a temple of the Holy Spirit should rejoice and join the current health trend. Parents who place a high priority on their own health and the health of their families will pass on this concern to their children. Thus, the next generation will continue this trend toward health.

Jesus commands us to love ourselves (Matthew 19:19). Therefore, Christians should be concerned about diet and exercise as well as their spiritual lives.

NO, Christians should not place a high priority on their health and physical appearance.

"You're getting the cottage cheese salad again? Are you on another one of your diets?"

"Yes, I have to watch what I eat. There's no use spending a lot of time working out if I don't watch my diet."

"Sharon, you look fine. I really mean it."

"Well thanks, Tina, but I know better. I saw myself in the mirror after our showers in gym class."

"You sure worry a lot about how you look. I thought Christians weren't supposed to be concerned about those kinds of things."

"Tina, God wants us to take care of our bodies. My church even has an aerobics class that is really popular with our members."

"But don't you think you're overdoing it a bit? Jesus didn't seem to worry much about such things. He specifically told his disciples not to be anxious about what they ate or drank or what they wore. I think his advice would extend to how fit they were, too."

Christians shouldn't be obsessed about their health. They should take normal precautions by avoiding harmful foods and substances, eating a wholesome diet and getting enough exercise and sleep. But they shouldn't join in the popular trend of buying expensive exercise clothes and equipment, joining health clubs and spending hours each day in elaborate exercise and dieting programs.

Many people have joined the health craze in an attempt to forestall old age and death. Some have a fixation on youth, good looks and sophisticated clothing. There is something narcissistic about so much emphasis on the body. The huge amount of time, energy and money that people spend on health clubs, diet programs, vitamins, cosmetics, workout clothing and equipment could be used in a more constructive way to improve the mind and spirit or to serve as a volunteer in church or community projects. Our society has a lot of beautiful, empty bodies, walking around trying to attract the attention of other beautiful, empty bodies, but inside there's very little soul or intellect to round out the personality. These healthy bodies have little sense of value or awareness of anything beyond the material or the what's-in-it-for-me attitude.

Although Jesus doesn't specifically deal with this issue, his advice about being overly concerned with ourselves definitely applies: "Therefore I tell you, do not worry about your life, what you will eat or drink; or about your body, what you will wear . . . " (Matthew 6:25). Jesus doesn't want his followers to be anxious about external concerns, in this case food and clothing. This same principle would apply to individuals' overconcern for the health of their physical bodies.

Few want to return to the medieval or Puritan practice of putting down the body and its needs. Such hatred of the flesh led people to punish their God-given bodies in ways that did not honor their Creator. But today's society has overemphasized the physical to the point it actually worships the body. Posters of half-nude men and women, crowded health spas, body-building centers, large numbers of diet and health books, tanning parlors plus the influx of new and increasingly expensive health gadgets and specialized clothing reflect the unhealthy concern people have with their physical appearance. The Preacher who wrote Ecclesiastes would no doubt sum up all of this emphasis on the body with his terse remark, "Vanity of vanities . . . all is vanity" (Ecclesiastes 1:2).

Programming Ideas for Issue 39

Preparation—The week before this session ask the kids to bring some of their posters or calendars of good-looking guys and gals. Tape the posters on the meeting room wall. Ask the kids to bring their magazines that offer health tips, ads and articles on aerobics, cosmetics and exercise equipment. Borrow or purchase at least five more magazines in case individuals forget. Some may have an aerobic record or even a workout videotape. Ask the kids to bring these items to share. Set up a record player, a tape player and a VCR with a monitor. Prepare a table at the front of the room for the items the kids will bring. Decorate the table with small pieces of exercise equipment such as leg and wrist weights, lightweight barbells, jogging shoes and a stopwatch.

Gather paper, pencils, markers, stamped envelopes and

Bibles for everyone. Purchase a box of Kodak's Ektagraphic Write-On slides from an educational supply store or a special photography shop. If you can't find these slides, bring one sheet of typing paper for each person.

Opening—Play a workout tape or an aerobic record as the group arrives. Begin this session by asking the kids: "Which picture do you like best? What makes these people attractive? What famous person would you like to look like if you could trade looks with anyone? Why? Do you think these individuals spend a lot of time and money on their looks and health? What makes you think the way you do?"

Presentation—Pass out paper and pencils. Ask each person to draw a picture of himself or herself. Remind the group members you know they are not artists, but you would like them to be as honest as possible as to what they think they look like. Let them know that no one will see this paper besides themselves.

After 10 minutes, have the group members each turn their paper over. On the back of their picture, ask them to make three columns. Have them write one of these three headings at the top of each column: Features I'm happy about, Features I'm unhappy with and Features I can work on. Take 10 minutes for kids to examine their drawings and make their lists under the first two headings. Spend the next five minutes working on the third heading. Tell the kids to list specific actions they could take to make the changes they desire. This list might include prayer, seeking help from a friend or a doctor, dieting, special exercises, giving up certain foods or harmful practices, joining a YMCA, YWCA or other type of exercise program and so on.

Pass out the envelopes and have each person address an envelope to himself or herself. Ask the kids to put their papers in their envelopes, seal them and give them to you. Tell them: "I will send these back to each of you after 30 days. At that time you can examine what you wrote and see if you are continuing to work on those features you want to change.

"Think about what we just did, about the commitment

you are making to work on personal features you would like to change. How can this kind of concern get out of hand?" Have one of your young people read Matthew 6:25-34. Ask, "How does this passage apply to our concerns for health and good looks?"

Divide kids into small groups of four to five people. Pass out the magazines that deal with physical fitness and beauty. Give each group two sheets of newsprint and a marker. Ask the groups to select someone from their group to record their findings.

Have the groups go through the magazines. Tell them to use the first sheet of newsprint to note the types of articles they find and list the advice given. Ask the groups to examine the ads, too. Use the second sheet of newsprint to describe what the ads are like. What kinds of promises do they make? Study the ads to figure out how much a person could spend on a collection of items to be healthy and good-looking—vitamins and dietary supplements, exercise equipment, membership in health clubs, aerobic clothing, cosmetics, hair products and so on. Do you think these items and activities would really make a big difference in a person's longevity? Would simple living, careful eating and maintaining a close walk with God do the same thing? Explain your answer.

Call the groups back together to share their insights. After each group has shared its findings, read Exodus 20:3-6. Ask the groups: "If you were to take all these ads and advice seriously, what would your lifestyle be like? What kinds of things would you do? How much time would you spend concentrating on your health and looks? How expensive would it be? How do God's first two commandments relate to this issue?"

Read Matthew 19:19. Tell the group: "Jesus commanded us to love our neighbors as ourselves. What does this say about a proper self-love? Is it possible to love our neighbors if we don't love ourselves? Explain your answer."

Response—Pass each person a Write-On slide and a marker or pencils. Ask each person to create a slide that expresses thanks for something about his or her health or personal appearance. The kids can use a word, a small picture, a symbol or whatever else they can think of to symbolize this physical blessing. Collect the slides and place them in a slide tray. If you were unable to find Kodak's Ektagraphic Write-On slides in your area, have the group draw on sheets of typing paper.

Form a circle. Have each person turn to the right and give that person a back rub. After one minute have each person turn to the left and give that person a back rub. Ask the group, "How does that feel?" Remind the group: "God did create us as physical beings, as well as spiritual ones. Feeling good and looking good are both important. Our bodies are gifts from God and are to be treated with respect. Let's celebrate our physical blessings as we recognize their source."

Share the slides or have each member share his or her picture. Ask the group to sing the doxology together as their prayer, and close with a group hug.

Options:
1. If your cable system carries the service called "Lifetime," ask group members to watch several programs. Some programs feature high-powered speakers who talk to gatherings of people who sell certain health products. Discuss how these programs are like a gathering of Christians. If some of your group members don't have cable, tape one of the programs and play it back at a meeting. Ask individuals to point out examples of how these meetings operate like church meetings.

2. Assign several members to go to local bookstores and make a list of the self-help books on health and physical appearance. Have them look through the books and make notes.

Ask others to explore the library. Does it contain any self-help books? How big is the health-and-good-looks industry? What are some of its main teachings? Are these teachings overemphasized?

ISSUE 40
Should Christians listen to rock music?

YES, Christians may listen to any kind of music they like, even rock music.

"Hi, Meryl. Want to join us? We're on our way to Record Shack to get Springsteen's new album; it's supposed to be out today."

"No, I don't think I'd better, Bev. I'd be too tempted . . . "

"Yeah, I know what you mean. I always want to buy at least a dozen albums. I'm a little short on cash too, but I've got enough to buy this one album."

"No, it's not that. It's just that . . . well . . . I'm not supposed to buy any more rock albums, or even listen to rock."

"What? You must be kidding! Who's on your case?"

"My folks . . . and my church, too! We had one of those traveling evangelists a few weeks ago, and he preached a real 'fire-and-brimstone' sermon on how evil rock music is."

"Is he the one I read about in the newspaper? The guy who told all the teenagers to bring their albums to the big bonfire?"

"Yes, he's the one. He did present a pretty good case when I listened to him. He talked about the rock stars' use of drugs and all the references to drugs in their music. He also explained how many groups use Satanism, witchcraft and free sex and how they promote these things through their music. He raised a lot of questions I'd never thought of."

"Satanism, witchcraft and drugs? I wonder if he's ever listened to Bruce, U2, Sting or Billy Joel. Meryl, you know as well as I do that there isn't anything like that in their stuff! I'm sure there might be in some of the music of the crazies, but he shouldn't put down all rock music just because of a few weirdos!"

"Yeah, I know. I went home and played some of my albums to see if what he was saying was true. I did have a few older albums that were like he said, but most weren't like that at all.''

"Gosh, Meryl, I'm sorry. That's tough to have both your parents and your church against your music. What are you going to do?''

"I don't know. I do know they're not getting *my* albums for a bonfire. We'll just have to see what happens. Darn it, why do adults have to make things so complicated?''

Not everyone likes rock music, but then not everyone likes jazz, classical, country, Broadway, opera, folk or the other forms of music. We should be able to listen to any kind of music that pleases us. Some rock music is poor, both from a musical and a moral standpoint. But that's true for other music as well. Numerous popular songs from the '30s and '40s were suggestive, urging listeners to "do it" tonight with no thought of the consequences. The songs didn't come right out and say what "it" was, but the meaning was as corrupt as anything today. Many operas have heroes who live immoral lives and burn with desire for bloody vengeance, yet we call these creations "great works of art.'' Those who criticize the private lives of rock stars would be surprised to study the great composers of the past. One look at the personal lives of Wagner and Mozart would help the critic see that God is able to use all kinds of people to create beautiful and lasting works of art.

Many rock songs are beautiful and moving. Some challenge listeners. In "I Am a Rock," Simon and Garfunkel point out the folly of withdrawing from human contact. The Beatles urge those who sit on life's sidelines to get involved in "Nowhere Man." In "Eleanor Rigby," they also lament the lonely, lost lives of little people. Sting reminds us that the Russians are human, too, in his song "The Russians,'' while Bruce Springsteen protests what's happening to America's blue-collar workers and veterans in songs like "My Hometown" and "Born in the USA." Many of Stevie Wonder's songs celebrate life and the joy of love and friendship.

When the rock operas *Jesus Christ Superstar* and *Godspell*
swept the country in the early '70s, many people examined
Jesus' life more closely. Since then many Christian musicians have learned to "sing unto the Lord a new song," one
with a distinct beat. Some Christian bands are just as good
(or better) musicians than those in the higher-paid secular
bands. But these groups sing about God, Christ and the call
to discipleship. Their songs lift up the issues of faith and
doubt, trial and temptation. Those who dismiss their music
simply because of its rock format are missing out on a dy-
namic and satisfying expression of faith.

Every new musical form meets with those who resist it.
Some label it as "of the devil." Queen Elizabeth referred
disdainfully to the hymn "All People That on Earth Do
Dwell" as a "Geneva jig" because it was imported from
John Calvin's Geneva. She felt it should never be sung in
church. Jazz was looked down on as sensual "Negro music"
and associated with the bars and brothels where it was
played. Our parents had to endure their parents' insults
when they began to listen to the swing music of Benny
Goodman's and Glen Miller's bands or the crooning music
of "that skinny kid," Frank Sinatra. The same resistance exists today with rock music. Immoral rock songs do exist,
and Christians should avoid these. But this concern should
not blind us to the possibilities of rock music, secular or
sacred.

NO, Christians should not listen to rock music in any
form, Christian or otherwise.

"Bryan, have you heard about Vic?"

"I saw him yesterday in math class. Why? What's he
done this time? Let loose another skunk in the principal's
office?"

"No, he's dead!"

"What? You're kidding! That can't be!"

"I'm afraid it's true. His parents found him in his room
last night. His mom was upset because he had his stereo on
so loud. When she went in to ask him to turn it down, she

found him on the floor with a needle beside him."

"Vic . . . mainlining? I knew he was playing around with drugs a little, especially when he'd go to the rock concerts. But I didn't realize he was using a needle."

"Me neither. He showed me some coke yesterday. Said he'd picked it up from a friend. I tried to talk him out of using it, but ever since 10th-grade when he started listening to the hard rock groups and trying to imitate his favorite rock stars, he's gone overboard on drugs. He got worse when he started playing sax in that rock group. He didn't think he was cool unless he was high or drinking something. His mom said he was even getting into witchcraft and other strange stuff."

"Yeah, I think he started that after that group—what's their name?—the ones with the weird costumes and blazing fires on stage—came to town."

Secular rock music is especially evil in its imagery, words and associations. Drugs, free sex, bad language and rebellion against authority go with the rock scene and are just a few of the reasons why Christians should shun such music. Rock music is a bad influence on today's young people.

Many rock songs praise and promote drug use. This shouldn't surprise anyone, since many professional band members use drugs and talk freely about using them. Marijuana is bad enough, but rock musicians merely start out on this weed. They prefer to get high on the hard stuff that is currently in fashion such as heroine and cocaine. "I get high with a little help from my friends" was a line from one of the Beatles' songs that seduced teenagers into seeing drug use as okay. Hundreds of rock songs have similar phrases that support this habit. Anyone who attends a rock concert can see and smell drugs being used and sold throughout the audience.

Many rock stars and their songs embrace the strange and forbidden world of the occult and demonic. Album covers feature lurid paintings of the devil, witches, foreign idols and vile practices condemned by the Bible and the church. To gain notoriety, rock groups dress outlandishly and perform such disgusting acts as twisting the head off a chicken, drinking blood, destroying their instruments or making lewd gestures at the audience.

The philosophy of many rock groups is total rebellion against any order or authority. Pink Floyd attacked education and urged students to tear down their schools. Parents, police, government, the church, marriage, rules and ethics are all under attack by the dark forces behind the rock music industry.

Some groups who aren't content to spread their anti-Christian beliefs and values in a straightforward way are using sneaky tactics such as back masking. To do this, they record some awful message urging the listener to sin, incorporate it into their music, but play the music backward so that the conscious mind doesn't pick it up. But the message is still received by the listeners and affects the unconscious portion of their minds.

In light of the many disreputable and obnoxious stories that have come out of rock music, why would any Christian want to associate with this phenomenon? Peer pressure regards fellow teenagers as "square" if they don't listen to what is popular. But it seems best to be pegged as "not cool" rather than pollute the mind with such filth. Paul told believers to avoid even the appearance of evil; this is a good principle to use in regard to rock music. There's plenty of good music to listen to without supporting such a decadent industry and a mind-poisoning form of entertainment.

Programming Ideas for Issue 40

Preparation—Invite the group to bring posters and album covers of rock musicians to decorate the walls of the youth meeting room. The kids might not be willing to bring some of the more outlandish album covers. You may need to check with friends outside the church or record collections at the public library. You can also purchase copies of older albums at the Salvation Army or Goodwill Industries stores.

Invite group members to bring an album or single of their favorite song. Set up a record player and a tape player.

Gather paper and pencils and pass these out as the members arrive. Tape three sheets of newsprint to the wall. Bring 3×5 cards, a basket and a marker.

Opening—Play a familiar rock song as the group arrives. When it's meeting time, turn down the volume and read Deuteronomy 32:4. Tell the group, "Tonight we will be looking at rock music and the Rock described in this Bible verse." Ask, "What objections have you heard to rock music?" Record these on the first sheet of newsprint you taped to the wall. Some objections you may hear include language; sex and nudity; drugs; violence; the occult; glorification of Satanism or witchcraft; and so on.

Program—After the group has listed the objections to rock music, ask the following questions and record the answers on the second sheet of newsprint.

1. How many of you listen to music?

2. How many of you listen to a radio? a stereo? tapes? a video? How many of you play in a band?

3. How many concerts do you attend each year? zero? one? two? (and so on, up to 10)

4. How many of you buy records or tapes? How many buy rock music? How many buy other kinds of music besides rock?

5. About how many singles or albums do you buy a year? zero? one? two? three? four? five? 10? 15? more than 20?

6. On the paper you received as you entered the room, list the names of three songs you really like. List three or four of your favorite groups or bands. Why do you like the songs and groups you listed? Be specific about your answer.

7. On the same sheet of paper, complete the following statements:

My music tells me that life is . . .

If I could talk to adults about my music, I would say . . .

Tell the members to look for a partner and share their

favorite songs and completed statements. (If there's an odd number of people, ask the extra person to join with one of the pairs.) The only ground rule is that there will be no put-downs of others' musical choices; each person's taste is okay.

As people complete their sharing, pass out album covers to each pair and ask the individuals to review the objections to rock music listed on the newsprint at the front of the room.

Ask each pair to pay special attention to the words included on the sleeve or back cover.

Many rock songs are about "love." If love is mentioned in the song you selected, could "lust" be substituted? Is this love other-centered or self-centered? Is this love merely a feeling or is there something more permanent about it? Compare the song's concept of love with 1 Corinthians 13 or Philippians 2:1-8.

Have each pair, on the back of one person's sheet of paper, make a list of things people might find offensive. After five minutes, call the groups together and let each pair report on either a song from the album, the cover or the group itself—its costumes, actions, publicity, the staging, etc. As people report their findings, check the list on the newsprint and write the name of the rock group next to the objection. If one group has offensive actions in more than one area, write the name of the group next to each objection. If new objections are discovered, add these to the list along with the groups who are guilty of these offensive actions.

After the pairs and small groups have finished sharing, ask everyone to look at the list of objections again. Ask: "Which groups have the most objections? Do you listen to these groups? What do you think about the objections to these groups? Should Christians listen to these songs or these groups?" On the third sheet of newsprint, list reasons "For" and "Against" listening to such music. What are some of the dangers? What positive things can happen by listening to this music? Ask people to be specific in their answers.

Have someone read 1 Corinthians 10:23-24 aloud to the rest of the group. Ask: "How can these verses help us decide whether a song or album is suitable for Christians? Explain what Paul means by 'Nobody should seek his own good, but the good of others.' How can this passage support listening to rock music? How can it support not listening to rock music?"

Response—As time permits, listen to songs brought by group members. Let the person who brought each song introduce it by name and artist and tell why it's a favorite. Remind the group again that no one will put down the choice of another.

After each song ask: "What is the song about? Is this a song that just celebrates the goodness of being alive or does it have another message? Does it reflect anything objectionable from our earlier discussions?"

Obviously, there won't be time to listen to and discuss each person's favorite music. Arrange for another session to listen to more songs. Some groups choose to have a listening and discussion session periodically since songs quickly come and go. By approaching rock music objectively and showing that you can learn from your young people, they may open up in revealing ways. When teenagers find they can trust you to listen to them, they will begin to listen in return. You can help your young people apply the insights of their faith to a pastime that fills many hours of their weekly schedule.

Pass out 3×5 cards. Have a member of the group read 1 Corinthians 10:31-33. Ask each person to write a way he or she has caused others to stumble. Pass a basket around the group. As each person drops his or her card in the basket, ask the others to pray for that person. Remind the group members to be selective about what kind of music they listen to or spend their money on. Close by singing the prayer "Day by Day" from *Songs* (Songs and Creations).

Options:

1. Use the "MediaWatch" section of GROUP Magazine to explore current songs.

2. Invite a radio station disc jockey or a member of a rock group to speak to your group. Let the speaker know the group would like to ask questions, too. Include questions like these: "Why are you drawn to certain music? Do you look for specific values in the music you use? How do you respond to criticism of the music you use? Does public opinion make a difference to you?"

3. If parents approve, take your kids to a rock concert and plan an overnighter to talk about the total experience. (If this isn't possible, watch a segment of MTV or a televised concert and talk about it.)

4. Rent the video of *Footloose* and talk about the different attitudes toward rock music and dancing as they are expressed in the film. Ask the group: "What does rock mean to the teenagers? to parents? to the minister and his church leaders?" For more discussion questions see the discussion guide in the May 1984 issue of GROUP Magazine.

5. Many teenagers haven't heard much Christian rock. Invite those who own Christian rock albums to bring them to your next meeting. Play such Christian videos as Steve Taylor's *Meltdown* or Petra's *The Whole World*. Ask the group: "How is Christian rock like hard rock? What differences do you see?"

6. Decide on a theme like caring, sharing, what is love, etc., and select several songs you could use. Create a script to tie the songs together and record the songs on tape. Take slide pictures to interpret the lyrics or the mood of the music. The pictures can be of group members, neighborhood scenes or community activities. Use a camera with a close-up lens to take slide pictures from books or magazines. When all the slides come back from the lab, have the group meet to sort the slides to match the lyrics of the songs. Use two projectors to create a mixture of sight and sound. Preview the show to see if there are spots where you need to add slides or delete others. If your group is

large, divide into small groups with each subgroup working on a specific song.

Show the finished product to an adult Sunday school class or at a church supper. Let area service clubs know that your young people have a program they are willing to share. After each showing, ask the audience to respond with what *their* parents thought of their favorite music when they were teenagers. Let your young people talk about objections to their music. This exchange will facilitate mutual sharing and understanding between generations.

HOW TO CONDUCT A DEBATE

The formal debate, popular both in high school and college, is an excellent learning method for dealing with issues that are "too hot" to handle in ordinary discussions. This technique provides an organized forum in which debaters learn to research facts and arguments, build and organize their cases, and make presentations in opposition to another team. The group would select one of the issues in the book and restate the question as a proposition. For example, if the group wanted to talk about the question "Does God use illness to punish his people for their sins?" then the group would restate this issue as "Resolved, God does use illness as a punishment for people's sin" or "Resolved, God does not use illness as a punishment for people's sin."

Four volunteers would agree to study the question and be ready to debate it the following week (or later, if you want to give each side time to get together to practice). Two individuals would make up the "Pro" or Affirmative team and two would be on the "Con" or Negative team. If your teenagers have never experienced debate at school, it is unlikely they will volunteer easily; however, let them know you expect effort, not expertise, in this first attempt.

Organizing Facts and Arguments

Encourage your young people to use the skills they
have learned in their English classes. Their knowledge of
how to locate materials in the library, how to interview
knowledgeable people, how to make note cards and how to
properly acknowledge sources will be extremely helpful.
You may need to work with them on how to organize their
materials and how to open and close their cases effectively.
If you are uncertain about the debate procedure yourself,
there are books in the library that can help. You could also
check with a high school speech or English teacher in your
community.

In a formal debate, facts and evidence are very important for supporting each major argument. Opinions of the
debaters are not enough, even though the opinion of an
expert is. There are numerous sources for facts and evidence, including books and magazines in the church, school
and public libraries. To find articles on any topic, the Readers' Guide To Periodical Literature is a must. Find out if the
students have been taught how to use this reference tool. If
they haven't, go with them to the library and show them.

Debaters should outline the main arguments or points
of their cases and then look for facts or evidence to support
them. When they find such evidence, the fact or quotation
should be written on a file card (using one file card for
each fact). At the top of the card, they should list the debate topic, and on another line, the argument. Then they
should print or type the fact or quotation. At the bottom it
is important to give the exact source, including the title of
the article, the author, magazine or book, publisher, date
and page number.

The teams should also examine the possible cases their
opponents might use to support their position. This research
will help them preview the main points their opposition
will probably use. It will help them support their cases and
prepare arguments against their opponents. When they
come across evidence that an opponent will probably use,
they should copy this down on a card for future study and

possible use. For instance, an opponent might use only part of a quote and leave out something that isn't as supportive. During a debate, the opponent would point to this tactic as a way of offsetting the evidence. This preparation will also lessen the possibility of a team being taken by surprise with an opponent's argument.

Experienced debaters organize their file cards in a file box under main points and arguments. The cards they will use are put in the order they plan to refer to them. The box is kept at hand during the debate so that when an opponent comes up with an argument or demands further evidence, the debater can go through the file box and pull out a card with pertinent information. For example, a debate topic might be "Should church bulletins be used?" A speaker might want to record the results of his or her team's survey about local churches that use bulletins. The cards might look like the following:

Card 1

Debate topic: Should church bulletins be used?
Cost of bulletins—First United Methodist, New Haven
    Budget item: $125 in 1987
    Total budget: $47,875
    0.26 percent of budget
Source: Phone interview with Geraldine Mickey, financial
        secretary
        Page 16 of the annual report for First United Methodist

---

Card 2

Debate topic: Should church bulletins be used?
Cost of bulletins—Calvary Baptist Church, New Haven
    Budget item: $265 in 1987
    Total budget: $87,560
    0.3 percent of budget
Source: Phone interview with Casey Painter, associate pastor
        Page 27 of the annual report for Calvary Baptist Church

---

Other cards might contain a relative scripture passage, a set of statistics or a quotation from an authority that supports the position taken. Be sure to include the credentials of the expert and the source for any statistics or facts you might want to use.

It's often good for young people to pick a side of an issue they don't favor. Their preparation for the debate will force them to stretch their minds when they look at the issue from a different perspective. Their research may reinforce their present position, but they will be forced to rethink their position when they have to deal with the arguments and facts of which they are unaware or have previously ignored.

A Debate Format

At the youth meeting, the moderator, who could be the youth leader or preferably one of the young people in the group, would give a brief statement about the issue and why it is important for the group to consider it. He or she would introduce the debaters and give final instructions for timing the debate. The question would be introduced, and the debate would begin. The debate would follow this format:

First presentation by the Affirmative . . . . . . four minutes
First presentation by the Negative . . . . four minutes
Second presentation by the Affirmative . . . four minutes
Second presentation by the Negative . . . . . four minutes
First rebuttal by the Affirmative . . . . two minutes
First rebuttal by the Negative . . . . two minutes
Second rebuttal and summary by
    the Affirmative . . . . two minutes
Second rebuttal and summary by
    the Negative . . . . two minutes

The amount of time listed above is shorter than that allowed for college debates, but you can extend the time if the group members wish to do so. They probably will once they discover how short four minutes really are. Nevertheless, a total of 24 minutes allows plenty of time for the debate to fit into most any schedule.

An official timekeeper should use a stopwatch to time the speakers carefully. The timekeeper will hold up a card to warn the speakers when they have exactly 30 seconds left. This warning should give the speakers time to make one last point or to summarize their arguments. The timer will then signal when time is up. If the speakers try to continue, the timer should cut them off with, "Thank you, it's now time for our next speaker."

A Sample Debate

A sample debate might work like this: The president of the youth group would serve as moderator and introduce the issue by asking the question, "Should churches use printed bulletins for their worship services?" After a brief explanation of why it is important for the group to consider this issue, he or she would introduce the debaters and the debate would begin.

The first Affirmative speaker would repeat the question in an affirmative resolved format: "Resolved, churches *should* use bulletins for their people to follow the service of worship.

"The majority of churches today use bulletins. Since this is so, there must be some good reasons for this practice. We will show you that there are indeed good reasons for using bulletins.

"Church bulletins make it possible for *all* people to be involved in the service, not just the pastor and the choir. Printing unison prayers and anthems in the bulletin make it easier for all to see and join in. Some may even take these home and think about them during the week.

"The church bulletin also provides an order everyone can see so they will not be caught unprepared for what comes next. This kind of preparation supports Paul's stance that everything should be done 'decently and in order.' People will know when to sing the hymns without having them announced, and they will also realize when to have their money ready for the offering. For these reasons and others my partner will state, we believe that churches should continue to use printed bulletins."

The first Negative speaker responds to the issue from his or her perspective: "No, churches should *not* use printed bulletins.

"Just because lots of people agree on something is no reason to continue a practice that can be wrong for many reasons. And we intend to prove this in the case of church bulletins.

"Church bulletins are an unnecessary expense of both money and time. The cost of preparing a four-color bulletin plus its duplication is $_____ per 100 bulletins. Aside from the cost of the bulletins themselves is the time required for a secretary or pastor to type and prepare the copy for duplication. Such money and time could be better spent for missions or other needs.

"Church bulletins also stifle the movement of the Spirit among the people gathered for worship. Everyone is tied to the bulletin so there is little room for momentary inspiration, especially if it would upset the schedule.

"Printed prayers are also a poor substitute for people offering their own prayers. A recent survey of local churches indicated that few congregations call on their membership anymore to pray spontaneously as was done in the early church.

"For these and other reasons, my colleague and I will show you why we believe bulletins should be omitted from church worship services."

In the second Affirmative speech, the speaker should repeat the two points of the first Affirmative speech. Then the speaker should offer a rebuttal of the points of the first Negative speaker. For example, he or she might say: "The cost of church bulletins is just a small fraction of the church's total budget. In a recent survey my colleague and I discovered that the cost of bulletins constitutes less than three-tenths of 1 percent in the two largest churches here in New Haven. First United Methodist reported a cost of 0.26 percent of the total budget, and Calvary Baptist's expenses ran 0.3 percent of the total budget.

"The Spirit of God is not stifled by a bulletin, but by rigid, inflexible attitudes on the part of church leaders and members. Many so-called 'free churches' can be just as closed to the Spirit as those that use bulletins. Also, most church leaders feel free to change the order of their service if something unexpected comes along.

"In addition to the affirmative points previously mentioned, church bulletins actually save time since important announcements and news can be printed. In this way the pastor or some other church leader doesn't have to disturb the worship experience by mentioning the announcement or explaining necessary details.

"Bulletins are also an excellent means of communication for shut-ins, visitors and prospective members. They offer a profile of the church, both by presenting the order of service and by listing the announcements and church activities. They can also serve as an inexpensive form of advertising for the church. Therefore, we are confident you will agree that churches should continue to use church bulletins because of all the good they do."

At this point the second Negative speaker will briefly restate the negative points previously presented, plus add further rebuttal to the Affirmative position. He or she might say: "As my partner has shown, church bulletins are definitely a waste of time and money. And even worse, they tend to shut out the Holy Spirit from a rigidly conceived worship service. This, I contend, has not been disproved by my worthy opponent.

"My opponent has stated that the actual cost of bulletins is just a fraction of a church's total budget. This may be true, but our point is that even that small fraction of a church's budget shouldn't be wasted but should be better spent! Our opponent also failed to respond to the number of hours required to produce a bulletin that could be better used by those trained for ministry.

"Rigid attitudes tend to keep out the Spirit, and we contend that rigid attitudes are fostered by a printed bulletin. People tend to regard something in print as unalterable, a schedule cast in concrete. This is why we believe it would be better not to risk this rigidity by using printed bulletins. Also, the time saved by using a bulletin and the souvenir value of a church bulletin are so insignificant that they aren't even worth arguing about.

"In addition to the negative arguments already presented, it should be noted that a printed bulletin tends to lead a group into spiritual pride and ostentation. Once a church starts with a simple, mimeographed bulletin in black and white, someone notices that other churches have decorative covers. Later someone else notices that a printer can produce a much better-looking copy than the mimeograph machine. Bigger churches feel a need to spend more and more on impressive bulletins, and their membership becomes more and more prideful over things that represent the church rather than the church itself. Therefore, we believe that the practice of using church bulletins should be stopped so that the money and time required to produce them can be spent on more worthwhile matters."

In the rebuttal speeches, the first Negative speaker will deal with the main points of the Affirmative speakers and point out any objections raised that were not dealt with in either of the Affirmative speeches. The first Affirmative speaker will want to spend the time refuting the arguments of the Negative speakers. He or she should also address only the major points since there isn't time to deal with minor issues.

The second Negative speaker will quickly add any further rebuttals and then summarize the Negative case as strongly as possible. The second Affirmative speaker will also make a quick final rebuttal and then close with a speech that summarizes the main points. The moderator will then thank the debaters and recess the meeting to give the group or judge time to arrive at a decision.

After the first few debates, have the group members talk about what they heard and how the information was presented. Here are some questions for them to discuss

after they listen to the debate:
- How well were the cases prepared?
- How much real evidence did each side present?
- Did the presentations follow a logical order? Explain.
- Were the courtesies of debate followed? Explain.
- Did either side resort to emotional arguments and attacks on its opponent? Explain.

After a few practice sessions ask a teacher or another adult to serve as a judge. Try to use someone who has had debating experience and knows what to look for in judging a debate. Remind this individual to consider these factors:
- Are the arguments logical?
- Are the arguments presented clearly and in order?
- Is the evidence used to support the arguments credible and from recognized authorities?
- If the evidence is from the Bible, are the scripture passages used in correct context? Or are passages lifted out of context in an attempt to manipulate their meaning?
- Are the arguments presented courteously? Do the speakers put down their opponents in any way?
- Do the speakers make good use of their voices?
- Do the speakers use devices such as humor effectively?

Work out a scoring system with points for each of the above criteria. At the end of the debate the judge will merely add up the points and announce the winners.

While the judge tabulates the scores, encourage the audience to ask questions and express comments like they did after the practice debates. Most issues in this book include questions you can use to stimulate discussion.

Members of the youth group might also discuss who they thought the winner might be and why. Young and inexperienced audiences are often swayed by popular personalities or smooth-talking individuals who use little logic or faulty evidence to back their cases. By discussing different people's observations, individuals may learn *why* their personal opinions differ or agree with the judge. This discussion process also offers an opportunity for the group to learn more about the fundamentals of debate.

Many of the topics in this book represent complex issues and could easily fill several sessions if you explore them thoroughly. Your group might use debate to introduce the topic at the first session and then have a film and a discussion session the next week. Speakers and (or) a field trip might provide the educational experience, followed by group role plays as a response. If the group then feels a need to examine the issue further, a closing debate would offer a natural opportunity to share what individuals have learned.

Other practical resources from

TRAINING VOLUNTEERS IN YOUTH MINISTRY

Video Kit

Give your volunteer youth workers a deeper understanding of youth ministry. You'll get expert, in-depth education with the **Training Volunteers in Youth Ministry** video kit. The nation's top authorities on youth ministry and teenagers provide solid, practical information. Your complete kit includes four 30-minute videotapes and 128-page leaders guide packed with tons of volunteer-building help . . .

Video 1: Youth Ministry Basics   Video 3: Building Relationships
Video 2: Understanding Teenagers   Video 4: Keys for Successful
                                                      Meetings

You'll use this valuable resource again and again, sharpening the skills of your volunteer team. Design a training plan to meet your needs using helpful tips from the leaders guide. You'll discover how to find, motivate and keep volunteers. Plus, get ready-to-copy worksheets to enhance your training program. Strengthen your youth ministry team with practical, affordable youth ministry training.

ISBN: 0931-529-59-X
$98.00

DETERMINING NEEDS IN YOUR YOUTH MINISTRY

by Dr. Peter L. Benson and Dorothy L. Williams
Foreword by George Gallup, Jr.

Identify and respond to the specific needs and concerns of your young people. **Determining Needs in Your Youth Ministry** helps you get honest answers to important questions. You'll zero in on the needs of any group of young people. Sunday school classes. Youth choir and more. Your complete survey includes . . .

- 20 questionnaires and answer sheets
- Survey administration and scoring guide
- Interpretation guide
- Programming suggestions

Open new, positive lines of communication with your kids. And plan programming to better meet their needs with this professional ministry tool.

ISBN: 0931-529-56-5
$19.95

WHY TEENAGERS ACT THE WAY THEY DO

by Dr. G. Keith Olson

What makes your teenagers tick?
- Why does Ann seem unable to take responsibility?
- Why does Johnny act like a klutz—always injuring himself?
- Why does Karen always put herself down?

Why Teenagers Act the Way They Do helps you unravel the mystery of personality development. You'll discover how each young person is unique with different wants, needs and urges. Learn ways to turn your teenagers' weaknesses into strengths. You'll help your young people mature into Christian adults.

ISBN: 0931-529-17-4
$15.95

YOUTH MINISTRY CARE CARDS

Here's a quick, colorful and low-cost way to build attendance and give affirmation. **Youth Ministry Care Cards** are inspiring post cards your kids will love to get. Each card includes a meaningful Bible verse and zany cartoon.

Affirmations—positive, encouraging messages to let your kids know you're thinking about them.

Attendance Builders—unforgettable reminders to attract more kids to your meetings, retreats and special events.

Each 30-card pack contains 6 different messages.

Affirmations
ISBN: 0931-529-28-X
$3.95/pack

Attendance Builders
ISBN: 0931-529-36-0
$3.95/pack

GROUP'S BEST JR. HIGH MEETINGS, Vol. 1

edited by Cindy Parolini

Save time with 58 of the best ready-to-use meetings from **Group's Best Jr. High Meetings, Volume 1.** You'll get complete meetings to help your young people . . .

- Develop self-esteem
- Build strong, positive friendships
- Improve decision-making skills
- Communicate with parents and more

Your young people will love lively meetings packed with activities, games and Bible studies. Create an encouraging time of growth for your junior highers with faith-building programs.

ISBN: 0931-529-58-1
$18.95